The Atlantic Slave Trade

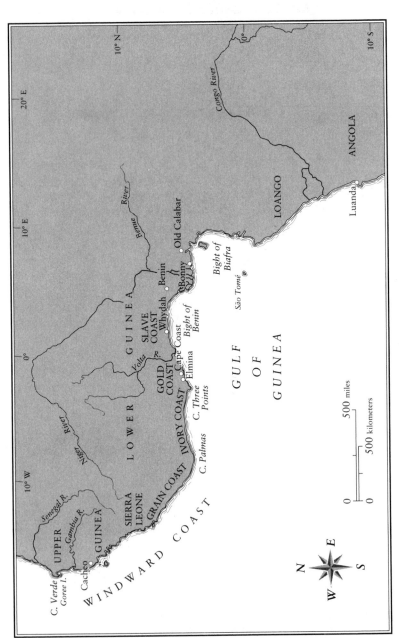

Western Africa, c. 1640–1750 (showing places mentioned in the text).

PROBLEMS IN WORLD HISTORY

The Atlantic Slave Trade

Edited by

David Northrup

Boston College

D. C. Heath and Company
Lexington, Massachusetts   Toronto

Address editorial correspondence to:
D. C. Heath and Company
125 Spring Street
Lexington, MA 02173

Acquisitions Editor: James Miller
Developmental Editor: Sylvia Mallory
Production Editor: Carolyn Ingalls
Designer: Henry Rachlin
Photo Researcher: Martha Shethar
Production Coordinator: Michael O'Dea
Permissions Editor: Margaret Roll

Published simultaneously in Canada.

Printed in the United States of America.

International Standard Book Number: 0-669-33145-7

Library of Congress Catalog Number: 92-75216

10 9 8 7 6 5 4 3 2 1

For Nancy

Preface

The past three decades have witnessed a lively new interest in the slave trade from Africa to the Americas. Grounded in immense new research and sophisticated new techniques of interpretation, recent studies have explored new issues, proposed new answers to old questions, and provided the basis for a much more precise understanding of this important and sensitive subject. *The Atlantic Slave Trade* brings together a representative sample of this new scholarly writing by historians from the four continents affected by the trade. It also places the modern works in a larger historical context by including a substantial number of records from contemporary eyewitnesses, both black and white, along with selections from influential older histories of the Atlantic slave trade.

Part I probes the reasons why Africans became the dominant labor force for European settlers in some parts of the Americas. Part II presents new estimates of the volume of the Atlantic slave trade and of its different sectors, as well as the disputes such research has generated. Parts III and IV look at how the slave trade was organized and conducted, first through the eyes of contemporary participants and then through the works of modern historians. The effects of the slave trade on Africa are explored in Part V. Finally, Part VI examines the forces that brought the trade to an end.

The first volume in D. C. Heath's new Problems in World History series, *The Atlantic Slave Trade* treats a subject whose scope extends beyond the limits of any single continent or nation. During the four centuries of the Atlantic slave trade, Europeans (and European-Americans) transported Africans to the Caribbean, South America, and North America, establishing indelible links among these once separated lands. For this reason this volume can be a useful addition to courses treating either global interactions or the separate histories of the lands the slave trade affected.

I am grateful for the constructive comments of the following historians, who reviewed the table of contents at various stages: Mavis C. Campbell, Amherst College; David Eltis, Queens University;

Joseph E. Inikori, University of Rochester; Patrick Manning, Northeastern University; Robert M. Maxon, West Virginia University; Jessie Gaston Mulira, California State University, Sacramento; Robert L. Paquette, Hamilton College; and Jerome Wood, Swarthmore College.

D. N.

CONTENTS

VI. Abolition   175

INTRODUCTION

The forced migration of enslaved Africans across the Atlantic marked the beginning neither of slavery nor of the trade in slaves. Slavery has been widespread since ancient times, and many different peoples have been its victims. Centuries before the first Africans crossed to the New World in chains, Asian, European, and African slaves were sold among the Old World's continents. Prior to the fifteenth century most enslaved persons were not Africans. Even the plantation system, so central to the slave experience in the Americas, first appeared in the Mediterranean world.

Yet the Atlantic commerce in African slaves has attracted more attention than any other slave trade because of the magnitude of its historical legacies. First, it brought many millions of Africans to the Americas (four times the number of European immigrants who settled there down to about 1820), leaving a permanent cultural and genetic imprint on many parts of the New World. Second, the creation of slave-labor systems in the New World was associated with the first phase of European expansion and the rise of capitalism. Third, the end of the slave trade was the subject of a massive abolitionist campaign that scholars widely have seen as one of the great turning points in Western moral consciousness. Finally, the Atlantic slave trade has been seen not only as affecting Africa during the four centuries of its existence but also as leading to the later European takeover of the continent and causing its present-day underdevelopment.

From the early days of Spanish colonization, African slaves played important roles in the conquest and economic development of the Americas. They were also the base upon which Portuguese Brazil became the world's major sugar producer in the early seventeenth century. However, the Atlantic slave trade's greatest importance in the development of the New World and a vital South Atlantic economy dates from the mid-seventeenth century, when Dutch capitalists transferred the sugar-plantation economy from northern Brazil to the West Indies. Wresting Caribbean islands from Spanish control, the English established sugar plantations in Barbados and

Jamaica, the French in Saint Domingue, and other nations elsewhere, significantly increasing the demand for slave labor.

The Atlantic slave trade expanded rapidly because it was put on a firm business footing. Most of the growing number of slaving ships crossing the Atlantic belonged to European trading companies that had established permanent outposts and other contacts along the African coast. Large sums of capital from private investors financed the great trading circuit that ran from Europe to Africa, from Africa to the Americas, and back to Europe. European factories turned out special guns and other goods that were used to buy slaves in Africa, supplemented by cotton textiles brought from India and rum and tobacco from the Americas. European governments protected these profitable commercial empires from outside competition.

The search for slaves opened more and more parts of Africa to the trade. Angola and the adjoining coast north of the Congo River composed the most important trading area overall, whereas the infamous Slave Coast and the Bight of Biafra on the Gulf of Guinea dominated slave trade north of the equator during the century after 1740. For a time in the nineteenth century, even far distant parts of southeastern Africa were tapped for the Atlantic slave trade. Slaving became a business in Africa, too. In some places networks of slave markets fed victims to the coast, where they were sold by professional African traders and by powerful rulers, who successfully drove up the prices and fees paid by European slave dealers. Yet at its base the trade rested on violence that spread farther and farther inland from the coast. Ultimately, most of those sold into slavery were the victims of war, kidnapping, famine, debt, and social oppression.

By 1700 the West Indies had surpassed Brazil in sugar production, but Portugal's giant South American colony retained its importance as the major destination of the transatlantic slave trade for two more centuries. As Brazil's sugar industry felt the impact of competition, slaves were diverted to almost every sort of job imaginable—they worked as miners, cowboys, stevedores, and factory laborers. In the nineteenth century investment in new sugar plantations made Cuba a major importer of slaves. The territories that became part of the United States imported a modest share of the slave trade (comparable to that of the Dutch Caribbean colonies), but on the eve of emancipation, the United States had the largest slave population the Western world ever had seen.

In the eighteenth century slavery came under mounting attack by philosophical and religious thinkers as well as by slave rebels. Antislavery societies sprang up in many Western countries. Ironically it was in Great Britain, whose traders dominated the carrying of slaves across the Atlantic, that the largest and most influential abolitionist movement arose. Led by religious idealists—Quakers, Methodists, and evangelical Anglicans—the British abolitionist movement also gained the support of a new industrial middle class, whose members identified slavery with the outmoded political economy of the old colonial system. For both ethical and economic reasons, these people supported the abolition of the slave trade as the first step toward ending slavery.

In 1808 a new law prohibited the participation of British subjects in the Atlantic slave trade. That same year, the expiration of a twenty-year ban written into the Constitution permitted the United States Congress to enact similar legislation with regard to American citizens. Other Western nations followed suit: the Netherlands in 1814, France in 1831, Spain (under great pressure from Great Britain) in 1835, Portugal in 1846, and Brazil in 1850. Despite these laws and the enforcement measures spearheaded by the British, the Atlantic slave trade remained vigorous as long as a strong demand for slaves existed. Only after slavery finally was outlawed in the United States, the French and Dutch colonies, and the former Spanish colonies, did the last known slave ships make their crossings in 1866. Brazil and Cuba ended slavery in 1886 and 1888.

For a long time the history of the slave trade was dominated by the writings of the British abolitionists who gathered data on sailings, interviewed sailors and captains in the British slaving ports, and encouraged participants and victims to publish accounts of their experiences. Because their evidence faced close scrutiny from the vested interests in Parliament who defended the slave trade, these abolitionist accounts generally were highly accurate. However, because their intention was not the objective analysis of the operations of the slave trade but a propaganda campaign to move the hearts and minds of members of Parliament and their constituents to end the trade, they concentrated on incidents of such extreme inhumanity that even the most hard-hearted would be moved to act.

Understanding of the Atlantic slave trade continues to be shaped by the abolitionist tradition, but two influential works of modern scholarship have directed attention to issues besides the trade's immorality and cruelties. *Capitalism and Slavery*, a brief and readable survey published in 1944 by the young West Indian historian Eric Williams, focused attention on the trade's economic importance. Williams, who later became prime minister of Trinidad and Tobago, argued that the slave trade was of central importance to the rise of commercial capitalism in the seventeenth and eighteenth centuries and that the end of the slave trade was linked intimately with the emergence of the new industrial capitalists, who had good economic reasons for seeking its demise. He also argued that the end of slavery had as much to do with changes in economics as with changes in ideas of morality.

The Atlantic Slave Trade: A Census, published in 1969 by historian Philip D. Curtin, profoundly altered slave-trade historiography by examining a different topic. The foremost American-born specialist in the emerging field of African history and later the president of the American Historical Association, Curtin sought the answer to a simple factual question: how many slaves were transported from Africa to the Americas? His estimate, based on published sources then available, was lower than the figure commonly accepted and set off new research and controversy. The careful sifting of archival records by other scholars has improved many of Curtin's original estimates, but his work remains central in defining areas in need of further study and in providing a model for amalgamating separate research findings. Such statistical research also has permitted more precise assessments of the effects of the slave trade in different parts of Africa, of the profits received by different carriers, of the causes of the mortality during the middle passage, and of the reasons why slave populations multiplied or failed to multiply in different parts of the Americas.

The growing interest in the Atlantic slave trade in recent decades has not been stimulated simply by new historical works. In the United States the successes of the civil-rights and black-power movements has sparked interest in African-American history, including the slave trade and its legacy. The postwar decolonization of Africa has kindled new interest in African history in African, European, and American universities, including a reexamination of the role of the slave trade in African history. Indeed, most recent writing on the Atlantic slave trade is the work of scholars who have specialized in African history, and it reflects the scholarly developments in that field. Finally, the end of colonial empires in Asia, Africa, and the West Indies has generated a debate over the persistence of Western economic imperialism and the role of the Atlantic slave trade in the creation of underdevelopment and neocolonialism.

In light of the complexities of the long history of the Atlantic slave trade and of the questions asked by modern constituencies, it is not surprising that many historical controversies remain unresolved. Still, the readings in this volume also document recent advances in knowledge about the Atlantic slave trade and show how historical debates can refine our understanding of important issues.

PART I

Why Were Africans Enslaved?

VARIETY OF OPINION

Slavery was not born of racism: rather, racism was the consequence of slavery. . . . The origin of Negro slavery was economic, not racial; it had to do not with the color of the laborer, but the cheapness of the labor.

ERIC WILLIAMS

Rather than slavery causing "prejudice," or vice versa, they seem to have generated each other . . . , dynamically joining hands to hustle the Negro down the road to complete degradation.

WINTHROP D. JORDAN

It is simplistic to assume that [negative color] symbolism accounts for the growing Muslim and Christian conviction that black Africans were in some way "made" to be slaves. . . . For the Africanization of large parts of the New World was the result not of concerted planning, racial destiny, or immanent historical design but of innumerable local and pragmatic choices.

DAVID BRION DAVIS

Because of the high level of prejudice against blacks during and after slavery, many persons have suspected that the enslavement of Africans must have arisen as the result of racism. A half-century ago, the influential West Indian historian Eric Williams forcefully argued that this was not the case. Slavery caused racism, but economic motives, not racial impulses, caused slavery. The rise of plantation slavery was tied to the development of capitalism; the capitalists' decision to import large numbers of Africans and to hold them in hereditary bondage was based on the fact that enslaved Africans were cheaper than any other available form of labor. In the West Indies and other parts of the Americas, a second cold-blooded financial calculation—that it was cheaper to import a young adult slave than to raise one born in slavery on a plantation—necessitated continuous fresh shipments of enslaved Africans.

In his study of colonial Virginia and Maryland, historian Winthrop D. Jordan of the University of Mississippi examines the reasons why the indentured servitude of Europeans and the bondage of Africans, which had existed side by side, gradually developed in opposite directions, with European bondage coming to an end as African slavery increased. While not disagreeing with Williams that slavery had an economic base, Jordan stresses slavery's intellectual and psychological roots. He shows that over time the religious, physical, and cultural differences that distinguished Africans from Europeans came to be perceived primarily in terms of appearance, and specifically of color. He traces the negative associations that "black" had for English persons long before a trade in black Africans came about, and argues that because Africans were not Christians and practiced (or were believed to practice) customs repugnant to the English, the negative associations multiplied. Jordan stops short of contending that these negative preconceptions caused slavery. Rather, he argues that, at least in Virginia and Maryland, color prejudice and African slavery developed hand in hand.

In two prize-winning earlier works Yale historian David Brion Davis traced the intellectual roots of slavery in the West. In the excerpt from his *Slavery and Human Progress,* he approaches the subject from a broader perspective than either Williams or Jordan, both of whom concentrate on the development of slavery in English colonies. Davis examines the role of color and religious prejudice in the enslavement of Africans in the medieval Mediterranean. He shows that although very similar racial stereotypes of black Africans existed among contemporary Muslims and Christians before the discovery of the Americas, slavery in the medieval Mediterranean was by no means exclusively African: negative physical stereotypes also were applied to non-African slaves.

In tracing the beginning of African slavery in the New World, Davis refrains from assigning paramount importance to prejudice or to economic factors. Following a pattern familiar to historians, if frustrating to those who want simpler answers from the past, he stresses the chronological and coincidental interaction of many different factors: the spread of slave-grown sugar plantations from Mediterranean islands down the coast of West Africa and then across the Atlantic to Brazil and the West Indies; a critical cutoff of Europe from slaves from the eastern Mediterranean, leading to a growing concentration of black Africans as a slave labor force that was transferred to the New World by the Portuguese; and the economic and intellectual connection between the transsaharan slave trade and the transatlantic.

If these three authors were asked to explain their differences, they might attribute them to their different areas of emphasis: Williams to the English West Indies, Jordan to Chesapeake Bay, Davis to the long sweep of the Mediterranean and South Atlantic worlds. But is that a sufficient explanation?

Economics, not Racism, as the Root of Slavery

ERIC WILLIAMS

Slavery in the Caribbean has been too narrowly identified with the Negro. A racial twist has thereby been given to what is basically an economic phenomenon. Slavery was not born of racism: rather, racism was the consequence of slavery. Unfree labor in the New World was brown, white, black, and yellow; Catholic, Protestant and pagan.

The first instance of slave trading and slave labor developed in the New World involved, racially, not the Negro but the Indian. The

Source: From *Capitalism and Slavery* by Eric Williams, 1944, excerpts from pp. 7–14, 16–23, 29, 126–27, 135–36, 169–73, 178–92. Copyright © 1944 Renewed 1972 by The University of North Carolina Press. Reprinted by permission of the publisher.

Indians rapidly succumbed to the excessive labor demanded of them, the insufficient diet, the white man's diseases, and their inability to adjust themselves to the new way of life. Accustomed to a life of liberty, their constitution and temperament were ill-adapted to the rigors of plantation slavery. As Fernando Ortíz writes: "To subject the Indian to the mines, to their monotonous, insane and severe labor, without tribal sense, without religious ritual, . . . was like taking away from him the meaning of his life. . . . It was to enslave not only his muscles but also his collective spirit.". . .

England and France, in their colonies, followed the Spanish practice of enslavement of the Indians. There was one conspicuous difference—the attempts of the Spanish Crown, however ineffective, to restrict Indian slavery to those who refused to accept Christianity and to the warlike Caribs on the specious plea that they were cannibals. From the standpoint of the British government Indian slavery, unlike later Negro slavery which involved vital imperial interests, was a purely colonial matter. As Lauber writes: "The home government was interested in colonial slave conditions and legislation only when the African slave trade was involved. . . . Since it (Indian slavery) was never sufficiently extensive to interfere with Negro slavery and the slave trade, it never received any attention from the home government, and so existed as legal because never declared illegal."

But Indian slavery never was extensive in the British dominions. Ballagh, writing of Virginia, says that popular sentiment had never "demanded the subjection of the Indian race *per se,* as was practically the case with the Negro in the first slave act of 1661, but only of a portion of it, and that admittedly a very small portion. . . . In the case of the Indian . . . slavery was viewed as of an occasional nature, a preventive penalty and not as a normal and permanent condition." In the New England colonies Indian slavery was unprofitable, for slavery of any kind was unprofitable because it was unsuited to the diversified agriculture of these colonies. In addition the Indian slave was inefficient. The Spaniards discovered that one Negro was worth four Indians. A prominent official in Hispaniola insisted in 1518 that "permission be given to bring Negroes, a race robust for labor, instead of natives, so weak that they can only be employed in tasks requiring little endurance, such as taking care of maize fields or farms." The future staples of the New World, sugar and cotton, required strength which the Indian lacked, and demanded the robust "cotton nigger" as sugar's need of strong mules produced in Louisiana the epithet "sugar mules." According to Lauber, "When compared with sums paid for Negroes at the same time and place the prices of Indian slaves are found to have been considerably lower."

The Indian reservoir, too, was limited, the African inexhaustible. Negroes therefore were stolen in Africa to work the lands stolen from the Indians in America. The voyages of Prince Henry the Navigator complemented those of Columbus, West African history became the complement of West Indian.

The immediate successor of the Indian, however, was not the Negro but the poor white. These white servants included a variety of types. Some were indentured servants, so called because, before departure from the homeland, they had signed a contract, indented by law, binding them to service for a stipulated time in return for their passage. Still others, known as "redemptioners," arranged with the captain of the ship to pay for their passage on arrival or within a specified time thereafter; if they did not, they were sold by the captain to the highest bidder. Others were convicts, sent out by the deliberate policy of the home government, to serve for a specified period.

This emigration was in tune with mercantilist theories of the day which strongly advocated putting the poor to industrious and useful labor and favored emigration, voluntary or involuntary, as relieving the poor rates and finding more profitable occupations abroad for idlers and vagrants at home. "Indentured servitude," writes C. M. Haar, "was called into existence by two different though complementary forces: there was both a positive attraction from the New World and a negative repulsion from the Old." In a state paper delivered to James I in 1606 Bacon emphasized that by emigration England would gain "a double commodity, in the avoidance of people here, and in making use of them there.". . .

A regular traffic developed in these indentured servants. Between 1654 and 1685 ten thousand sailed from Bristol alone, chiefly for the West Indies and Virginia. In 1683 white servants represented one-sixth of Virginia's population. Two-thirds of the immigrants to Pennsylvania during the eighteenth century were white servants; in four years 25,000 came to Philadelphia alone. It has been estimated that more than a quarter of a million persons were of this class during the colonial period, and that they probably constituted one-half of all English immigrants, the majority going to the middle colonies.

As commercial speculation entered the picture, abuses crept in. Kidnaping was encouraged to a great degree and became a regular business in such towns as London and Bristol. Adults would be plied with liquor, children enticed with sweetmeats. The kidnapers were called "spirits," defined as "one that taketh upp men and women and children and sells them on a shipp to be conveyed beyond the sea." The captain of a ship trading to Jamaica would visit the Clerkenwell House of Correction, ply with drink the girls who had been imprisoned there as disorderly, and "invite" them to go to the West Indies. The temptations held out to the unwary and the credulous were so attractive that, as the mayor of Bristol complained, husbands were induced to forsake their wives, wives their husbands, and apprentices their masters, while wanted criminals found on the transport ships a refuge from the arms of the law. . . .

Convicts provided another steady source of white labor. The harsh feudal laws of England recognized three hundred capital crimes. Typical hanging offences included: picking a pocket for more than a shilling; shoplifting to the value of five shillings; stealing a horse or a sheep; poaching rabbits on a gentleman's estate. Offences for which the punishment prescribed by law was transportation comprised the stealing of cloth, burning stacks of corn, the maiming and killing of cattle, hindering customs officers in the execution of their duty, and corrupt legal practices. Proposals made in 1664 would have banished to the colonies all vagrants, rogues and idlers, petty thieves, gipsies, and loose persons frequenting unlicensed brothels. A piteous petition in 1667 prayed for transportation instead of the death sentence for a wife convicted of stealing goods valued at three shillings and four pence. In 1745 transportation was the penalty for the theft of a silver spoon and a gold watch. One year after the emancipation of the Negro slaves, transportation was the penalty for trade union activity. It is difficult to resist the conclusion that there was some connection between the law and the labor needs of the plantations, and the marvel is that so few people ended up in the colonies overseas.

Benjamin Franklin opposed this "dumping upon the New World of the outcasts of the Old" as the most cruel insult ever offered by one nation to another, and asked, if England was justified in sending her convicts to the colonies, whether the latter were justified in sending to England their rattlesnakes in exchange? It is not clear why Franklin should have been so sensitive. Even if the convicts were hardened criminals, the great increase of indentured servants and free emigrants would have tended to render the convict influence innocuous, as increasing quantities of water poured in a glass containing poison. Without convicts the early development of the Australian colonies in the nineteenth century would have been impossible. Only a few of the colonists, however, were so particular. The general attitude was summed up by a contemporary: "Their labor would be more beneficial in an infant settlement, than their vices could be pernicious." There was nothing strange about this attitude. The great problem in a new country is the problem of labor, and convict labor, as Merivale has pointed out, was equivalent to a free present by the government to the settlers without burdening the latter with the expense of importation. The governor of Virginia in 1611 was willing to welcome convicts reprieved from death as "a readie way to furnish us with men and not allways with the worst kind of men." The West Indies were prepared to accept all and sundry, even the spawn of Newgate and Bridewell, for "no goalebird [sic] can be so incorrigible, but there is hope of his conformity here, as well as of his preferment, which some have happily experimented."

The political and civil disturbances in England between 1640 and 1740 augmented the supply of white servants. Political and religious nonconformists paid for their unorthodoxy by transportation, mostly to the sugar islands. Such was the fate of many of Cromwell's Irish prisoners, who were sent to the West Indies. So thoroughly was this policy pursued that an active verb was added to the English language—to "barbadoes" a person. Montserrat became largely an Irish colony, and the Irish brogue is still frequently heard today in many parts of the British West Indies. The Irish, however, were poor servants. They hated the English, were always ready to aid England's enemies, and in a revolt in the Leeward Islands in 1689 we can already see signs of that burning indignation which, according to Lecky, gave Washington some of his best soldiers. The vanquished in Cromwell's Scottish campaigns were treated like the Irish before them, and Scotsmen came to be regarded as "the general travaillers and soldiers in most foreign parts." Religious intolerance sent more workers to the plantations. In 1661 Quakers refusing to take the oath for the third time were to be transported; in 1664 transportation, to any plantation except Virginia or New England, or a fine of one hundred pounds was decreed for the third offence for persons over sixteen assembling in groups of five or more under pretence of religion. Many of Monmouth's adherents were sent to Barbados, with orders to be detained as servants for ten years. The prisoners were granted in batches to favorite courtiers, who made handsome profits from the traffic in which, it is alleged, even the Queen shared. A similar policy was resorted to after the Jacobite risings of the eighteenth century.

The transportation of these white servants shows in its true light the horrors of the Middle Passage—not as something unusual or inhuman but as a part of the age. The emigrants were packed like herrings. According to Mittelberger, each servant was allowed about two feet in width and six feet in length in bed. The boats were small, the voyage long, the food, in the absence of refrigeration, bad, disease inevitable. A petition to Parliament in 1659 describes how seventy-two servants had been locked up below deck during the whole voyage of five and a half weeks, "amongst horses, that their souls, through heat and steam under the tropic, fainted in them." Inevitably abuses crept into the system and Fearon was shocked by "the horrible picture of human suffering which this living sepulchre" of an emigrant vessel in Philadelphia afforded. But conditions even for the free passengers were not much better in those days, and the comment of a Lady of Quality describing a voyage from Scotland to the West Indies on a ship full of indentured servants should banish any ideas that the horrors of the slave ship are to be accounted for by the fact that the victims were Negroes. "It is hardly possible," she writes, "to believe that human nature could be so depraved, as to treat fellow creatures in such a manner for so little gain.". . .

The status of these servants became progressively worse in the plantation colonies. Servitude, originally a free personal relation based on voluntary contract for a definite period of service, in lieu of transportation and maintenance, tended to pass into a property relation which asserted a control of varying extent over the bodies and liberties of the person during service as if he were a thing. Eddis, writing on the eve of the Revolution, found the servants groaning "beneath a worse than Egyptian bondage." In Maryland servitude developed into an institution approaching in some respects chattel slavery. Of Pennsylvania it has been said that "no matter how kindly they may have been treated in particular cases, or how voluntarily they may have entered into the relation, as a class and when once bound, indentured servants were temporarily chattels." On the sugar plantations of Barbados the servants spent their time "grinding at the mills and attending the furnaces, or digging in this scorching island; having nothing to feed on (notwithstanding their hard labour) but potatoe roots, nor to drink, but water with such roots washed in it, besides the bread and tears of their own afflictions; being bought and sold still from one planter to another, or attached as horses and beasts for the debts of their masters, being whipt at the whipping posts (as rogues), for their masters' pleasure, and sleeping in sties worse than hogs in England. . . ." As Professor Harlow concludes, the weight of evidence proves incontestably that the conditions under which white labor was procured and utilized in Barbados were "persistently severe, occasionally dishonourable, and generally a disgrace to the English name.". . .

Defoe bluntly stated that the white servant was a slave. He was not. The servant's loss of liberty was of limited duration, the Negro was slave for life. The servant's status could not descend to his offspring, Negro children took the status of the mother. The master at no time had absolute control over the person and liberty of his servant as he had over his slave. The servant had rights, limited but recognized by law and inserted in a contract. He enjoyed, for instance, a limited right to property. In actual law the conception of the servant as a piece of property never went beyond that of personal estate and never reached the stage of a chattel or real estate. The laws in the colonies maintained this rigid distinction and visited cohabitation between the races with severe penalties. The servant could aspire, at the end of his term, to a plot of land, though, as Wertenbaker points out for Virginia, it was not a legal right, and conditions varied from colony to colony. The serf in Europe could therefore hope for an early freedom in America which villeinage could not afford. The freed servants became small yeomen farmers, settled in the back country, a democratic force in a society of large aristocratic plantation owners, and were the pioneers in westward expansion. That was why Jefferson in America, as Saco in Cuba, favored the introduction of European servants instead of African slaves—as tending to democracy rather than aristocracy.

The institution of white servitude, however, had grave disadvantages. Postlethwayt, a rigid mercantilist, argued that white laborers in the colonies would tend to create rivalry with the mother country in manufacturing. Better black slaves on plantations than white servants in industry, which would encourage aspirations to independence. The supply moreover was becoming increasingly difficult, and the need of the plantations outstripped the English convictions. In addition, merchants were involved in many vexatious and costly proceedings arising from people signifying their willingness to emigrate, accepting food and clothes in advance, and then suing for unlawful detention. Indentured servants were not forthcoming in sufficient quantities to replace those who had served their term. On the plantations, escape was easy for the white servant; less easy for the Negro who, if freed, tended, in self-defence, to stay in his locality where he was well known and less likely to be apprehended as a vagrant or runaway slave. The servant expected land at the end of his contract; the Negro, in a strange environment, conspicuous by his color and features, and ignorant of the white man's language and ways, could be kept permanently divorced from the land. Racial differences made it easier to justify and rationalize Negro slavery, to exact the mechanical obedience of a plough-ox or a cart-horse, to demand that resignation and that complete moral and intellectual subjection which alone make slave labor possible. Finally, and this was the decisive factor, the Negro slave was cheaper. The money which procured a white man's services for ten years could buy a Negro for life. As the governor of Barbados stated, the Barbadian planters found by experience that "three blacks work better and cheaper than one white man."

But the experience with white servitude had been invaluable. Kidnaping in Africa encountered no such difficulties as were encountered in England. Captains and ships had the experience of the one trade to guide them in the other. Bristol, the center of the servant trade, became one of the centers of the slave trade. Capital accumulated from the one financed the other. White servitude was the historic base upon which Negro slavery was constructed. The felon-drivers in the plantations became without effort slave-drivers. "In significant numbers," writes Professor Phillips, "the Africans were latecomers fitted into a system already developed."

Here, then, is the origin of Negro slavery. The reason was economic, not racial; it had to do not with the color of the laborer, but the cheapness of the labor. As compared with Indian and white labor,

Negro slavery was eminently superior. "In each case," writes Bassett, discussing North Carolina, "it was a survival of the fittest. Both Indian slavery and white servitude were to go down before the black man's superior endurance, docility, and labor capacity." The features of the man, his hair, color and dentifrice, his "subhuman" characteristics so widely pleaded, were only the later rationalizations to justify a simple economic fact: that the colonies needed labor and resorted to Negro labor because it was cheapest and best. This was not a theory, it was a practical conclusion deduced from the personal experience of the planter. He would have gone to the moon, if necessary, for labor. Africa was nearer than the moon, nearer too than the more populous countries of India and China. But their turn was to come.

This white servitude is of cardinal importance for an understanding of the development of the New World and the Negro's place in that development. It completely explodes the old myth that the whites could not stand the strain of manual labor in the climate of the New World and that, for this reason and this reason alone, the European powers had recourse to Africans. The argument is quite untenable. A Mississippi dictum will have it that "only black men and mules can face the sun in July." But the whites faced the sun for well over a hundred years in Barbados, and the Salzburgers of Georgia indignantly denied that rice cultivation was harmful to them. The Caribbean islands are well within the tropical zone, but their climate is more equable than tropical, the temperature rarely exceeds 80 degrees though it remains uniform the whole year round, and they are exposed to the gentle winds from the sea. The unbearable humidity of an August day in some parts of the United States has no equal in the islands. Moreover only the southern tip of Florida in the United States is actually tropical, yet Negro labor flourished in Virginia and Carolina. The southern parts of the United States are not hotter than South Italy or Spain, and de Tocqueville asked why the European could not work there as well as in those two countries? . . .

Negro slavery, thus, had nothing to do with climate. Its origin can be expressed in three words: in the Caribbean, Sugar; on the mainland, Tobacco and Cotton. A change in the economic structure produced a corresponding change in the labor supply. The fundamental fact was "the creation of an inferior social and economic organization of exploiters and exploited." Sugar, tobacco, and cotton required the large plantation and hordes of cheap labor, and the

small farm of the ex-indentured white servant could not possibly survive. The tobacco of the small farm in Barbados was displaced by
the sugar of the large plantation. The rise of the sugar industry in the
Caribbean was the signal for a gigantic dispossession of the small
farmer. Barbados in 1645 had 11,200 small white farmers and 5,680
Negro slaves; in 1667 there were 745 large plantation owners and
82,023 slaves. In 1645 the island had 18,300 whites fit to bear arms,
in 1667 only 8,300. . . .

Negro slavery therefore was only a solution, in certain historical
circumstances, of the Caribbean labor problem. Sugar meant labor—
at times that labor has been slave, at other times nominally free; at
times black, at other times white or brown or yellow. Slavery in no
way implied, in any scientific sense, the inferiority of the Negro.
Without it the great development of the Caribbean sugar plantations,
between 1650 and 1850, would have been impossible.

The Simultaneous Invention of Slavery and Racism

WINTHROP D. JORDAN

English voyagers did not touch upon the shores of West Africa until
after 1550, nearly a century after Prince Henry the Navigator had
mounted the sustained Portuguese thrust southward for a water passage to the Orient. Usually Englishmen came to Africa to trade goods
with the natives; the principal hazards of these ventures proved to
be climate, disease, and the jealous opposition of the "Portingals"
who had long since entrenched themselves in forts along the coast.
The earliest English descriptions of West Africa were written by ad-
venturous traders, men who had no special interest in converting the
natives or, except for the famous Hawkins voyages, in otherwise lay-

Source: From *White Over Black: American Attitudes Toward the Negro, 1550–
1812*, by Winthrop D. Jordan, excerpts from pp. 3–9, 20–26, 28, 80–81, 91–96.
Published for the Institute of Early American History and Culture, Williamsburg,
Virginia. Copyright © 1968 by The University of North Carolina Press. Used by
permission of the publisher.

ing hands on them. Extensive English participation in the slave trade did not develop until well into the seventeenth century. The first permanent English settlement on the African coast was at Kormantin in 1631, and the Royal African Company was not chartered for another forty years. Initially, therefore, English contact with Africans did not take place primarily in a context which prejudged the Negro as a slave, at least not as a slave of Englishmen. Rather, Englishmen met Negroes merely as another sort of men.

Englishmen found the natives of Africa very different from themselves. Negroes looked different; their religion was un-Christian; their manner of living was anything but English; they seemed to be a particularly libidinous sort of people. All these clusters of perceptions were related to each other, though they may be spread apart for inspection, and they were related also to circumstances of contact in Africa, to previously accumulated traditions concerning that strange and distant continent, and to certain special qualities of English society on the eve of its expansion into the New World.

The most arresting characteristic of the newly discovered African was his color. Travelers rarely failed to comment upon it; indeed when describing Negroes they frequently began with complexion and then moved on to dress (or rather lack of it) and manners. At Cape Verde, "These people are all blacke, and are called Negros, without any apparell, saving before their privities.". . .

Englishmen actually described Negroes as *black*—an exaggerated term which in itself suggests that the Negro's complexion had powerful impact upon their perceptions. Even the peoples of northern Africa seemed so dark that Englishmen tended to call them "black" and let further refinements go by the board. Blackness became so generally associated with Africa that every African seemed a black man. In Shakespeare's day, the Moors, including Othello, were commonly portrayed as pitchy black and the terms *Moor* and *Negro* used almost interchangeably. With curious inconsistency, however, Englishmen recognized that Africans south of the Sahara were not at all the same people as the much more familiar Moors. Sometimes they referred to Negroes as "black Moors" to distinguish them from the peoples of North Africa. During the seventeenth century the distinction became more firmly established and indeed writers came to stress the difference in color, partly because they delighted in correcting their predecessors and partly because Negroes were being taken up as slaves and Moors, increasingly, were not. In the more detailed and accurate reports about West Africa of the seventeenth century, moreover, Negroes in different regions were described as varying considerably in complexion. In England, however, the initial impression of Negroes was not appreciably modified: the firmest fact about the Negro was that he was "black.". . .

In England perhaps more than in southern Europe, the concept of blackness was loaded with intense meaning. Long before they found that some men were black, Englishmen found in the idea of blackness a way of expressing some of their most ingrained values. No other color except white conveyed so much emotional impact. As described by the *Oxford English Dictionary,* the meaning of *black* before the sixteenth century included, "Deeply stained with dirt; soiled, dirty, foul. . . . Having dark or deadly purposes, malignant; pertaining to or involving death, deadly; baneful, disastrous, sinister. . . . Foul, iniquitous, atrocious, horrible, wicked. . . . Indicating disgrace, censure, liability to punishment, etc." Black was an emotionally partisan color, the handmaid and symbol of baseness and evil, a sign of danger and repulsion.

Embedded in the concept of blackness was its direct opposite—whiteness. No other colors so clearly implied opposition, "beinge coloures utterlye contrary"; no others were so frequently used to denote polarization:

> *Everye white will have its blacke,*
> *And everye sweete its sowre.*

White and black connoted purity and filthiness, virginity and sin, virtue and baseness, beauty and ugliness, beneficence and evil, God and the devil.

Whiteness, moreover, carried a special significance for Elizabethan Englishmen: it was, particularly when complemented by red, the color of perfect human beauty, especially *female* beauty. This ideal was already centuries old in Elizabeth's time, and their fair Queen was its very embodiment: her cheeks were "roses in a bed of lillies." (Elizabeth was naturally pale but like many ladies then and since she freshened her "lillies" at the cosmetic table.) An adoring nation knew precisely what a beautiful Queen looked like.

> *Her cheeke, her chinne, her neck, her nose,*
> *This was a lillye, that was a rose;*

> Her hande so white as whales bone,
> Her finger tipt with Cassidone;
> Her bosome, sleeke as Paris plaster,
> Held upp twoo bowles of Alabaster.

Shakespeare himself found the lily and the rose a compelling natural coalition.

> 'Tis beauty truly blent, whose red and white
> Nature's own sweet and cunning hand laid on.

By contrast, the Negro was ugly, by reason of his color and also his "horrid Curles" and "disfigured" lips and nose. As Shakespeare wrote apologetically of his black mistress,

> My mistress' eyes are nothing like the sun;
> Coral is far more red than her lips' red:
> If snow be white, why then her breasts are dun;
> If hairs be wires, black wires grow on her head.
> I have seen roses damask'd, red and white,
> But no such roses see I in her cheeks.

. . . While distinctive appearance set Africans over into a novel category of men, their religious condition set them apart from Englishmen in a more familiar way. Englishmen and Christians everywhere were sufficiently acquainted with the concept of heathenism that they confronted its living representatives without puzzlement. Certainly the rather sudden discovery that the world was teeming with heathen people made for heightened vividness and urgency in a long-standing problem; but it was the fact that this problem was already well formulated long before contact with Africa which proved important in shaping English reaction to the Negro's defective religious condition. . . .

Considering the strength of the Christian tradition, it is almost startling that Englishmen failed to respond to the discovery of heathenism in Africa with at least the rudiments of a campaign for conversion. Although the impulse to spread Christianity seems to have been weaker in Englishmen than, say, in the Catholic Portuguese, it cannot be said that Englishmen were indifferent to the obligation imposed upon them by the overseas discoveries of the sixteenth century. While they were badly out of practice at the business of conversion (again in contrast to the Portuguese) and while they had never before been faced with the practical difficulties involved in Christianizing entire continents, they nonetheless were able to contemplate with equanimity and even eagerness the prospect of converting the heathen. Indeed they went so far as to conclude that converting the natives in America was sufficiently important to demand English settlement there. As it turned out, the well-publicized English program for converting Indians produced very meager results, but the avowed intentions certainly were genuine. It was in marked contrast, therefore, that Englishmen did not avow similar intentions concerning Africans until the late eighteenth century. Fully as much as with skin color, though less consciously, Englishmen distinguished between the heathenisms of Indians and of Negroes. . . .

Although Englishmen failed to incorporate Negroes into the proselytizing effort which was enjoined by the Christian heritage, that heritage did much to shape the English reaction to Negroes as a people. Paradoxically, Christianity worked to make Englishmen think of Negroes as being both very much like themselves and very different. The emphasis on similarity derived directly from the emphatic Christian doctrine which affirmed that mankind was one. . . .

At the same time, Christianity militated against the unity of man. Because Englishmen were Christians, heathenism in Negroes was a fundamental defect which set them distinctly apart. However much Englishmen disapproved of Popery and Mahometanism, they were accustomed to these perversions. Yet they were not accustomed to dealing face to face with people who appeared, so far as many travelers could tell, to have no religion at all. Steeped in the legacy and trappings of their own religion, Englishmen were ill prepared to see any legitimacy in African religious practices. Judged by Christian cosmology, Negroes stood in a separate category of men. . . .

Indeed the most important aspect of English reaction to Negro heathenism was that Englishmen evidently did not regard it as separable from the Negro's other attributes. Heathenism was treated not so much as a specifically religious defect but as one manifestation of a general refusal to measure up to proper standards, as a failure to be English or even civilized. There was every reason for Englishmen to fuse the various attributes they found in Africans. During the first century of English contact with Africa, Protestant Christianity was an important element in English patriotism; especially during the struggle against Spain the Elizabethan's special Christianity was interwoven into his conception of his own nationality, and he was therefore inclined to regard the Negroes' lack of true religion as part of theirs. Being a Christian was not merely a matter of subscribing to certain doctrines; it was a quality inherent in oneself and in one's society. It was interconnected with all the other attributes of normal and proper men: as one of the earliest English accounts distinguished Negroes from Englishmen, they were "a people of beastly living, without a God, lawe, religion, or common wealth"—which was to say that Negroes were not Englishmen. Far from isolating African heathenism as a separate characteristic, English travelers sometimes linked it explicitly with barbarity and blackness. They already had in hand a mediating term among these impinging concepts—the *devil*. As one observer declared, Negroes "in colour so in condition are little other than Devils incarnate," and, further, "the Devil . . . has infused prodigious Idolatry into their hearts, enough to rellish his pallat and aggrandize their tortures when he gets power to fry their souls, as the raging Sun has already scorcht their cole-black carcasses." "Idolatry" was indeed a serious failing, but English travelers in West Africa tended to regard defect of true religion as an aspect of the Negro's "condition." In an important sense, then, heathenism was for Englishmen one inherent characteristic of savage men.

The condition of savagery—the failure to be civilized—set Negroes apart from Englishmen in an ill-defined but crucial fashion. Africans were *different* from Englishmen in so many ways: in their clothing, huts, farming, warfare, language, government, morals, and (not least important) in their table manners. Englishmen were fully aware that Negroes living at different parts of the coast were not all alike; it was not merely different reactions in the observers which led one to describe a town as "marveilous artificially builded with mudde walles . . . and kept very cleane as well in their streetes as in their houses" and another to relate how "they doe eate" each other "alive" in some places but dead in others "as we wolde befe or mutton." No matter how great the actual and observed differences among Negroes, though, none of these black men seemed to live like Englishmen. . . .

As with skin color, English reporting of African customs constituted an exercise in self-inspection by means of comparison. The necessity of continuously measuring African practices with an English yardstick of course tended to emphasize the differences between the two groups, but it also made for heightened sensitivity to instances of similarity. Thus the Englishman's ethnocentrism tended to distort his perception of African culture in two opposite directions. While it led him to emphasize differences and to condemn deviations from the English norm, it led him also to seek out similarities (where perhaps none existed) and to applaud every instance of conformity to the appropriate standard. Though African clothing and personal etiquette were regarded as absurd, equivalents to European practices were at times detected in other aspects of African culture. Particularly, Englishmen were inclined to see the structures of African societies as analogous to their own, complete with kings, counselors, gentlemen, and the baser sort. Here especially they found Africans like themselves, partly because they knew no other way to describe a society and partly because there was actually good basis for such a view in the social organization of West African communities.

Most English commentators seem to have felt that Negroes would behave better under improved circumstances; a minority thought the Africans naturally wicked, but even these observers often used "natural" only to mean "ingrained." (English accounts of West Africa did not emphasize ingrained stupidity in the natives; defect of "Reason" was seen as a function of savagery.) Until well into the eighteenth century there was no debate as to whether the Negro's non-physical characteristics were inborn and unalterable; such a question was never posed with anything like sufficient clarity for men to debate it. There was no precise meaning in such statements about the Africans as, "Another (as it were) innate quality they have [is] to Steal any thing they lay hands of, especially from Foreigners . . . this vicious humor [runs] through the whole race of *Blacks*," or in another comment, that "it would be very surprizing if upon a scrutiny into their Lives we should find any of them whose perverse Nature would not break out sometimes; for they indeed seem to be born and bred Villains: All sorts of Baseness having got such sure-footing in them, that 'tis impossible to lye concealed." These two vague suggestions concerning innate qualities in the Negro were among the most precise in all the English accounts of West Africa. It was sufficient to depict and describe. There might be disagreement as to the exact measure of tenacity with which the African clung to his present savage character, but this problem would yield to time and accurate description. . . .

It would be a mistake, however, to slight the importance of the Negro's savagery, since it fascinated Englishmen from the very first. English observers in West Africa were sometimes so profoundly impressed by the Negro's deviant behavior that they resorted to a powerful metaphor with which to express their own sense of difference from him. They knew perfectly well that Negroes were men, yet they frequently described the Africans as "brutish" or "bestial" or "beastly." The hideous tortures, the cannibalism, the rapacious warfare, the revolting diet (and so forth page after page) seemed somehow to place the Negro among the beasts. The circumstances of the Englishman's confrontation with the Negro served to strengthen this feeling. Slave traders in Africa handled Negroes the same way men in England handled beasts, herding and examining and buying. The Guinea Company instructed Bartholomew Haward in 1651 "to buy and put aboard you so many negers as yo'r ship can cary, and for what shalbe wanting to supply with Cattel, as also to furnish you with victualls and provisions for the said negers and Cattel." Africa, moreover, teemed with strange and wonderful animals, and men that killed like tigers, ate like vultures, and grunted like hogs seemed indeed to merit comparison with beasts. In making this instinctive analogy, Englishmen unwittingly demonstrated how powerfully the African's different culture—for Englishmen, his "savagery"—operated to make Negroes seem to Englishmen a radically different kind of men. . . .

From the surviving evidence, it appears that outright enslavement and these other forms of debasement appeared at about the same time in Maryland and Virginia. Indications of perpetual service, the very nub of slavery, coincided with indications that English settlers discriminated against Negro women, withheld arms from Negroes, and—though the timing is far less certain—reacted unfavorably to interracial sexual union. The coincidence suggests a mutual relationship between slavery and unfavorable assessment of Negroes. Rather than slavery causing "prejudice," or vice versa, they seem rather to have generated each other. Both were, after all, twin aspects of a general debasement of the Negro. Slavery and "prejudice" may have been equally cause and effect, continuously reacting upon each other, dynamically joining hands to hustle the Negro down the road to complete degradation. Much more than with the other English colonies, where the enslavement of Negroes was to some extent a borrowed practice, the available evidence for Maryland and Virginia points to less borrowing and to this kind of process: a mutually interactive growth of slavery and unfavorable assessment, with no cause for either which did not cause the other as well. If slavery caused prejudice, then invidious distinctions concerning working in the fields, bearing arms, and sexual union should have appeared *after* slavery's firm establishment. If prejudice caused slavery, then one would expect to find these lesser discriminations preceding the greater discrimination of outright enslavement. Taken as a whole, the evidence reveals a process of debasement of which hereditary lifetime service was an important but not the only part.

White servants did not suffer this debasement. Rather, their position improved, partly for the reason that they were not Negroes. By the early 1660s white men were loudly protesting against being made "slaves" in terms which strongly suggest that they considered slavery not as wrong but as inapplicable to themselves. The father of a Maryland apprentice petitioned in 1663 that "he Craves that his daughter may not be made a Slave a tearme soe Scandalous that if admitted to be the Condicon or tytle of the Apprentices in this Province will be soe distructive as noe free borne Christians will ever be induced to come over servants." An Irish youth complained to a Maryland court in 1661 that he had been kidnapped and forced to sign for fifteen years, that he had already served six and a half years and was now twenty-one, and that eight and a half more years of service was "contrary to the lawes of God and man that a Christian Subject should be made a Slave." (The jury blandly compromised the dispute by deciding that he should serve only until age twenty-one, but that he was now only nineteen.) Free Negro servants were generally increasingly less able to defend themselves against this insidious kind of encroachment. Increasingly, white men were more clearly free because Negroes had become so clearly slave.

Certainly it was the case in Maryland and Virginia that the legal enactment of Negro slavery followed social practice, rather than vice versa, and also that the assemblies were slower than in other English colonies to declare how Negroes could or should be treated. These two patterns in themselves suggest that slavery was less a matter of previous conception or external example in Maryland and Virginia than elsewhere. . . .

In scanning the problem of *why* Negroes were enslaved in America, certain constant elements in a complex situation can be readily, if roughly, identified. It may be taken as given that there would have been no enslavement without economic need, that is, without persistent demand for labor in underpopulated colonies. Of crucial importance, too, was the fact that for cultural reasons Negroes were relatively helpless in the face of European aggressiveness and technology. In themselves, however, these two elements will not explain the enslavement of Indians and Negroes. The pressing exigency in America was labor, and Irish and English servants were available. Most of them would have been helpless to ward off outright enslavement if their masters had thought themselves privileged and able to enslave them. As a group, though, masters did not think themselves so empowered. Only with Indians and Negroes did Englishmen attempt so radical a deprivation of liberty—which brings the matter abruptly to the most difficult and imponderable question of all: what was it about Indians and Negroes which set them apart, which rendered them *different* from Englishmen, which made them special candidates for degradation?

To ask such questions is to inquire into the *content* of English attitudes, and unfortunately there is little evidence with which to build an answer. It may be said, however, that the heathen condition of the Negroes seemed of considerable importance to English settlers in America—more so than to English voyagers upon the coasts of Africa—and that heathenism was associated in some settlers' minds with the condition of slavery. This is not to say that the colonists enslaved Negroes because they were heathens. The most clear-cut positive trace of such reasoning was probably unique and certainly far from being a forceful statement: in 1660 John Hathorne declared, before a Massachusetts court in partial support of his contention that an Indian girl should not be compelled to return to her master, that "first the law is undeniable that the indian may have the same distribusion of Justice with our selves: ther is as I humbly conceive not the same argument as amongst the negroes[,] for the light of the gospell is a begineing to appeare amongst them—that is the indians."

The importance and persistence of the tradition which attached slavery to heathenism did not become evident in any positive assertions that heathens might be enslaved. It was not until the period of legal establishment of slavery after 1660 that the tradition became manifest at all, and even then there was no effort to place heathenism and slavery on a one-for-one relationship. Virginia's second statutory definition of a slave (1682), for example, awkwardly attempted to rest enslavement on religious difference while excluding from possible enslavement all heathens who were not Indian or Negro. Despite such logical difficulties, the old European equation of slavery and religious difference did not rapidly vanish in America, for it cropped up repeatedly after 1660 in assertions that slaves by becoming Christian did not automatically become free. By about the end of the seventeenth century, Maryland, New York, Virginia, North and South Carolina, and New Jersey had all passed laws reassuring masters that conversion of their slaves did not necessitate manumission. These acts were passed in response to occasional pleas that Christianity created a claim to freedom and to much more frequent assertions by men interested in converting Negroes that nothing could be accomplished if masters thought their slaves were about to be snatched from them by meddling missionaries. This decision that the slave's religious condition had no relevance to his status as a slave (the only one possible if an already valuable economic institution was to be retained) strongly suggests that heathenism was an important component in the colonists' initial reaction to Negroes early in the century.

Yet its importance can easily be overstressed. For one thing, some of the first Negroes in Virginia had been baptized before arrival. In the early years others were baptized in various colonies and became more than nominally Christian; a Negro woman joined the church in Dorchester, Massachusetts, as a full member in 1641. With some Negroes becoming Christian and others not, there might have developed a caste differentiation along religious lines, yet there is no evidence to suggest that the colonists distinguished consistently between the Negroes they converted and those they did not. It was racial, not religious, slavery which developed in America.

Still, in the early years, the English settlers most frequently contrasted themselves with Negroes by the term *Christian,* though they also sometimes described themselves as *English;* here the explicit religious distinction would seem to have lain at the core of English reaction. Yet the concept embodied by the term *Christian* embraced so much more meaning than was contained in specific doctrinal affirmations that it is scarcely possible to assume on the basis of this linguistic contrast that the colonists set Negroes apart because they were heathen. The historical experience of the English people in the sixteenth century had made for fusion of religion and nationality; the qualities of being English and Christian had become so inseparably blended that it seemed perfectly consistent to the Virginia Assembly in 1670 to declare that "noe negroe or Indian though baptised and enjoyned their owne Freedome shall be capable of any such purchase of christians, but yet not debarred from buying any of their owne nation." Similarly, an order of the Virginia Assembly in 1662 revealed a well-knit sense of self-identity of which Englishness and Christianity were interrelated parts: "METAPPIN a Powhatan Indian being sold for life time to one Elizabeth Short by the king of Wainoake Indians who had no power to sell him being of another nation, *it is ordered* that the said Indian be free, he speaking perfectly the English tongue and desiring baptism."

From the first, then, vis-à-vis the Negro the concept embedded in the term *Christian* seems to have conveyed much of the idea and feeling of *we* as against *they*: to be Christian was to be civilized rather than barbarous, English rather than African, white rather than black. The term *Christian* itself proved to have remarkable elasticity, for by the end of the seventeenth century it was being used to define a species of slavery which had altogether lost any connection with explicit religious difference. In the Virginia code of 1705, for example, the term sounded much more like a definition of race than of religion: "And for a further christian care and usage of all christian servants, *Be it also enacted, by the authority aforesaid, and it is hereby enacted,* That no negroes, mulattos, or Indians, although christians, or Jews, Moors, Mahometans, or other infidels, shall, at any time, purchase any christian servant, nor any other, except of their own complexion, or such as are declared slaves by this act." By this time "Christianity" had somehow become intimately and explicitly linked with "complexion." The 1705 statute declared "That all servants imported and brought into this country, by sea or land, who were not christians in their native country, (except Turks and Moors in amity with her majesty, and others that can make due proof of their being free in England, or any other christian country, before they were shipped, in order to transportation hither) shall be accounted and be slaves, and as such be here bought and sold notwithstanding a conversion to christianity afterwards." As late as 1753 the Virginia slave code anachronistically defined slavery in terms of religion when everyone knew that slavery had for generations been based on the racial and not the religious difference.

It is worth making still closer scrutiny of the terminology which Englishmen employed when referring both to themselves and to the two peoples they enslaved, for this terminology affords the best single means of probing the content of their sense of difference. The terms *Indian* and *Negro* were both borrowed from the Hispanic languages, the one originally deriving from (mistaken) geographical locality and the other from human complexion. When referring to the Indians the English colonists either used that proper name or called them *savages,* a term which reflected primarily their view of Indians as uncivilized, or occasionally (in Maryland especially) *pagans,* which gave more explicit expression to the missionary urge. When they had reference to Indians the colonists occasionally spoke of themselves as *Christians* but after the early years almost always as *English.*

In significant contrast, the colonists referred to *Negroes* and by the eighteenth century to *blacks* and to *Africans,* but almost never to Negro *heathens* or *pagans* or *savages.* Most suggestive of all, there seems to have been something of a shift during the seventeenth century in the terminology which Englishmen in the colonies applied to themselves. From the initially most common term *Christian,* at mid-century there was a marked drift toward *English* and *free.* After about 1680, taking the colonies as a whole, a new term appeared— *white.*

So far as the weight of analysis may be imposed upon such terms, diminishing reliance upon *Christian* suggests a gradual muting of the specifically religious element in the Christian-Negro disjunction in favor of secular nationality: Negroes were, in 1667, "not in all respects to be admitted to a full fruition of the exemptions and impunities of the English." As time went on, as some Negroes became assimilated to the English colonial culture, as more "raw Africans" arrived, and as increasing numbers of non-English Europeans were attracted to the colonies, the colonists turned increasingly to the striking physiognomic difference. By 1676 it was possible in Virginia to assail a man for "eclipsing" himself in the "darke imbraces of a Blackamoore" as if "Buty consisted all together in the Antiphety of Complections." In Maryland a revised law prohibiting miscegenation (1692) retained *white* and *English* but dropped the term *Christian*—a symptomatic modification. As early as 1664 a Bermuda

statute (aimed, ironically, at protecting Negroes from brutal abandonment) required that the "last Master" of senile Negroes "provide
for them such accomodations as shall be convenient for Creatures of
that hue and colour untill their death." By the end of the seventeenth
century dark complexion had become an independent rationale for
enslavement: in 1709 Samuel Sewall noted in his diary that a "Span-
iard" had petitioned the Massachusetts Council for freedom but that
"Capt. Teat alledg'd that all of that Color were Slaves." Here was a
barrier between "we" and "they" which was visible and permanent:
the Negro could not become a white man. Not, at least, as yet.

Sugar and Slavery from the Old to the New World

DAVID BRION DAVIS

In some ancient languages the word "slave" simply connoted labor
or service. In other languages, however, the word referred at first to
the foreign origin of captives, even if it later extended, as in the Third
Dynasty of Ur (2345–2308 B.C.), to in-group debt slaves and children who had been sold by their parents. In ancient India the word
dasa originally referred to the dark-skinned Dravidian people conquered by Aryan invaders. It later came to mean "slave," even though
fewer Dravidians seem to have ended up in slavery than in the lowest
rungs of the caste system or, worst of all, in the ritually unclean category of untouchables. By the Buddhist period slavery had lost its
ethnic connotations and a *dasa* could well be light-skinned.

The origin of the European variants of "slave" presents a somewhat different transition from ethnic reference to a generalized category of "enslavable barbarian." During the late Middle Ages, the
Latin *servus* and other ethnically neutral terms gradually gave way
to *sclavus*, the root of *schiavo, esclavo, esclave, sclau, Sklave,* and
"slave," all meaning a person of "Slavic" origin. According to
Charles Verlinden, *sclavus* had as early as the tenth century become

Source: Excerpted from *Slavery and Human Progress* by David Brion Davis, pp.
32–39, 42–44, 51–52, 55–71. Copyright © 1984, by David Brion Davis. Reprinted
by permission of Oxford University Press, Inc.

legally synonymous with "slave" in the parts of Germany through which pagan Slavic captives were transported to Muslim Spain. But this usage virtually disappeared with the decline of the Umayyad dynasty and the eclipse of the overland trade in slaves to the west. Italian merchants continued to buy large numbers of genuinely Slavic prisoners along the Dalmatian coast, but only in the thirteenth century did they begin to tap one of the most continuously productive sources of slaves in human history—the peoples from Caucasia to the eastern Balkans who were repeatedly subjugated by invaders from Central Asia. Representing a multitude of languages and cultures, these captive Armenians, Circassians, Georgians, Abkhazians, Mingrelians, Russians, Tatars, Albanians, and Bulgarians were no more a distinct people than were the "Negroes" who later ended up as American slaves. By the early thirteenth century, however, these "Slavs," who were highly prized in Egypt, Syria, Cyprus, Sicily, Catalonia, and other Mediterranean markets, had begun to transform the European words for chattel slaves, as distinct from native serfs. Italian notaries applied the label *sclavus* not only to non-Slavic peoples from the Black Sea but also to Muslim captives from such reconquered regions as Majorca and Spain. In 1239 a Corsican notary used *sclava* in recording what Verlinden interprets as the sale of "une négresse captive." The rapid extension of *sclavus* to people of non-Slavic origin suggests a growing assumption that true slavery was appropriate only for pagans and infidels who shared the supposed characteristics of "Slavs," which were almost identical with the later "sambo" stereotype of North American blacks. Since Portugal remained on the periphery of the Slavic slave trade but became increasingly involved in religious warfare with Muslim North Africa, the word *escravo* had to compete with such terms as *mouro, guineu,* and *negro.* Later on, the French *noir* and English "black" became virtual synonyms for "slave." Much earlier, the Arabic word for slave, *'abd,* had come to mean only a black slave and, in some regions, to refer to any black whether slave or free.

In antiquity, however, bondage had nothing to do with physiognomy or skin color. It is true that various Greek writers insisted that slavery should be reserved for "barbarians," but they considered Ethiopians no more barbarous than the fair Scythians of the north. Skin color and other somatic traits they attributed to the effects of climate and environment. . . .

For early Christians, Ethiopia represented the most remote and dramatically "other" nation of the known world. In the New Testament the first baptism of a non-Jew occurs when Philip the deacon, traveling south through the Gaza desert, encounters an Ethiopian eunuch riding in a chariot. The eunuch, who held "great authority" under Ethiopia's Queen Candace and was in charge of her treasure, had been to Jerusalem to worship at the Temple. Philip's conversion and baptism of the Ethiopian became an enduring symbol for Christianizing the world. The theme appeared in Christian iconography from the third century on and was especially popular in northwestern Europe in the sixteenth and seventeenth centuries. The mixture of races in early Christian Egypt probably reinforced the appeal of universal evangelism. For example, Saint Menas, the patron saint of Alexandria, was sometimes depicted with "Negroid" features on the ampullae sold to pilgrims; in the Nubian states, which became Christianized during the seventh and eighth centuries, Menas appeared for a time as a black warrior-protector, similar to Saint George. By the end of the fourth century, Ethiopian Christians were making pilgrimages to the Holy Land. Ethiopian Christians also captured infidel white slaves in the Arabian Peninsula and supplied black slaves to the labor markets of the Lower Nile. By the seventh century, when Islam began expanding beyond Arabia, the presence of numerous black slaves in Egypt and the Mideast by no means suggested that bondage was becoming a racial institution. And for Muhammad and his early Arab followers, some of whom referred to themselves as "black," all human beings were potential converts and brethren; skin color could not signify either a sinful or a pious soul.

It is probable that color symbolism derived in part from astrology, alchemy, Gnosticism, or various forms of Manichaeism influenced Christian and Muslim attitudes toward black people. Until far more research has been done on this subject, one must be extremely cautious in relating black demonology to any changes in the actual enslavement or treatment of Africans. It is clear that patristic writers equated "Ethiopians" with the cosmic forces of sin and darkness and hence with the human struggle for redemption and salvation. Origen, the head of the catechetical school in Alexandria in the early third century, introduced into patristic literature the allegorical themes of Egyptian blackness and spiritual light. Didymus the Blind, who in the fourth century held the same position in Alexandria that Origen had previously occupied, asserted that "those who fall beneath the stroke of God's sword are the Ethiopians, because they all share in the malice and sin of the Devil, from whose blackness they take their name." He also spoke of the necessity of "wounding" the Ethiopians for their own good and pictured their loss of "sonship with the Devil" as a cleansing and washing that would make them "whiter than snow." Jean Marie Courtès and Jean Devisse have documented the prevalence in early Christian symbolism of Ethiopian demons and tempters, often described as ugly and evil smelling, who represented the spirit of vanity, idolatry, or fornication. . . .

But the association of blackness with death, danger, evil, and grief has been common to many cultures, and it is simplistic to assume that such symbolism accounts for the growing Muslim and Christian conviction that black Africans were in some way "made" to be slaves. The first objection, as we have already seen, is that "Slavs" and other light-skinned peoples were said to have all the slavish characteristics later attributed to black Africans. The second objection is that color symbolism is usually abstract, ambiguous, and reversible. The black devils and demons of early Christian iconography were usually pure fantasies, as devoid of ethnic traits as the medieval Black Madonnas; yet in medieval Europe, which Islam had largely sealed off from Africa, specifically "Negroid" blacks were depicted among the resurrected saints on the Day of Judgment and as camel drivers or attendants in scenes of the Adoration. By the early fifteenth century one of the Magi or Kings had become an ethnically recognizable "Negro," a transformation extended in the thirteenth century to Saint Maurice, protector of the Holy Roman Empire. . . .

With such cautionary points in mind, it still seems likely that the derogatory meanings of blackness were intensified by religious cosmologies that envisioned spiritual progress as the triumph of the children of light over the pagan or infidel children of darkness. Color symbolism, like the garbled interpretations of the biblical curse of Canaan, provided additional justification for new patterns of enslavement shaped by the Islamization of the trans-Saharan caravan trade. For devout Muslims the crucial and troublesome question was who could legally be enslaved. Apart from Christian enemies who might be ransomed by their brethren, the answer increasingly focused on pagan Africans or on blacks of presumably pagan origin. . . .

By the eighth and ninth centuries, Arabic literature was already merging blackness of skin with a variety of derogatory physical and characterological traits. . . . For medieval Arabs, as for later Europeans, the blackness of Africans suggested sin, damnation, and the devil. Although Arab and Iranian writers usually followed classical authorities in attributing the blacks' physical traits to climatic and other environmental forces, including the astrological effects of the planet Saturn, they increasingly invoked the biblical curse of Canaan to explain why the "sons of Ham" had been blackened and degraded to the status of natural slaves as punishment for their ancestor's sin. The precise origins of this argument, which was later taken up by European Christians and expounded as unshakable dogma in the nineteenth-century American South, are still obscure. . . .

From the accursed "sons of Ham" to the image of carefree blacks dancing an Arabic equivalent of "the long-tailed blue," one encounters in the Middle Ages the same stereotypes used to justify North American slavery to an age increasingly attuned to spurious connections between race and human progress. Or almost the same, since nineteenth-century Americans, unlike medieval Muslims, tried to deny recognition of the blacks' military and sexual capabilities. . . .

If one takes the New World as a whole, one finds that the importation of African slaves far surpassed the flow of European immigrants during the first three and one-third centuries of settlement. From Brazil and the Caribbean to Chesapeake Bay, the richest and most coveted colonies—in terms of large-scale capital investment, output, and value of exports and imports—ultimately became dependent on black slave labor. Yet the enslavement of whites persisted and at times even flourished on both Christian and Muslim shores of the Mediterranean and the Black seas, in eastern Europe and Russia, and even in western Europe, where lifelong sentences to the galleys became an acceptable and utilitarian substitute for capital punishment. And as David W. Galenson reminds us, "the use of bound white laborers preceded the use of black slaves in every British American colony, and it was only after an initial reliance on indentured servants for the bulk of their labor needs that the planters of the West Indies and the southern mainland colonies turned to slaves." Despite the gains of recent scholarship, a full explanation of the transition from white and Amerindian servitude to Afro-American slavery must await more detailed studies of every colony, of transatlantic transport, and of the changing labor markets in the Americas, Europe, and especially Africa. For the Africanization of large parts of the New World was the result not of concerted planning, racial destiny, or immanent historical design but of innumerable local and pragmatic choices made in four continents. The following discussion can do no more than trace some important continuities between such choices and point to the often bitterly ironic connections between the extension of black slavery and white concepts of progress.

The story begins, . . . with the revival of the ancient Mediterranean slave trade that accompanied the early expansion of western Europe. . . .

Slavery had always been pervasive and deeply entrenched in southern Italy, Sicily, Crete, Cyprus, Majorca, and Mediterranean Spain. These regions had all been subject to Muslim conquest and Christian reconquest; they remained frontier outposts, vulnerable to raids but also the closest beneficiaries of centuries of Christian-Muslim terrorism and trade. Sicily and the other Mediterranean islands were coveted prizes in the chesslike contests involving Normans, Germans, Aragonese, the Italian city-states, Byzantines, and the papacy. With respect to the history of "progress," these slaveholding and extraordinarily cosmopolitan societies were at the forefront of Western commercial, agricultural, and technological innovation, despite the ravages of war and political instability. . . .

The critical factor appears to have been the supply of labor available from regions that were ravaged by warfare or that lacked the political power and stability to protect their subjects. The plantation-oriented economies of the Mediterranean eagerly absorbed Moorish, Greek, and Caucasian slaves as long as they could be obtained at a tolerable price, though the price multiplied many times as a result of the demographic crisis and escalating labor costs of the fourteenth century. When Ottoman conquests later closed off the traditional sources of foreign labor, the Christian slaveholding regions turned to blacks from sub-Saharan Africa until that flow of labor was increasingly diverted to more profitable markets to the west. . . .

But apart from the temporary Iberian and Mediterranean demand for black slave labor, it was clearly sugar and the small Atlantic islands that gave a distinctive shape to New World slavery. Today it is difficult to appreciate the importance of the rugged, volcanic Atlantic islands as crucibles of New World institutions. The pattern of trade winds and ocean currents made all the islands crossroads of navigation, landmarks and stopovers for the ships of every maritime nation engaged legally or illegally in trade with West Africa, Asia, the West Indies, and Brazil. The Portuguese government understood the strategic value of permanent settlements along the vital sea lanes from the Azores to São Tomé, in the Gulf of Guinea close to the equator. The Cape Verdes and São Tomé were also ideal bases for trading ventures along the disease-ridden African coast. But in fifteenth-century Portugal, in contrast to England of the late sixteenth and early seventeenth centuries, there was no "excess" population of unemployed and dangerous laborers. Sidney M. Greenfield persuasively suggests that the only migrants who could be induced to settle Madeira were a few artisans and other workers who aspired to escape manual labor and achieve landholding and "noble" status. The colonists probably relied on captives from the Canary Islands to construct a system of irrigation canals from treacherous mountain ravines to the fertile but arid lands below. By the 1440s black slaves had begun to supplement or replace the Guanches. For some decades the colonists cultivated mainly cereals, but by the mid-fifteenth century there was sufficient sugar production to warrant the use of a hydraulic mill, or *engenho,* in place of hand presses. . . . By the 1490s Madeira had become a wealthy sugar colony wholly dependent on the labor of African slaves. As the first true colony committed to sugar monoculture and black slave labor, it was the transitional prototype for later mercantilist ideals of empire. Madeiran sugar, outstripping the production of the entire Mediterranean, was being shipped or reexported by the late 1490s to England, France, Italy, and even the eastern Mediterranean. Columbus, who lived for over a decade in Madeira, had the foresight to take sugar plants from the Canary Islands on his voyages to the "Indies."

. . . Even before English privateers saw Spanish sugar plantations in the Caribbean or began capturing cargoes of Brazilian sugar in the sea warfare of the late sixteenth century, northern Europeans had been directly involved in the Madeiran sugar boom. São Tomé occupied an equally strategic site, roughly one hundred miles west of Cape Gabon at the junction of wind systems that powered both northbound and southbound Atlantic traffic. After a long period of experiment and disappointment, Madeiran planters aided by the ubiquitous Genoese finally took advantage of São Tomé's fertile and well-watered soil. As early as 1495 Antwerp had begun receiving sugar from São Tomé, which during the first half of the sixteenth century imported more African slaves than Europe, the Americas, or the other Atlantic islands. The spectacular success of São Tomé and neighboring Príncipe made it clear that sugar and slaves could become the keys to imperial wealth and power.

. . . Black slavery took root in the Americas in a slow, spasmodic, and seemingly haphazard way, but even the last three-quarters of the sixteenth century gave ample and cumulative evidence that the fortunes of the New World depended on Africa. . . .

There can be no doubt that both the Spanish and Portuguese turned to African labor as a more reliable and durable substitute for captive aborigines, who seemed in the sixteenth century to be on the path to extinction. Philip D. Curtin notes that in the tropical lowlands such African diseases as malaria and yellow fever not only increased the mortality of Amerindians but also long prevented the formation of a self-sustaining population of European immigrants. "Slavery," he adds, "became the dominant form of labor organization wherever the impact of disease was most critical. . . . Non-European immigrants from Africa [became] epidemiologically preferable to Europeans." Peter H. Wood has also suggested that the English settlers in South Carolina found Africans particularly desirable for rice cultivation because of their relative immunity to malaria and yellow fever as well as their native experience in cultivating rice.

Without disputing the importance of epidemiology, one must be wary of a "medical" explanation of the New World's transition to black slavery. During the first centuries of colonization whites, blacks, and Amerindians all suffered extraordinary mortality rates, but certain peoples were always considered more expendable than others; much ultimately depended on the supply and cost of alternative forms of labor. For example, young British indentured workers flocked to Barbados during the colony's initial tobacco era of the late 1620s and 1630s. In 1640, just before Barbadian landowners began switching from tobacco to sugar, the island contained fewer than one thousand blacks and approximately nine thousand whites, mostly bound laborers; even this recently reduced estimate slightly exceeded the contemporary white population of Virginia, which had been settled twenty years earlier than Barbados and was populated mainly by the same kind of aspiring young indentured servants. Although mortality was generally much higher in the West Indies than on the North American mainland, Barbados was fairly salubrious by

seventeenth-century standards. Early colonists were relatively isolated from bubonic plague, smallpox, influenza, and other European
killers; malaria did not appear in the seventeenth century, and yellow
fever, possibly introduced by slave ships, did not strike until 1647.
There was also an abundance of food. Even in the sugar-boom decade of 1650–60, the net white migration to Barbados rose to 16,970,
only 553 below the combined net white migration to Virginia and
Maryland in the same decade. But in Barbados white workers were
increasingly displaced by black slaves. White workers began to avoid
the West Indies, and freed servants began an exodus to the North
American mainland, only after the islands were becoming wholly
transformed by sugar and black slaves.

The historical epidemiologists also tend to overlook the fact that
long before Virginia became committed to black slavery, the colony
had been a "death trap," as Edmund S. Morgan puts it, for Englishmen foolhardy enough to settle there. From 1625 to 1640 it probably
took fifteen thousand English immigrants to add fewer than seven
thousand to the cumulative white population. Yet a plantation economy developed and flourished with white indentured labor; planters
continued to favor importing white servants when an alternative supply of black slaves was available and after white mortality had been
significantly reduced. By the time Virginia turned decisively to African labor, in the 1680s, the colony had already overcome most of
the "seasoning" hazards for blacks as well as for whites.

The most telling point, however, is the mortality of African
slaves themselves in every colony south of the Chesapeake. While
Africans were not as vulnerable as Amerindians to Old World diseases, the Amerindians were not subjected to thousands of miles of
land and sea travel under the most oppressive conditions. The assumption that Africans were somehow "hardier" necessarily omits
the unrecorded death tolls from place of capture or initial sale even
to the African coast. Planters could disregard such losses unless the
cumulative costs inflated the price of slaves to a prohibitive level. But
from about 1680 to 1780, despite a fourfold rise in real prices offered
for slaves on the African coast, the tropical colonies affirmed that it
was cheaper to import a productive slave from Africa than to raise a
child to working age. Philip Curtin suggests that since African captors and middlemen could sell trade slaves for much less than the
cost of reproduction, the appropriate economic "model" is burglary,
and highly sophisticated burglary at that. Moreover, in the period

1640–1700 British planters in Barbados, Jamaica, and the Leeward Islands apparently accepted a loss of 164,000 slaves in order to increase their holdings by a bare 100,000. According to Richard S. Dunn, who works from Curtin's estimates, "between 1708 and 1735 the Barbadians imported 85,000 new slaves in order to lift the black population on this island from 42,000 to 46,000." While various factors accounted for the failure of slave populations to reproduce themselves, similar conditions prevailed throughout the Caribbean and Brazil. One can hardly conclude, therefore, that colonists chose African labor in order to minimize the loss of life.

In parts of the Old World, as we have seen, black slavery was an established institution by the beginning of the sixteenth century. There was nothing inevitable, however, about the transfer of the same institution to the various colonies of the New World. In view of the Iberians' extraordinary and unprecedented attempts to halt the enslavement of Amerindians, it was not inconceivable that African captives would eventually be accorded a protected status above chattel slavery. No one could have predicted that black chattel slavery would flourish in Mexico and Peru until the mid-seventeenth century and then gradually give way to other and more subtle forms of coerced labor; or that the institution would languish in Cuba until the sugar boom of the early nineteenth century. . . .

It was Brazil rather than Hispanic America that provided the model. Of the nearly ten million Africans who survived the voyage to the New World, well over one-third landed in Brazil and between 60 and 70 percent ended up in the sugar colonies. As early as the 1520s sugar cane was being cultivated in the Pernambuco region of Brazil, but despite the aid of experienced planters from Madeira and São Tomé, the industry developed very slowly. It took time for the Portuguese to clear the coast of French Huguenot settlers, to subdue hostile Amerindians, and to experiment with Amerindian slaves sold by the Paulista *bandeirantes* until an adequate supply of Africans became available. Sugar production, as we have noted, required a concentrated force of productive and dependable workers who had little opportunity to flee and join fellow tribesmen in the interior, as Amerindians were often able to do. It was only in the 1570s, after the growth of Portuguese influence in the Kongo Kingdom and the founding of Portuguese Luanda in Angola, that northeastern Brazil began to receive massive numbers of African slaves (some of whom managed to escape to *mocambos,* or organized settlements of fugitives). In 1570 Brazil was still producing less sugar than Madeira; thirty years later production had increased almost sevenfold, and Brazil had become one of the wealthiest colonies in human history.

PART II

How Many Were Enslaved?

━━━━━━━━━━ **VARIETY OF OPINION** ━━━━━━━━━━

One conclusion that might be drawn is that, in reducing the estimated total export of slaves from about twenty million to about ten million, the harm done to African societies is also reduced by half. This is obvious nonsense.

PHILIP D. CURTIN

Curtin's initial projection of total imports appears to have been remarkably accurate, despite numerous modifications in his partial figures.

PAUL E. LOVEJOY

No global estimate of the slave trade, or of any "underdevelopment" or "underpopulation" it may have caused, [is] possible. . . . To believe or advocate any particular set or range of figures becomes an act of faith rather than an epistemologically sound decision.

DAVID HENIGE

Many specialists believe that Curtin's original estimate has to be revised upward. . . . It seems probable that the ultimate figure is unlikely to be less than 12 million or more than 20 million.

JOSEPH E. INIKORI AND STANLEY L. ENGERMAN

Estimating the magnitude of the Atlantic slave trade has stirred immense controversies. In 1969, when Philip Curtin demonstrated that a widely accepted tally was based on the educated guess of "an obscure American publicist" and calculated a lower volume based on existing statistical evidence, some charged that by lowering the estimated volume of the slave trade, he was also diminishing its horrors. That was not Curtin's view. For him any understanding of the operation and effects of the slave trade must move beyond moral outrage to confront the verifiable data. Exaggerating the numbers will not make the slave trade worse, just as pinning them down, even if it results in a lower total, will not make it less bad. The evils of the trade are proven, but measuring its effects in Africa, the Americas, and the Atlantic economy requires believable sets of statistics, of which the estimated total is only the tip of the iceberg.

Curtin's book generated controversy but also stimulated much additional research in the subject of the numbers, which he had demonstrated were knowable but could be improved. By 1982 Paul Elijah Lovejoy, a former student of Curtin's who bears the name of his famous abolitionist ancestor, could summarize the results of many particular studies of the different archival sources of the slave trade. The much improved data led to corrections in nearly every part of Curtin's original estimate, but increased totals in some places were largely offset by decreases elsewhere. Although Lovejoy's total is somewhat higher than Curtin's, it still lies within the range of error that Curtin originally predicted.

Another North American historian, David Henige, founding editor of the journal *History in Africa,* approaches the issue differently. Henige's journal is subtitled *A Journal of Method,* and he long has urged more critical approaches to the study of African history. In a part of the article omitted here, he argued that there was little hope of finding additional sources of evidence for the Atlantic slave trade, and that it was impossible to calculate the number of people who died in wars fought in Africa to obtain slaves, en route to the coast or while crossing the Atlantic. In the excerpt included here, Henige criticizes attempts to calculate the population loss to West Africa owing to the slave trade, exposing both serious errors of method and flights of counterfactual fantasy. (*Counterfactual* refers to things that might have been, such as the population of West Africa if there had been no overseas slave trade.) Despite the shortage of verifiable evidence, many historians, among them Patrick Manning and Joseph

Miller, both included in this anthology, have continued to estimate the population losses in Africa stemming from the slave trade.

Joseph Inikori, a Nigerian-born scholar who teaches at the University of Rochester, has strongly challenged Curtin's calculations and is one of those criticized by Lovejoy and Henige. The excerpt below, from a new volume of essays on the slave trade that Inikori has edited along with his colleague Stanley Engerman, a distinguished historian of American slavery, gives Inikori the last word. Here, as in earlier works, he argues in favor of a total for the slave trade that is close to that refuted by Curtin, though based on a different reading of modern research on the subject. As he notes, not all would agree with this conclusion.

From Guesses to Calculations

Philip D. Curtin

This book . . . seeks to explore old knowledge, not to present new information. Its central aim is to bring together bits and pieces of incommensurate information already published, and to do this for only one aspect of the trade—the measurable number of people brought across the Atlantic. How many? When? From what parts of Africa? To what destinations in the New World? . . .

This book is . . . written with an implicit set of rules that are neither those of monographic research, nor yet those of a survey. Historical standards for monographic research require the author to examine every existing authority on the problem at hand, and every archival collection where part of the answer may be found. This has not been done. The rulebook followed here sets another standard. I have surveyed the literature on the slave trade, but not exhaustively. Where the authorities on some regional aspect of the trade have arrived at a consensus, and that consensus appears to be reasonable in the light of other evidence, I have let it stand. Where no consensus exists, or a gap occurs in a series of estimates, I have tried to

Source: From *The Atlantic Slave Trade: A Census* by Philip D. Curtin, 1969, excerpts from pp. xvi–xvii, 3–8, 265–273. Reprinted by permission of The University of Wisconsin Press.

construct new estimates. But these stop short of true research standards. I have not tried to go beyond the printed sources, nor into the relevant archives, even when they are known to contain important additional data. The task is conceived as that of building with the bricks that exist, not in making new ones. This often requires the manipulation of existing data in search of commensurates. In doing this, I have tried to show the steps that lead from existing data to the new synthesis. Not everyone will agree with all the assumptions that go into the process, nor with all the forms of calculation that have been used. But this book is not intended to be a definitive study, only a point of departure that will be modified in time as new research produces new data, and harder data worthy of more sophisticated forms of calculation. It will have served its purpose if it challenges others to correct and complete its findings.

This point is of the greatest importance in interpreting any of the data that follow. One danger in stating numbers is to find them quoted later on with a degree of certitude that was never intended. This is particularly true when percentages are carried to tenths of 1 per cent, whereas in fact the hoped-for range of accuracy may be plus or minus 20 per cent of actuality. Let it be said at the outset, then, that most of the quantities that follow are wrong. They are not intended to be precise as given, only approximations where a result falling within 20 per cent of actuality is a "right" answer—that is, a successful result, given the quality of the underlying data. It should also be understood that some estimates will not even reach that standard of accuracy. They are given only as the most probable figures at the present state of knowledge. These considerations have made it convenient to round out most quantities to the nearest one hundred, including data taken from other authors.

All of this may seem to imply estimates of limited value on account of their limited accuracy. For many historical purposes, greater accuracy is not required, and some of the most significant implications of this quantitative study would follow from figures still less accurate than these. Their principal value is not, in any case, the absolute number, an abstraction nearly meaningless in isolation. It is, instead, the comparative values, making it possible to measure one branch of the slave trade against another.

Some readers may miss the sense of moral outrage traditional in histories of the trade. This book will have very little to say about the evils of the slave trade, still less in trying to assign retrospective blame to the individuals or groups who were responsible. This omission in no way implies that the slave trade was morally neutral; it clearly was not. The evils of the trade, however, can be taken for granted as a point long since proven beyond dispute. . . .

The principal secondary authorities and the principal textbooks are, indeed, in remarkable agreement on the general magnitude of the [Atlantic slave] trade. Most begin with the statement that little is known about the subject, pass on to the suggestion that it may be impossible to make an accurate numerical estimate, and then make an estimate. The style is exemplified by Basil Davidson's *Black Mother,* the best recent general history of the slave trade.

> First of all, what were the round numbers involved in this forced emigration to which the African-European trade gave rise, beginning in the fifteenth century and ending in the nineteenth? The short answer is that nobody knows or ever will know: either the necessary records are missing or they were never made. The best one can do is to construct an estimate from confused and incomplete data.
>
> . . . For the grand total of slaves landed alive in the lands across the Atlantic an eminent student of population statistics, Kuczynski, came to the conclusion that fifteen millions might be "rather a conservative figure." Other writers have accepted this figure, though as a minimum: some have believed it was much higher than this.

Roland Oliver and J. D. Fage in their *Short History of Africa,* the most widely-read history of Africa to appear so far, are less concerned to express their uncertainty, and they too come to a total estimate in the vicinity of fifteen million slaves landed. They go a step farther, however, and subdivide the total by centuries. . . .

The total is again given as a minimum, and it is clearly derived from R. R. Kuczynski. Indeed, Professor Fage gave the same breakdown in his *Introduction to the History of West Africa* and in his *Ghana,* where the citation of Kuczynski is explicit. The estimate is repeated by so many other recent authorities that it can be taken as the dominant statement of present-day historiography. Some writers cite Kuczynski directly. Others, like Robert Rotberg in his *Political History of Tropical Africa,* strengthen the case by citing both Kuczynski and a second author who derived his data from Kuczynski.

Rotberg, however, improved on his authorities by raising the total to "at least twenty-five million slaves," an increase of two-thirds, apparently based on the general assurance that the fifteen-million figure was likely to be on the low side. Another alternative, chosen by D. B. Davis for his Pulitzer-Prize-winning *Problem of Slavery in Western Culture*, is not to bother with Kuczynski (who wrote, after all, more than thirty years ago), but to go directly to a recent authority—in this case to the words of Basil Davidson quoted above.

Since Kuczynski is at the center of this web of citations, quotations, and amplifications, it is important to see just how he went about calculating his now-famous estimates. The crucial passage in *Population Movements* does indeed present a general estimate of fifteen million or more slaves landed in the Americas, and it includes the distribution by centuries. . . . But Kuczynski himself shows no evidence of having made any calculation on his own. He merely found these estimates to be the most acceptable of those made by earlier authorities, and the particular authority he cited is none other than W. E. B. Du Bois.

Du Bois was, indeed, an eminent authority on Negro history, but Kuczynski's citation does *not* lead back to one of his works based on historical research. It leads instead to a paper on "The Negro Race in the United States of America," delivered to a semi-scholarly congress in London in 1911—a curious place to publish something as important as an original, overall estimate of the Atlantic slave trade—and in fact the paper contains no such thing. Du Bois's only mention of the subject in the place cited was these two sentences: "The exact number of slaves imported is not known. Dunbar estimates that nearly 900,000 came to America in the sixteenth century, 2,750,000 in the seventeenth, 7,000,000 in the eighteenth, and over 4,000,000 in the nineteenth, perhaps 15,000,000 in all."

The real authority, then, is neither Kuczynski nor Du Bois, but Dunbar. Though Du Bois's offhand statement was not supported by footnotes or bibliography, the author in question was Edward E. Dunbar, an American publicist of the 1860s. During the early part of 1861, he was responsible for a serial called *The Mexican Papers*, devoted to furthering the cause of President Juárez of Mexico and of the Liberal Party in that country. The Liberals had just won the War of the Reform against their domestic opponents, but they were hard pressed by European creditors and threatened with possible military intervention—a threat that shortly materialized in the Maximilian affair. Dunbar's principal task was to enlist American sympathy, and if possible American diplomatic intervention, in support of Juárez' cause. But Dunbar was a liberal, by implication an anti-slavery man in American politics, and he published *The Mexican Papers* during the last months of America's drift into civil war. It was therefore natural that he should write an article called "History of the Rise and Decline of Commercial Slavery in America, with Reference to the Future of Mexico," and it was there that he published a set of estimates of the slave trade through time. . . . He remarked that these were only his own estimates, and he made the further reservation (so often repeated by his successors) that they were probably on the low side. . . .

The sequence is an impressive tower of authority, though it also suggests that even the best historians may be unduly credulous when they see a footnote to an illustrious predecessor. Basil Davidson should have identified the original author as "an obscure American publicist," rather than "an eminent student of population statistics," but the *ad hominem* fallacy is present in either case. Dunbar's obscurity is no evidence that he was wrong; nor does Kuczynski's use of Dunbar's estimates make them correct. The estimates were guesses, but they were guesses educated by a knowledge of the historical literature. They earned the approval of later generations who were in a position to be still better informed. Even though no one along the way made a careful effort to calculate the size of the trade from empirical evidence, the Dunbar estimates nevertheless represent a kind of consensus. . . .

It is now possible to look at the long-term movement of the Atlantic slave trade over a period of more than four centuries. . . . [Figure 1] sums up the pattern of imports for each century, while . . . [Figure 2] shows the same data . . . [by destination]. Together, these data make it abundantly clear that the eighteenth century was a kind of plateau in the history of the trade—the period when the trade reached its height, but also a period of slackening growth and beginning decline. The period 1741–1810 marks the summit of the plateau, when the long-term annual average rates of delivery hung just above 60,000 a year. The edge of the plateau was reached, however, just after the Peace of Utrecht in 1713, when the annual deliveries began regularly to exceed 40,000 a year, and the permanent drop below 40,000 a year did not come again until after the 1840s. Thus

Figure 1. *Major trends of the Atlantic slave trade, in annual average number of slaves imported.*

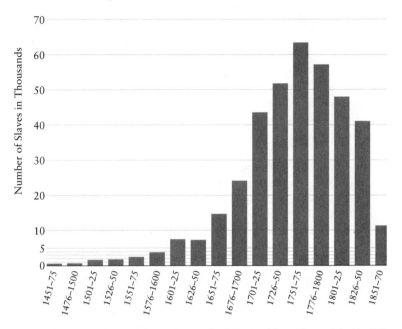

Source: Philip D. Curtin, *The Atlantic Slave Trade,* Figure 26. Adapted from original by UW Cartographic Lab. Data from Tables 33, 34, 65, 67.

about 60 per cent of all slaves delivered to the New World were transported during the century 1721–1820. Eighty per cent of the total were landed during the century and a half, 1701–1850.

The higher rates of growth, however, came at earlier phases of the trade. The highest of all may have been an apparent growth at the rate of 3.3 per cent per year between the last quarter of the fifteenth century and the first quarter of the sixteenth, but the data for this early period are too uncertain for confidence in this figure. In the smoothed-out long-term annual averages of the graph, the growth of the trade was remarkably constant at a remarkably uniform rate over more than two centuries. Two periods of stability or possible decline occur, one between the first and second quarters of the sixteenth century and again between 1601–25 and 1626–50. Aside from these periods, the growth rate was an overall 2.2 per cent

Figure 2. *Destinations of the Atlantic slave trade by importing regions, 1451–1870.*

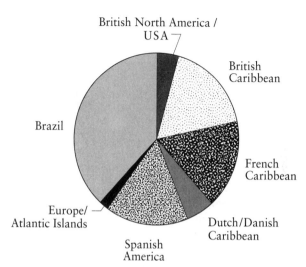

Source: Philip D. Curtin, *The Atlantic Slave Trade*, Table 77.

per year in the last half of the sixteenth century and the first quarter of the seventeenth, and at about the same rate during the equivalent period a century later. But during the first four decades of the eighteenth century, the growth rate was 0.7 per cent.

These trends are not surprising. They run parallel to the growth of the South Atlantic System traced in the literature on qualitative evidence. The nineteenth-century portion of the curve is less predictable from the present literature, but hardly surprising. The slave trade began to decline in the 1790s—not after 1808 with the legal abolition of the British trade. . . . One of the common older views of the slave trade holds that a last burst of imports took place between about 1802 and 1807, as planters sought to fill out their slave gangs before the trade became illegal. This pattern may be true of imports into the Anglo-Saxon territories, but not for the slave trade as a whole. Instead, the general trend shows a drop to the 1810's, then a rise in the 1820's. At first glance, the removal of British shipping from the trade in 1808 made no difference at all in the totals transported.

But this interpretation is probably mistaken. In the eighteenth century, warfare was the really important influence on the short-run rise and fall of the slave trade. There is no reason to expect this pattern to have changed at the end of the century. The drop of the 1790's seems to be accountable to the Napoleonic Wars, and it continued into the decade of the 1800's. After the wars, and especially after such a long period of warfare, an enormous backlog of demand would be expected, and the trade might well have shot up to meet that demand—had it not been for British abolition and the early work of the anti-slave-trade patrols at sea. The trade recovered somewhat in the 1820's, but the recovery was drastically dampened by the anti-slavery movement and by the shifts to new carriers (like Spain) and new sources (like Mozambique). In short, the quantitative impact of British abolition on the trade as a whole is obscured by other influences, but not completely missing.

The present projections also suggest a solution to some of the nineteenth-century controversies that still influence historical literature. Fig. [1] . . . shows a high and sustained level of annual average import from the 1810's through the 1840's—not a sharp drop as a result of abolition, nor yet a boom carrying the slave trade to new heights in the 1830's. Although an annual average export in excess of 135,000 a year is still mentioned by some authorities, it is clearly based on the Foreign Office estimate of 1848, apparently made without sufficient evidence and with a clear political interest in trying to show Parliament that the anti-slavery blockade had been effective. If the estimates here are correct, it *was* effective in diverting about 8 per cent of the trade, perhaps in keeping the trade from going even higher; but the trade nevertheless continued, at a level about a third less than its eighteenth-century peak. It was sustained first by the postwar boom of the 1820's, then by the sugar boom in Cuba and the coffee boom in Brazil. Really significant decline came only with the 1850's, when Brazil, the largest single importer, dropped from the trade. Steep as the final decline of the 1850's and 1860's appears to have been, the rate of import in the 1860's, the last important decade of the trade, nevertheless exceeded the rate for any period before the seventeenth century.

It would be premature to generalize about the impact of the slave trade on African societies over these four centuries. On the other hand, historians have already begun to do so. The range of opinion runs the gamut from the view that the slave trade was responsible for virtually every unfavorable development in Africa over these centuries, to the opposite position that even the slave trade was better than no trade, that it was therefore a positive benefit to the African societies that participated. Since the results of this survey could be brought into the argument on either side, it is appropriate to enter a few caveats.

One conclusion that might be drawn is that, in reducing the estimated total export of slaves from about twenty million to about ten million, the harm done to African societies is also reduced by half. This is obvious nonsense. The demographic consequences of moving any number of people from any society can have meaning only in relation to the size of the society, the time-period concerned, the age and sex composition of the emigrants and of the society from which they depart. Until we know at least the size of the African population that supplied the slaves, the demographic implications of the ten-million estimate are just as indeterminate as those of the twenty-million estimate. As for the social or political consequences of the slave trade to African societies, these would not necessarily vary directly with the number exported.

For that matter, the slave trade—even in its demographic consequences—was merely one aspect of the tightening web of intercommunication which followed the maritime revolution in the Atlantic basin. The new intensity of contact between Africa and Europe began to be felt by the 1480's, with the Americas entering shortly after 1500. The slave trade constituted a movement of people along these new lines of communication, but two other demographically important migrations took place along these same lines—the migration of diseases and the migration of food crops.

It is well known that the Old-World diseases virtually wiped out the American Indian populations of the tropical lowlands and caused a very sharp drop among other New-World populations. Given our present lack of knowledge about the epidemiological history of Africa, it is impossible to say what European (or even American) diseases were new to the tropical African disease environment—and hence what demographic consequences they may have had. For southern Africa, it seems clear that newly imported strains of smallpox and perhaps some other diseases effectively destroyed the integrity of the San or "Hottentot" community at the Cape. What similar events may have taken place in tropical Africa during the sixteenth and seventeenth centuries is not yet known.

As for the migration of food crops, at least two New-World crops were introduced into Africa by the sixteenth century: manioc and maize spread very widely and came to be two of the most important sources of food on that continent. If other factors affecting population size had remained constant, the predictable result would have been population growth wherever these crops replaced less efficient cultigens. Since this process took place over very large areas, it seems possible and even probable that population growth resulting from new food crops exceeded population losses through the slave trade. Whatever population loss may have followed the introduction of new diseases would have been temporary, while more efficient food crops tend to make possible a permanently higher level of population. It is even possible that, for sub-Saharan Africa as a whole, the net demographic effect of the three Atlantic migrations was population growth, not decline. Only further research in demographic and epidemiological history can give a firm answer.

But even if a firm answer were available, it would not solve the problem of assessing the impact of the slave trade on African societies. For statistics, "sub-Saharan Africa as a whole" is a useful entity, but not for this historical problem. People did not live in "sub-Saharan Africa as a whole." They lived in a series of particular African societies. The incidence of the slave trade was extremely variable, seriously affecting some regions while leaving others completely untouched. Useful analysis will therefore have to begin with particular societies, looking far beyond the narrowly demographic trends and seeing each society in its broader context. Only a systematic comparative study of the variety of different African responses to the European demand for slaves can expose the relevant evidence. The kind of quantitative evidence about the slave trade presented here is not completely irrelevant, but neither is it crucial.

One of the key questions to be answered, for example, is the possible role of the slave trade in social and political change. One model frequently found in the historical literature depicts the transformation of a previously peaceful peasant community into a militarized slave-catching society, where slave-raiding becomes an economic activity consciously pursued for the sake of the European imports that could be bought with slaves, and slaves alone. If the European demand for slaves did indeed force this kind of adaptation on African societies, the slave trade can be shown to have had disastrous consequences for the hunters as well as for the hunted. Alongside the destruction and death caused by the raids themselves, human resources and creative effort among the hunters must have been diverted from the pursuit of innovation and progress in other fields.

But another possibility, or model, is conceivable. African societies, like those of other people in other places, settled disputes by military means. Warfare produces prisoners-of-war, who can be killed, enslaved, or exchanged—but they may be a by-product of war, not its original cause. The African adaptation to the demand for slaves might be to change military tactics and strategy to maximize the number of prisoners, without actually increasing the incidence or destructiveness of warfare. In that case, the slave trade might have done little serious damage to the well-being of the African society.

Between these two extreme models, many mixed cases are obviously possible, and several of them appear to have existed historically. The crucial question is one of degree—which model was most common, or which tendency was dominant? The question asks for measurement, but the number of slaves exported (or even the ratio of slave exports to population) is no evidence of the way they were acquired. It tells even less about what might have happened if they had not been exported at all.

At best, the export data of the slave trade can be suggestive. If the dominant African pattern at the height of the slave trade was that of the militarized, slave-catching society, systematically preying on its neighbors, the export projections should show a relatively large and continuous supply of slaves from these hunter societies; and the slaves themselves should have been mainly from the less organized neighbors. This pattern does not emerge clearly from the slave-export data of eighteenth-century Africa. Some ports, notably the city-states of the Bight of Biafra, did produce a continuous supply that may imply slave-catching as an economic enterprise. Elsewhere, the rapid shift in sources of supply from one region to another suggests that by-product enslavement was the dominant feature, or that, if systematic slave-hunting were tried, it could not be maintained.

These weaknesses of quantitative evidence are important to keep in mind, if only because of a popular tendency to regard numbers as more "scientific" and reliable than other kinds of data. A great deal more could nevertheless be profitably done with the quantitative study of the slave trade. More and better samples of slave origins and better data on the numbers carried by the trade at particular times should make it possible to project the annual flow of slaves from particular societies, to take only one example. Even if the dimensions of the slave trade outlined here were as accurate as limited sources will ever allow—and they are not—still other dimensions of far greater significance for African and Atlantic history remain to be explored.

Curtin's Calculations Refined but Not Refuted

PAUL E. LOVEJOY

Since its publication in 1969, Philip D. Curtin's *The Atlantic Slave Trade: A Census* has been the subject of a lively debate. On the basis of published material, Curtin estimated that 9,566,100 slaves were imported into the Americas and other parts of the Atlantic basin from 1451 to 1870. Curtin intended his study as a "point of departure that will be modified in time as new research produces new data, and harder data worthy of more sophisticated forms of calculation. It will have served its purpose if it challenges others to correct and complete its findings." Scholars responded quickly to Curtin's challenge. Individuals working on specific sectors of the trade have used new data, gleaned from archives the world over, to modify Curtin's estimates for various portions of the trade. These revisions have even led one scholar—J. E. Inikori—to reject the validity of Curtin's entire census. Indeed Inikori states categorically that "there is now some consensus among specialists that Curtin underestimated the volume of Atlantic exports." Are Curtin's "global figures . . . much too low," as Inikori claims? This article is an attempt to synthesize the various revisions into a new global estimate. As such it provides both a re-

Source: From "The Volume of the Atlantic Slave Trade: A Synthesis" by Paul E. Lovejoy, in *Journal of African History* 23, 1982, excerpts from pp. 473–478, 494–500. Reprinted by permission of Cambridge University Press.

view of the literature since 1969 and presents a revised . . . [estimation of] the volume and direction of the slave trade across the Atlantic. On the basis of these revisions, it is clear that Inikori is premature in claiming the emergence of a consensus. Curtin's initial projection of total imports appears to have been remarkably accurate, despite numerous modifications in his partial figures.

The significance of these efforts to quantify the slave trade hardly needs to be mentioned. Ever since J. D. Fage first used Curtin's 1969 figures in his seminal article on the impact of the slave trade on West Africa, scholars have attempted to correspond export figures with political and economic developments in Africa. This literature in turn has spawned its own controversies. Curtin's *Census* lowered the estimate for the scale of the slave trade—which some scholars have taken to mean that the impact on Africa was less than previously thought. For example, Fage has argued that demographically, at least, the trade had a minimal impact, although politically and economically the trade had profound repercussions. Other scholars—notably Manning and Thornton—have shown that the demographic effects were significant, no matter what the absolute totals. Manning has postulated a demographic model which distinguishes between slave-depleted areas, slave-importing areas, and slave-trading areas, while Thornton has uncovered census data for late eighteenth-century Angola that confirm the sexual imbalance in local societies which matches the sex ratios in the trans-Atlantic trade. Finally, Inikori—using figures considerably higher than Curtin's *Census*—has argued that the demographic impact of slave exports had a retardative impact on African development. Hence the debate over the slave trade is far from a quibble over numbers; the debate ultimately relates to a major theme in the history of the Atlantic coastal basin and, also, southeastern Africa.

A number of Curtin's 1969 estimates have been revised upwards, some partial figures by substantial amounts, and consequently it is easy to see why Curtin's global estimate for the total volume of the trans-Atlantic trade has been challenged. Robert Stein, for example, has presented a figure for the eighteenth-century French trade which is 21.4 per cent higher than Curtin's figure. Roger Anstey reached a total for the British trade from 1761 to 1807 which was 10.3 per cent above Curtin's figure; subsequent revisions of Anstey's calculations increased the total still further—to a level 18.3 per cent higher than in the 1969 census. Enriqueta Vila Vilar took Curtin to task for his treatment of the early trade to Spanish America; new data showed that the figure Curtin used was wrong by 135,000 slaves in a forty-five-year period. David Eltis examined the nineteenth-century trade with a similar result: Curtin's data were 30 per cent too low for the period from 1821–43. In all fairness to these and other scholars who could be cited, these same individuals praised Curtin's efforts and accorded him the honour of providing the scholarly community with sets of figures which could be tested. They responded to Curtin's original challenge and generally adopted the same statistical methodology as Curtin in attempting to arrive at more accurate figures. Despite the upward revisions of different portions of the trade, however, none of these scholars attempted a reassessment of Curtin's global figure for the slave trade. The impression which gradually emerged was that Curtin must be wrong on that score too; after all, if the partial totals required upward revision, so must the global figure.

Leslie B. Rout Jr. was one of the first scholars to suggest that errors in the calculation of partial totals might indicate that Curtin's entire census was suspect. In 1973 he questioned "the credibility of Curtin's computations" for the volume of the slave trade to Spanish America before 1810. Rout considered Curtin's projection of 925,000 slave imports off by 62 per cent; instead he estimated a figure of 1.5–1.6 million slaves, although he did not add any new data of his own. Rout's claims are reminiscent of the projections of those scholars whom Curtin criticized in his discussion of the historiography of the slave trade. Rout favoured an educated guess to the detailed efforts at quantification represented in Curtin's study. His figure is also important because Inikori—Curtin's most serious critic—relies on it.

Inikori's challenge came at a conference in 1975; the revised paper was subsequently published in the *Journal of African History* in 1976 and resulted in a series of exchanges involving Inikori, Curtin, Anstey and Seymour Drescher. Inikori used a straightforward (but dubious) method of adjusting Curtin's global figure upwards by 4,400,000, obtaining a figure of 15,400,000 slaves exported from Africa and 13,392,000 slaves imported into the Americas. The method is dubious because Inikori transformed Curtin's estimate for imports into the Americas into an export figure—which Curtin did not do—using a percentage of approximately 13 per cent to allow for losses in transit. Inikori thereby arrived at an estimate for exports from Africa of 11,000,000 slaves, which he effectively attributes to Curtin. Inikori then added his own projection for the eighteenth-century British trade (49.2 per cent higher than Curtin's estimate for British exports), with Eltis's revision for the period of 1821–43 (34.4 per cent higher than Curtin's estimate), and Robert Stein's reassessment of the eighteenth-century French trade (21.4 per cent higher than Curtin's figure). These modifications accounted for an additional 1,800,000 slaves, or so Inikori claimed. He also accepted Rout's "correction" of the Spanish-American import figure, even though Rout's figure was only a "guesstimate." Presumably, Inikori also converted Rout's import estimate into an export figure by allowing for losses in transit of 13 per cent, thereby accounting for approximately 660,000 more slaves. Finally, Inikori allowed a correction of almost 2,000,000 for other slaves which he claimed were exported to the Americas in the sixteenth and seventeenth centuries or otherwise were unrecorded in Curtin's estimates for the Portuguese trade. As will be demonstrated below, this kind of manipulation of statistics cannot be accepted. Inikori makes a basic mistake in mixing different sets of data without accounting for the duplication resulting from such a mixture.

James Rawley, following a different procedure, makes the same mistake of mixing data which overlap. His computation of a global figure for the slave trade is also considerably higher than Curtin's estimate for imports into the Americas (11,345,000 compared to Curtin's figure of 9,566,100). Rawley's method is more reliable than Inikori's, if the errors are corrected, and the results can be used as an alternative to the method employed in this article in reaching a global estimate. Rawley basically employs the same procedure as Curtin did in 1969—he estimates total slave imports into the Americas, attempting to bypass shipping data. Unfortunately, he did not remain true to this procedure in estimating the volume of imports into the British Caribbean, and he made a serious mathematical error in computing the Brazilian sector. These errors alone account for an excess of 1,110,000 slaves, so that an adjustment for these sectors alone reduces Rawley's global estimate to 10,235,000, which is well within range of Curtin's original projection. Rawley also makes allowance for 122,000 slaves shipped to other parts of the Atlantic basin, other than the Americas after 1600, which Curtin did not record. An adjustment in Curtin's global figure for this trade would bring Rawley's and Curtin's estimates even more into line.

The procedure I have followed differs from the methods employed by Curtin, Inikori and Rawley, although there is invariably some overlap between all approaches. I have essentially used Curtin's findings—with minor adjustments—before 1700 and have used the partial totals of a variety of scholars for the eighteenth and nineteenth centuries. For 1701–1810, these partial totals are based on the different sectors of the carrying trade, rather than on estimates for imports into different colonies. For most of the nineteenth century, my estimates are based on shipping data as analysed by David Eltis. The details of my calculations are discussed below, but it should be pointed out that when the revisions of the scholars who have worked on the various sectors of the trade are analysed, it becomes clear that the claims of Inikori, Rout and Rawley are indeed extreme. The volume of the Atlantic slave trade is here estimated at 11,698,000 slaves exported from Africa between 1450 and 1900 (Table 1). This total estimate for the export trade is then used to derive a figure for the number of slaves imported into the Americas and other parts of the Atlantic basin between 1450 and 1867 (excluding the offshore islands after 1600), which I calculate as 9,778,500 slaves. My import figure is then compared with the import estimates of Curtin, Inikori, Rawley and other scholars, and it is shown that my estimate is remarkably close to Curtin's original global estimate of 9,566,100. . . .

Table 1. *Slave exports from Africa: the Atlantic trade.*

Period	Volume	Per cent
1450–1600	367,000	3.1
1601–1700	1,868,000	16.0
1701–1800	6,133,000	52.4
1801–1900	3,330,000	28.5
Total	11,698,000	100.0

The Volume of Slave Imports into the Americas and Atlantic Basin

The impression that Curtin's census has been steadily revised upwards is based on a serious misunderstanding of the debate which has arisen since 1969. As I have demonstrated, many of the partial totals that Curtin developed have been revised, indeed some of them upwards by substantial amounts, but such increases in single components of the trade do not necessarily modify Curtin's original estimate of the total number of slaves imported into the Americas. Although his figure of 9,566,100 is often used for convenience, Curtin states that the total was "about ten million," with an allowance for error of several hundred thousand. He claimed that "it is extremely unlikely that the ultimate total will turn out to be less than 8,000,000 or more than 10,500,000." My synthesis of the partial totals supports Curtin's total estimate for imports into the Americas and the islands of the Atlantic basin.

The misunderstanding has arisen from a failure to distinguish between Curtin's various estimates for different portions of the export trade from Africa, on the one hand, and his overall projection for total imports into the Americas, on the other hand. Curtin did not attempt to reach a figure for total exports from Africa based on export data because of gaps in his material, although, as is evident from the preceding section of this article, it is now possible to calculate a figure which is based largely on export data. Revisions of Curtin's census have concentrated on partial totals, and the unwary scholar may well have been fooled by these revisions. After all, there is a logical connexion between the export trade and the level of imports—the difference being losses in transit. Nonetheless, upward revisions of the partial figures for slave exports do not necessarily affect Curtin's total estimate for slave imports, since revisions can cancel each other or fill in gaps in the export data. . . .

A comparison of Curtin's *Census* and the figures derived from the revisions suggests that Curtin's overall estimate was probably too high for the eighteenth century and too low for the nineteenth century, but the differences almost cancel each other. The difference for the whole trade is 212,000 slaves . . . and given the quality of the data, this difference is not very significant. Because the gross figures for slave imports are based on a combination of estimated slave populations in the Americas and shipping data, the difference between Curtin's 1969 *Census* and later revisions cannot be compared in a simple, straightforward way. Stein, Drescher, Anstey and Inikori appear to increase Curtin's estimate for 1701–1810 by several hundred thousand slaves, but Curtin's import-based estimates appear to have been too high by almost that amount. In order to estimate imports between 1701 and 1810, I have taken my figure for total exports and allowed for losses at sea on the order of 15 per cent. At the height of the British trade in the last three decades of the eighteenth century, losses were considerably less; hence a figure of 12 or 13 per cent may be more accurate. If 13 per cent is used, then the number of imports would have been 5,872,500 slaves, which would be closer to Curtin's original estimate for the volume of imports in this period. The difference between Curtin's original estimate and my revision would be 179,200 instead of 314,100 slaves. This change would mean that my estimate for imports would be 347,300 slaves greater than Curtin's figure—a global estimate of 9,913,000. Other changes in the estimates for losses at sea would affect the global figure, too; for this reason all that I am claiming is that the revisions made since 1969 do not significantly alter Curtin's original global estimate. The changes do require adjustments in the distribution of exports over time, however.

Revisions for the nineteenth century, for example, balance Curtin's overestimation for the eighteenth century. In reaching a total for the period after 1810, I have estimated imports for three distinct periods: firstly, 1811–20; secondly, 1821–43, and thirdly, 1844–67. In the first period 441,000 slaves were imported. This figure is derived as follows. Curtin estimated 127,700 slaves imported into Spanish America, the French Caribbean and the United States. Another 45,000 slaves came from Mozambique, primarily to Brazil (allowance is made for 25 per cent losses at sea). Another 218,000 slaves came from West-Central Africa, while 50,000 slaves were imported into Brazil from the Bight of Benin on Portuguese ships. In the 1821–43 period, following the work of Eltis, 1,300,000 slaves were imported, which allows for losses at sea of 10 per cent, and accounts for slaves who were liberated before reaching the Americas. Finally, 512,300 slaves were imported between 1844 and 1867. The period after 1820 is particularly well documented, and while Eltis has shown that Curtin's estimates need to be raised for the years

1821–43, the estimate for the last twenty-four years of the trade requires virtually no adjustment. As Eltis has noted for these years:

> the aggregate picture, for . . . African exports, is uncannily close to that drawn by Curtin. The latter estimated total imports in this period at 510,000 compared to estimates here of 511,750. But then the present researcher is not alone in having toiled through the archives only to finish up with data which largely confirm the broad estimates contained in the *Census*.

I have added another few hundred to account for Dutch exports from the Gold Coast, but such a minor adjustment only serves to confirm Eltis's sense of the uncanny.

Another way to estimate the total volume of imports is to adjust Curtin's original projection by incorporating the revisions of those scholars who have presented alternative figures for imports into the different receiving areas in the Americas. Rawley attempted to follow this procedure, but he confused the import totals for different colonies with the carrying trade of the various European countries. Nonetheless, if the figures for North America, Spanish America and Brazil are adjusted according to the findings of Fogel and Engerman, Vila Vilar and Eltis, a more accurate revision of Curtin's census can be obtained. At present, however, this revision must be considered tentative, for I have not attempted to assess the volume of imports into the majority of receiving areas. Inikori criticized Curtin's estimates for French Saint-Domingue, and it may well be that a thorough investigation of imports into the French Caribbean will result in an upward revision of Curtin's estimate. On the other hand, a review of Spanish America from 1640 to 1773 may require a downward revision of Curtin's estimate, despite Rout's claim to the contrary.

Present revisions of the estimates for slave imports into different receiving areas suggest that Curtin's figure should be raised by 600,000 slaves. Vila Vilar has accounted for an additional 135,600 slaves imported into Spanish America between 1595 and 1640. Fogel and Engerman have established that North American imports were probably 168,000 higher than Curtin allowed. Finally, Eltis has suggested that Curtin's import data for 1821–43 is too low, although it is difficult to establish a figure, since Curtin and Eltis made estimates for different periods. Eltis has estimated 511,750 slaves imported from 1844–67 and just under 1.3 million slaves from 1821–43, for a total of over 1.8 million for 1821–67. Curtin estimated 1,898,400 slaves imported from 1811 to 1870. As discussed above, I have estimated that 441,000 slaves were imported in the second decade of the nineteenth century; hence the difference between the revisions of Eltis and Curtin's original calculation is about 340,000 additional slaves.

As a rough guide, therefore, an estimate for the slave trade derived from import-based data is approximately 10,210,000 slaves, which is very close to the estimate suggested in Rawley's calculation, once his tables are corrected for errors. This rough estimate is, of course, still within the range of Curtin's original projection, and it provides some confirmation that my global total is of the right order of magnitude. Until additional research is done on the volume of imports into the different receiving areas, however, my global estimate for imports (9.8–9.9 million slaves) is preferred. Further revisions could well require the addition of another hundred thousand slaves or so in order to allow for the trade of the minor ports in France, Britain and elsewhere in the eighteenth century and the trade to the offshore islands (Madeira, Cape Verde, etc.) after 1600. Again it must be stressed, therefore, that my synthesis is only the next stage in the continuing effort to calculate the volume of the Atlantic slave trade.

Conclusion

There is no question that the Atlantic slave trade had a tremendous impact on Africa. Despite the probable error in the regional breakdown of slave shipments, this impact can be quantified in broad outline for virtually the whole of the trade. Western central Africa (the Angolan coast north to Cabinda) was drawn into the trade on a significant scale in the sixteenth century and remained a major exporting region until the end of the trade in the nineteenth century. The Bight of Benin became a second major source of slaves in the second half of the seventeenth century, and from there the trade spread westward to the Gold Coast by 1700 and eastward to the Bight of Biafra by the 1740s. The Sierra Leone coast, including the rivers to the north, was another focal point of the export trade, although the expansion of slave exports there grew relatively slowly until the middle of the eighteenth century, when for two decades exports were very large. Senegambia entered the trade early and retained a relatively fixed, but small, place in total exports until the nineteenth century. Southeast Africa, by contrast, was drawn in relatively late; only after the movement to end the slave trade began to have an impact was it advantageous to seek slaves so far from the Americas. The decline of slave exports occurred in parallel stages to the rise of the trade. The Gold Coast ceased to supply large numbers of slaves by the first decade of the nineteenth century, while the supplies from the Bight of Biafra fell off in the 1830s. The Bight of Benin and western-central Africa remained important sources of slaves until the 1850s, and southeastern Africa also continued to supply exports until the end.

While these broad patterns have been understood for some time, it is now possible to analyse internal African developments much more fully, now that Curtin's export figures have been revised and tested. Scholars are likely to modify these estimates further. For the time being, however, it can be expected that detailed studies of political, economic and social changes will attempt to correlate the volume of exports with local developments. Because slaves were a peculiar commodity, representing labour power lost to local societies as well as a commodity whose value could be exchanged on the international market, the export trade distorted the historical process in an equally peculiar way. Various scholars have attempted to analyse the nature of this distortion: Walter Rodney talked about the process in terms of underdevelopment; Fage has emphasized the political impact while attempting to minimize the demographic consequences; Inikori has argued that the trade retarded economic development, particularly because of severe demographic losses. I have argued that the growth of the export trade was related to the consolidation of a mode of production based on slavery. These examples are but a few of the many studies which take the "numbers game" seriously. Slaves were more than commodities and numbers, of course, which is a major reason why the study of slavery retains its significance.

A Skeptical View of How Much Can Be Known

DAVID HENIGE

No problem has exercised Africanists for so long and so heatedly as the slave trade. Now that any difference of opinion as to its morality has ended, debate tends to concentrate on its economic and political aspects, particularly on its magnitude and regional characteristics. In the past few scholarly generations, sophisticated statistical manipulations have supplied more evidence, but it has been concentrated on the number of slaves who arrived in the New World. Nonetheless, dearth of evidence (sometimes total) regarding the other components of the trade has not seemed to discourage efforts to arrive at global figures and, by extension, to determine its effects on African societies.

The present paper asks why this should be so, and wonders how any defensible conclusions can ever be reached about almost any facet of the trade that can go beyond ideology or truism. It concludes that no global estimate of the slave trade, or of any "underdevelopment" or "underpopulation" it may have caused, are possible, though carefully constructed micro-studies might provide limited answers. Under the circumstances, to believe or advocate any particular set or range of figures becomes an act of faith rather than an epistemologically sound decision. . . .

. . . Historians of the [slave] trade are more frequently succumbing to the temptation to widen their field of vision by contemplating the effects of the trade on West Africa, both *en gros* and in its parts. Success in this particular enterprise depends on a concomitant success in estimating the facets of the trade already discussed, as well as several others (e.g. ratio of males to females; differential regional impact of the trade within West Africa; the counter-active role of newly introduced New World food crops). Both with and without

---

Source: From "Measuring the Immeasurable: The Atlantic Slave Trade, West African Population and the Pyrrhonian Critic" by David Henige, in *Journal of African History* 27.2 (1986) excerpts from pp. 303–309, 312–313. Reprinted by permission of Cambridge University Press.

regard to the degree of that success, we can consider what the possibility might be of determining with any useful precision the impact of the trade on West Africa.

The obverse to knowing the number of West Africans killed or transported is to know how many were not, entailing some effort to determine the population of West Africa (or parts of it) during the centuries in question, as well as any trends in it that might be discernible or inferable. If it should be possible to do this, we could at least begin to assess the purely demographic implications of the trade. . . .

The usual procedure for determining both the levels of and trends in the historical population of West Africa has been to accept figures in colonial censuses and to project them backwards, in the process assuming various rates of natural increase (fertility less mortality) on the one hand, and rates of unnatural decrease (losses from the slave trade) on the other, with each tailored to fit the thrust of particular arguments. Three hypotheses have been mooted: that population remained fairly stable during the period; that it declined slightly in the eighteenth century before recovering slowly; and that it declined continuously throughout. In its own way each of these lines of thought illustrates the ultimate deficiency of the evidence on which it is based.

The argument of long-term equilibrium is of longest standing. It proceeds from belief in a figure of about 100 million for all of sub-Saharan Africa in the sixteenth century, of which West Africa is held to have constituted perhaps one-quarter to one-third. Both of these figures and the idea of stability have been borrowed from the literature of historical demography, where it seems not to be very firmly based. Caldwell has shown, for instance, that at least the figure is no more than a latter-day repetition of a hazard by a seventeenth-century author who, for his part, based it on nothing tangible at all. In turn Caldwell suggests a much lower figure, perhaps no more than 50 million, or about the same as Niane believes Mali alone possessed.

That West African population declined to one degree or another during the course of the eighteenth century is an almost inevitable conclusion from the fact that the Atlantic slave trade in that century constituted fully one-half of its whole. In hopes that technology might be made to intervene between the historian and his evidence to the advantage of the former, Patrick Manning has attempted to estimate what the extent of this decline might have been. Manning does not pretend that the task he has set is a simple one and is careful to make explicit both his postulates and their problematic aspects. In general none of his assumptions is inherently impossible, although some might quibble with at least his premise that males and females were captured in roughly equal numbers and that two of every three females remained in Africa whereas two of every three men did not. At any rate, Manning concludes that West Africa suffered a loss of in the neighbourhood of eight million persons from the slave trade, a figure that could not have been offset by natural growth rates.

If Manning's conclusions do not fly in the face of any known evidence, it is more difficult to characterize the views of the advocates of a continuous and even precipitate decline in West African population from the middle of the sixteenth century through the middle of the nineteenth. This argument has been championed most persistently by Inikori, who decides (there is no other word for it) that the mid-nineteenth-century population of West Africa was actually much lower than usually estimated, while that of three centuries earlier was even larger than Riccioli had imagined. Inikori goes so far as to argue that the earlier population was as large as it was because West Africa's land was fertile and its productivity high; its inhabitants were healthy and fecund and serious encounters with disease, famine, and drought were infrequent. On the other hand its later population was as low as it was *because* high levels of natural increase must be projected as far back as the middle of the nineteenth century. Those who feel that they detect a whiff of circularity in all this are not likely to be mistaken.

Indeed, all arguments dealing with West African population trends base themselves to one degree or another on adopting natural growth rates, which tend to be concocted to taste from ranges putatively provided by other pre-industrial societies or by twentieth-century Africa. In no other aspect of West African historical demography does argumentation beg the question more obstinately by confounding what is to be proved with what is to do the proving. The notion that West African population declined dramatically, whether or not as a result of the slave trade, is reminiscent of the current rage to attribute an even more dramatic depopulation to the post-contact New World. Both hypotheses are supported by the same amount of evidence: none.

On the other hand, it is only fair to point out that any other particular interpretation suffers from much the same handicap, and it becomes a nice question whether we are more justified to be moderate without cause than to be extreme without it. The unpalatable truth is that we have not the slightest idea (nor any hope of gaining it) of the population of any part of tropical Africa in the sixteenth or the seventeenth or the eighteenth centuries. Such ineffable ignorance is ordinarily considered an unpromising point from which to move on towards other hypotheses which require just the knowledge we lack.

However, this is clearly not the only recognized view of the appropriate relationship between hypothesis and evidence. A contrary methodology seeks to go beyond reconstructing what was, to dwell on what might have been; we see counterfactual argument recurring more frequently in this field (as in others). Based on widely divergent views of the number of individuals physically lost to West Africa (X in our equation) and linked to determining (for instance) what proportion of these were female, estimates of what *potential* losses resulted inevitably range widely.

The work of M.-L. Diop exemplifies one locus of this argument. Diop believes that on the eve of the slave trade Africa (and certainly West Africa) was able to (and therefore did) sustain populations more dense than that of contemporaneous western Europe and nearly as dense as those of "monsoon Asia" and that the population of the continent might have been as great as 270 million if not greater. Startling as this thesis is, even more startling is the manner in which Diop arrives at it. Her conclusion stated, Diop seeks to legitimate it by arguing that such a dense population *must have* been predicated on agrotechnological capabilities on a par with those of Europe at the time. She supplements this reasoning by arguing that "if [*sic*] the slave trade involved a loss on the order of 100,000,000 persons," then Africa's population "must have surpassed" the commonly cited figure of 100 million in the seventeenth century.

This dizzying confusion between cause and effect in argument serves as a prelude for her major counterfactual hypothesis: without the slave trade the population of Africa would now be about 1,800 million, or as much as eight times what it actually seems to be. In a similar vein, if on a somewhat smaller scale, Inikori adopts similar arguments for West Africa, concluding that the slave trade resulted in the (potential) loss of nearly 50 million people.

These breezy exercises in helical thinking ignore other constraints on population growth or dismiss them as "Malthusian" and therefore inappropriate. Both Diop and Inikori stoutly deny that disease played an important role in limiting West Africa's population growth before the seventeenth century, and even contend that the well-known climatic constraints of today were all but unknown earlier.

Conversely, taking advantage of the opportunity to base himself on actual evidence, Miller argues that, for West Central Africa at least, drought, famine, and disease were, in aggregate, more effective constraints on population growth than the slave trade. It does appear that from the sixteenth century West Africa became more humid, which should have (and maybe did) reduce the probability of frequent and severe droughts and famines. But any such blessing was not likely to have been unmixed since higher levels of humidity frequently bring with them a higher incidence of such diseases as malaria and plague.

It is no more easy to accept Inikori's contention that the centuries of the slave trade coincided with (and not accidentally) an increasing tempo of warfare in West Africa. To advance this argument is to turn a decidedly blind eye to the evidence of the *ta'rikhs* and other sources for the earlier history of the western Sudan, which are replete with accounts of warfare. Inikori's intuition of a *"Pax Askiana,"* rudely broken at the end of the sixteenth century, is ludicrously at odds with this evidence, which Inikori must impeach if he is to carry his point.

One taste of the heady heights of counterfactual reasoning often leads to another. The slave trade and its possible effects have come to be a cornerstone for those who wish to extend the concept of "underdevelopment" back beyond the colonial period. By lexicography "underdevelopment" is a counterfactual concept, and its proponents necessarily rely on their instincts as to what would have happened had Africa been allowed to proceed untouched through (in this case) the centuries of the slave trade. Inikori and Suret-Canale have criticized Fage and Curtin for failing to venture suitable opinions on this aspect of the trade, as though such silence constitutes more than a realization of the limitations in pressing such counterfactual arguments. One such misbegotten effort to do just this personifies well the inescapable hazards of adopting a form of argumentation which cannot be linked to evidence in any way.

A Skeptical View of Curtin's and Lovejoy's Calculations

JOSEPH E. INIKORI AND STANLEY L. ENGERMAN

Probably the aspect of the Atlantic slave trade that has received the most lively debate is its impact on African populations. The controversy begins with the numbers actually exported and ends with the interpretation of these numbers in terms of African historical demography. Disagreement about the numbers exported revolves around the estimate published over two decades ago by Philip Curtin based on the published data available at the time. Curtin's work served to raise questions about the then-available estimates based on earlier pamphleteers. Since 1969, detailed archival researches have been conducted on the volume of the traffic from particular ports, nations, and regions during particular time periods. Most of these researches have revised upward Curtin's original estimates, some by small, others by large margins. Nearly a decade ago, Paul Lovejoy provided a controversial synthesis of these researches, arriving at a global figure only slightly higher than Curtin's original estimate. However, further estimates since then, some still quite controversial, include those by Charles Becker, who has raised the estimate of the French trade by over 50 percent to about 1.5 million in total. Ivana Elbl presents an estimate for the Portuguese slave trade of the fifteenth and early sixteenth centuries (132,880 for 1450–1521) that suggests a doubling of Curtin's figures for the early period, raising the possibility of a further upward revision of his estimate. And David Richardson has raised Lovejoy's figures for the British trade in the eighteenth century by 342,700, although the magnitude of Richardson's adjustment is itself contested by Joseph Inikori. Inikori is now working on an estimate of the entire British trade from the seventeenth century to abolition. On the basis of these and other archival researches, many specialists believe that Curtin's original estimate has to be revised upward, but important disagreements on the magnitude of such revision remain; Lovejoy says that "the acceptable figures for the volume of the trade seem to inch upwards." But how fast is the movement, and what final level can we expect? Making inferences based on the results of archival researches since 1976, Joseph Inikori has suggested a global figure of 15.4 million. This figure has been contested by some scholars, and while the process of revision continues, it seems probable that the ultimate figure is unlikely to be less than 12 million or more than 20 million captives exported from Africa in the transatlantic slave trade.

Interpreting the export figures in terms of African historical demography has posed as much of a problem as the computation of the export volume. For many years scholars were uncertain about the age and sex ratios of the exported population. That issue is now very much settled. The overall female ratio turned out to be higher than many had thought: over 35%. But the magnitude of the mortality between the time of capture and the final departure of slave ships from the African coast, as well as the numbers of deaths occurring during the process of capture, and the magnitude of further deaths caused by sociopolitical upheavals associated with the procurement of captives remain uncertain. The demographic consequences of the Moroccan invasion of 1591 in the Niger Bend of the Western Sudan have been used as one gauge of the effects of sociopolitical upheavals on populations of precapitalist agricultural societies. Ultimately the main source of disagreement on the subject is the differing conceptual frameworks employed by the scholars. Some have used models, such as the Malthusian population theory, claiming that the populations of tropical African societies had reached the limit permissible by available resources by 1400. The demographic effects of the Atlantic slave trade have even been compared with the effects of emigration in the late nineteenth and early twentieth centuries from capitalist and semi-capitalist industrial countries. These kinds of comparison were criticized by Joseph Inikori over a decade ago, who argued that each mode of production has a demographic law specific to it, and that it is therefore unwise to compare demographic behavior in precapitalist, preindustrial agricultural societies with that of capitalist and industrial societies. It is also contended that tropical African societies were land-surplus (open resource) between 1400 and 1850, under the existing agricultural technology.

PART III

Contemporary Views of Slaving and Slavers

---------------- **VARIETY OF OPINION** ----------------

*With the help of the king ... [we] assaulted the town ...
[and] took 250 persons.*

JOHN HAWKINS, 1568

*For you ought to be informed, that markets of men are here
kept in the same manner as those of beasts with us.*

WILLEM BOSMAN, 1700

*One day, when ... only I and my dear sister were left to
mind the house, two men and a woman got over our walls,
and in a moment seized us both and ... ran off with us into
the nearest wood.*

OLAUDAH EQUIANO, C. 1756

*[Africans] are considered as a people to be robbed and
spoiled with impunity. ... [They] are cheated ... in every
possible way.*

JOHN NEWTON, C. 1745–1754

*They wanted to take the Dutch longboat, and kill the crew
[because] a Dutch ship some few days before had taken four
[of their] men.*

RICHARD STORY, 1767–1768

I cannot make war to catch slaves in the bush, like a thief.
OSEI BONSU, KING OF ASANTE, 1820

The king of a town sells whom he dislikes or fears; his wives and children are sold in turn by his successor.
EYO HONESTY II, KING OF CREEK TOWN,
OLD CALABAR, 1850

The words of eyewitnesses, the raw material from which history is crafted, can vividly evoke the times and places of the slave trade. The selections that follow, while including the views of European and African slave traders as well as of a person who was enslaved, are not numerous enough to document the entire scope of the slave trade but do suggest the range of its historical circumstances. These selections record the different ways in which people were enslaved—by capture in war, by kidnapping, by sale. They describe the bargaining for slaves along the African coast and the anguished circumstances of the "middle passage" from Africa to the Americas. For all their rich detail, such accounts must be used with care because they also may include distortions caused by the witnesses' prejudices or lapses of memory.

The oldest account is by John Hawkins (1532–1595) of Plymouth, England, who, backed by powerful investors, made three profitable slaving voyages to Guinea (as West Africa was then called) in the 1560s before becoming a member of Parliament and treasurer of the Royal Navy. This excerpt from his third voyage shows how trading and raiding were closely associated in the early decades of the English slave trade. Because Hawkins's force was not strong enough to attack an African community alone, success depended on finding an African ally who would cooperate with him—up to a point.

By 1700 slaving was a well-established business for both Europeans and Africans. Willem Bosman, the chief agent on the African coast of the important Dutch West India Company, wrote a series of letters about his experiences to a friend in Holland. The excerpt included here recounts how Europeans obtained slaves at Whydah, an important city-state on the Slave Coast, and how the enslaved Africans reacted to their treatment.

The eighteenth century is represented by two memoirs that were written decades after the events described and were published as part of the campaign against the slave trade. Olaudah Equiano's vivid autobiography, a rare account from the African side of the Atlantic slave trade, narrates how he was sold from hand to hand during the six months between his kidnapping (c. 1756) from his home among the Ibo people of southeastern Nigeria and his sale to white slavers at the coast. Transported to Barbados when about twelve years old, he was sold in rapid succession to a planter in Virginia and then to a British naval officer, who gave him to a British sea captain from whom Equiano learned the seaman's trade. After a decade in slavery, he bought his freedom with money he had earned from trading between different ports, and then he worked on voyages to Turkey, Greenland, and the Arctic. In later life he married and settled in England, where he actively pursued abolitionist causes.

At about the same time that Equiano was sold from Lower Guinea, the young Englishman John Newton was working on slaving ships trading up the coast at Sierra Leone. He later underwent a religious conversion and, at the time of his writing, served as rector of an Anglican parish in England. In the passages reprinted here, Newton describes the physical and moral effects of the trade on the whites who participated in it, the sharp dealing in the buying of slaves, the foul conditions aboard the ships, and the risks of insurrection.

A third eighteenth-century account is from the testimony of Richard Story, a lieutenant in the Royal Navy, to a parliamentary committee investigating the slave trade in 1791. His memories of voyages in West Africa in 1766–1770 remind us that the violent seizures and reprisals of Hawkins's era did not disappear from slaving, however much buying and selling slaves came to predominate.

The nineteenth century is represented by two West African rulers' reflections on the slave trade that had just been brought to an end by British actions. Osei Bonsu, king of the powerful Asante empire that dominated the hinterland of the Gold Coast, expresses puzzlement to the British representative Joseph Dupuis at Britain's motives for stopping the purchase of slaves, and Bonsu comments on the proper role of a king in selling slaves. Three decades later, similar views are voiced by King Eyo Honesty II, the head of Creek Town and the most powerful man in the three Efik trading communities known to Europeans as Old Calabar. Well familiar with the conduct

of the slave trade, Eyo describes the personal horrors of the strong
preying on the weak. Eyo is responding to criticisms made about
slavery's continuation in Old Calabar by a resident Scottish missionary, Hope Waddell, a close friend who recorded Eyo's words in his
journal.

An Alliance to Raid for Slaves, 1568

JOHN HAWKINS

The ships departed from Plymouth, the second day of October, Anno
1567 and . . . arrived at Cape Verde, the eighteenth of November:
where we landed 150 men, hoping to obtain some Negroes, where
we got but few, and those with great hurt and damage to our men,
which chiefly proceeded of their envenomed arrows: and although
in the beginning they seemed to be but small hurts, yet there hardly
escaped any that had blood drawn of them, but died in strange sort,
with their mouths shut some ten days before they died, and after
their wounds were whole; where I myself had one of the greatest
wounds, yet thanks be to God, escaped. From thence we passed the
time upon the coast of Guinea, unto Sierra Leone, till the twelfth of
January, in which time we had not gotten together a hundred and
fifty Negroes: yet notwithstanding the sickness of our men, and the
late time of the year commanded us away; and thus having nothing
wherewith to seek the coast of the West Indies, I was with the rest of
the company in consultation to go to the coast of the Mine [i.e., the
Gold Coast], hoping there to have obtained some gold for our wares,
and thereby to have defrayed our charge. But even in that present
instant, there came to us a Negro, sent from a king, oppressed by
other kings, his neighbors, desiring our aid, with [the] promise that
as many Negroes as by these wars might be obtained, as well of his
part as of ours, should be at our pleasure; whereupon we concluded
to give aid, and sent 120 of our men, which the 15 of January, as-

Source: From "The third troublesome voyage . . . to the parts of Guinea, and the
West Indies, in the yeeres 1567 and 1568 by M. John Hawkins," in *The Principal
Navigations, Voyages, Traffiques and Discoveries of the English Nation,* pp. 53–
55, by Richard Hakluyt, New York, 1928. Spelling has been modernized.

saulted a town of the Negroes of our ally's adversaries, which had in it 8,000 inhabitants, being very strongly impaled and fenced after their manner, but it was so well defended, that our men prevailed not, but lost six men and forty hurt: so that our men sent forthwith to me for more help: whereupon considering the good success of this enterprise might highly further the commodity of our voyage, I went myself, and with the help of the king of our side, assaulted the town, both by land and sea, and very hardly with fire (their houses being covered with dry palm leaves) obtained the town, put the inhabitants to flight, where we took 250 persons, men, women, & children, and by our friend the king of our side, there were taken 600 prisoners, whereof we hoped to have our choice: but the Negro (in whose nation is seldom or never found truth) meant nothing less: for that night he removed his camp and prisoners, so that we were fain to content us with those few which we had gotten ourselves.

Trading on the Slave Coast, 1700

WILLEM BOSMAN

The first business of one of our factors [agents] when he comes to Fida [Whydah], is to satisfy the customs of the king and the great men, which amounts to about a hundred pounds in Guinea value, as the goods must yield there. After which we have free license to trade, which is published throughout the whole land by the crier.

But yet before we can deal with any person, we are obliged to buy the king's whole stock of slaves at a set price, which is commonly one third or one fourth higher than ordinary; after which, we obtain free leave to deal with all his subjects, of what rank soever. But if there happen to be no stock of slaves, the factor must then resolve to run the risk of trusting the inhabitants with goods to the value of one or two hundred slaves; which commodities they send into the inland country, in order to buy with them slaves at all markets, and

Source: From *A New and Accurate Description of the Coast of Guinea, Divided into the Gold, Slave, and the Ivory Coasts,* pp. 339–345, by William Bosman, translated from the Dutch, 2nd edition, London, 1721. Spelling and some punctuation have been modernized.

that sometimes two hundred miles deep in the country. For you ought to be informed, that markets of men are here kept in the same manner as those of beasts with us.

Not a few in our country fondly imagine that parents here sell their children, men their wives, and one brother the other. But those who think so, do deceive themselves; for this never happens on any other account but that of necessity, or some great crime; but most of the slaves that are offered to us, are prisoners of war, which are sold by the victors as their booty.

When these slaves come to Fida, they are put in prison all together; and when we treat concerning buying them, they are all brought out together in a large plain; where, by our surgeons, whose province it is, they are thoroughly examined, even to the smallest member, and that naked both men and women, without the least distinction or modesty. Those that are approved as good, are set on one side; and the lame or faulty are set by as invalids, which are here called *mackrons:* these are such as are above five and thirty years old, or are maimed in the arms, legs or feet; have lost a tooth, are grey-haired, or have films over their eyes; as well as all those which are affected with any venereal distemper, or several other diseases.

The invalids and the maimed being thrown out, as I have told you, the remainder are numbered, and it is entered who delivered them. In the meanwhile, a burning iron, with the arms or name of the companies, lies in the fire, with which ours are marked on the breast. This is done that we may distinguish them from the slaves of the English, French, or others (which are also marked with their mark), and to prevent the Negroes exchanging them for worse, at which they have a good hand. I doubt not but this trade seems very barbarous to you, but since it is followed by mere necessity, it must go on; but we yet take all possible care that they are not burned too hard, especially the women, who are more tender than the men.

We are seldom long detained in the buying of these slaves, because their price is established, the women being one fourth or fifth part cheaper than the men. The disputes which we generally have with the owners of these slaves are, that we will not give them such goods as they ask for them, especially the *boesies* [cowry shells] (as I have told you, the money of this country) of which they are very fond, though we generally make a division on this head, in order to make one part of the goods help off another; because those slaves which are paid for in *boesies,* cost the company one half more than those bought with other goods. . . .

When we have agreed with the owners of the slaves, they are returned to their prison; where, from that time forwards, they are kept at our charge, cost us two pence a day a slave; which serves to subsist them, like our criminals, on bread and water: so that to save charges, we send them on board our ships with the very first opportunity, before which their masters strip them of all they have on their backs; so that they come to us stark-naked, as well women as men: in which condition they are obliged to continue, if the master of the ship is not so charitable (which he commonly is) as to bestow something on them to cover their nakedness.

You would really wonder to see how these slaves live on board; for though their number sometimes amounts to six or seven hundred, yet by the careful management of our masters of ships, they are so [well] regulated, that it seems incredible. And in this particular our nation exceeds all other Europeans; for as the French, Portuguese, and English slave-ships are always foul and stinking; on the contrary, ours are for the most part clean and neat.

The slaves are fed three times a day with indifferent good victuals, and much better than they eat in their own country. Their lodging place is divided into two parts; one of which is appointed for the men, the other for the women, each sex being kept apart. Here they lie as close together as it is possible for them to be crowded.

We are sometimes sufficiently plagued with a parcel of slaves which come from a far inland country, who very innocently persuade one another, that we buy them only to fatten, and afterwards eat them as a delicacy. When we are so unhappy as to be pestered with many of this sort, they resolve and agree together (and bring over the rest of their party) to run away from the ship, kill the Europeans, and set the vessel ashore; by which means they design to free themselves from being our food.

I have twice met with this misfortune; and the first time proved very unlucky to me, I not in the least suspecting it; but the uproar was timely quashed by the master of the ship and myself, by causing the abettor to be shot through the head, after which all was quiet.

But the second time it fell heavier on another ship, and that chiefly by the carelessness of the master, who having fished up the anchor of a departed English ship, had laid it in the hold where the male slaves were lodged, who, unknown to any of the ship's crew, possessed themselves of a hammer, with which, in a short time they broke all their fetters in pieces upon the anchor: After this, they came above deck, and fell upon our men, some of whom they grievously wounded, and would certainly have mastered the ship, if a French and English ship had not very fortunately happened to lie by us; who perceiving by our firing a distressed-gun, that something was in disorder on board, immediately came to our assistance with shallops and men, and drove the slaves under deck: notwithstanding which, before all was appeased, about twenty of them were killed.

The Portuguese have been more unlucky in this particular than we; for in four years time they lost four ships in this manner.

Kidnapped, Enslaved, and Sold Away, c. 1756

OLAUDAH EQUIANO

That part of Africa, known by the name of Guinea, to which the trade for slaves is carried on, extends along the coast above 3,400 miles from Senegal to Angola, and includes a variety of kingdoms. Of these the most considerable is the kingdom of Benin, both as to extent and wealth. . . . This kingdom is divided into many provinces or districts: in one of the most remote and fertile of which I was born, in the year 1745, situated in a charming fruitful vale, named Essaka. The distance of this province from the capital of Benin and the sea coast must be very considerable; for I had never heard of white men or Europeans, nor of the sea. . . .

I have already acquainted the reader with the time and place of my birth. My father, besides many slaves, had a numerous family, of which seven lived to grow up, including myself and a sister, who was the only daughter. As I was the youngest of the sons, I became the favourite with my mother, and was always with her; and she used to take particular pains to form my mind. I was trained up from my earliest years in the arts of agriculture and war: my daily exercise was shooting and throwing javelins; and my mother adorned me with emblems, after the manner of our greatest warriors. In this way I grew up till I was turned the age of eleven, when an end was put

Source: Excerpts from *The Interesting Narrative of the Life of Olaudah Equiano, or Gustavus Vassa, the African*, 6th edition, London, 1793, pp. 3–4, 31–33, 41, 45–49, 51–53.

Olaudah Equiano. From the 1793 edition of his autobiography. (Royal Albert Memorial Museum, Exeter, England)

to my happiness in the following manner:—Generally, when the grown people of the neighbourhood were gone far in the fields to labour, the children assembled together in some of the neighbours [*sic*] premises to play; and commonly some of us used to get up a tree to look out for any assailant, or kidnapper, that might come upon us; for they sometimes took those opportunities of our parents' absence, to attack and carry off as many as they could seize. . . . One day, when all our people were gone out to their works as usual, and only I and my dear sister were left to mind the house, two men and a woman got over our walls, and in a moment seized us both and, without giving us time to cry out, or to make resistance, they stopped our mouths, and ran off with us into the nearest wood. Here they tied our hands, and continued to carry us as far as they could, till night came on, when we reached a small house, where the robbers halted for refreshment, and spent the night. We were then unbound, but were not able to take any food; and, being quite overpowered by fatigue and grief, our only relief was some sleep, which allayed our misfortune for a short time. The next morning we left the house, and continued travelling all the day. For a long time we had kept to the woods, but at last we came to a road which I believed I knew. I now had some hopes of being delivered; for we had advanced but a little way before I discovered some people at a distance, on which I began to cry out for their assistance; but my cries had no other effect than to make them tie me faster and stop my mouth, and then put me in a large sack. They also stopped my sister's mouth, and tied her hands, and in this manner we proceeded till we were out of the sight of these people. When we went to rest the following night they offered us some victuals; but we refused them; and the only comfort we had was in being in one another's arms all that night, and bathing each other with our tears. But alas! we were soon deprived of even the smallest comfort of weeping together. The next day proved a day of greater sorrow than I had yet experienced; for my sister and I were separated, while we lay clasped in each other's arms: it was in vain that we besought them not to part us: she was torn from me, and immediately carried away, while I was in such a state of distraction not to be described. I cried and grieved continually; and for several days did not eat any thing but what they forced into my mouth. At length, after many days travelling, during which I had often changed masters, I got into the hands of a chieftain, in a very pleasant country. . . .

I was again sold and carried through a number of places, till, after travelling a considerable time, I came to a town called Timneh, in the most beautiful country I had yet seen in Africa. It was extremely rich, and there were many rivulets which flowed through it, and supplied a large pond in the centre of the town, where the people washed. Here I first saw and tasted cocoa nuts, which I thought superior to any nuts I had ever tasted before; and the trees, which were loaded, were also interspersed among the houses, which had commodious shades adjoining and were in the same manner as ours, the insides being neatly plastered and whitewashed. Here I also saw and tasted for the first time sugar-cane. Their money consisted of little white shells the size of a finger nail. I was sold here for one hundred seventy-two of them by a merchant who lived and brought me there. . . .

At last I came to the banks of a large river, which was covered with canoes in which the people appeared to live with their household utensils and provisions of all kinds. I was beyond measure astonished at this, as I had never before seen any water larger than a pond or a rivulet; and my surprise was mingled with no small fear when I was put into one of those canoes, and we began to paddle and move along the river. We continued going on thus till night; and when we came to land, and made fires on the banks. . . . Thus I continued to travel, sometimes by land, sometimes by water, through several different countries, and various nations, till, at the end of six months after I had been kidnapped, I arrived at the sea coast. . . .

The first object which saluted my eyes when I arrived on the coast was the sea, and a slave ship, which was then riding at anchor, and waiting for its cargo. These filled me with astonishment, which was soon converted into terror, which I am yet at a loss to describe nor the then feelings of my mind. When I was carried on board I was immediately handled, and tossed up, to see if I were sound by some of the crew; and I was now persuaded that I had got into a world of bad spirits, and that they were going to kill me. Their complexions too differing so much from ours, their long hair, and the language they spoke, which was very different from any I had ever heard, united to confirm me in this belief. Indeed, such were the horrors of my views and fears at the moment, that, if ten thousand worlds had been my own, I would have parted with them all to have exchanged my condition with that of the meanest slave in my own country. When I looked around the ship too, and saw a large furnace or copper boiling, and a multitude of black people of every description chained together, every one of their countenances expressing dejection and sorrow, I no longer doubted of my fate; and, quite overpowered with horror and anguish, I fell motionless on the deck and fainted. When I recovered a little, I found some black people about me, who, I believed were some of those who brought me on board, and had been receiving their pay; they talked to me in order to cheer me, but all in vain. I asked them if we were not to be eaten by those white men with horrible looks, red faces, and long hair? They told me I was not; and one of the crew brought me a small portion of spirituous liquor in a wine glass; but, being afraid of him, I would not take it out of his hand. One of the blacks therefore took it from him, and gave it to me, and I took a little down my palate, which, instead of reviving me, as they thought it would, threw me into the greatest consternation at the strange feeling it produced, having never tasted any such liquor before. Soon after this, the blacks who brought me on board went off, and left me abandoned to despair. I now saw myself deprived of any chance of returning to my native country, or even the least glimpse of hope of gaining the shore, which I now considered as friendly; and I even wished for my former slavery, in preference to my present situation, which was filled with horrors or every kind, still heightened by my ignorance of what I was to undergo. I was not long suffered to indulge my grief; I was soon put down under the decks, and there I received such a salutation in my nostrils as I had never experienced in my life; so that, with the loathsomeness of the stench, and crying together, I became so sick and low that I was not able to eat, nor had I the least desire to taste any thing. I now wished for the last friend, Death, to relieve me; but soon, to my grief, two of the white men offered me eatables; and, on my refusing to eat, one of them held me fast by the hands, and laid me across, I think, the windlass, and tied my feet, while the other flogged me severely. I had never experienced any thing of this kind before; and, although not used to the water, I naturally feared that element the first time I saw it, yet, nevertheless, could I have got over the nettings, I would have jumped over the side, but I could not; and, besides, the crew used to watch us very closely who were not chained down to the decks, lest we should leap into the water: and I have seen some of these poor African prisoners severely cut for attempting to do so, and hourly whipped for not eating. This indeed was often the case with myself. In a little time after, amongst the poor chained men I found some of my own nation, which in a small degree gave ease to my mind. I inquired of them what was to be done with us? They gave me to understand we were to be carried to these white people's country to work for them. I was then a little revived, and thought if it were no worse than working, my situation was not so desperate: but still I feared I should be put to death, the white people looked and acted, as I thought, in so savage a manner; for I had never seen among any people such instances of brutal cruelty; and this not only shewn toward us blacks, but also to some of the whites themselves. One white man in particular I saw, when we were permitted [*sic*] to be on deck, flogged so unmercifully that he died in consequence of it; and they tossed him over the side as they would have done to a brute. This made me fear these people the more; and I expected nothing less than to be treated in the same manner. . . .

The stench of the hold while we were on the coast was so intolerably loathsome, that it was dangerous to remain there for any time, and some of us had been permitted to stay on the deck for the fresh air; but now that the whole ship's cargo were confined together, it became absolutely pestilential. The closeness of the place, and the heat of the climate, added to the number in the ship, which was so crowded that each had scarcely room to turn himself, almost suffocated us. This produced copious perspirations, so that the air became unfit for respiration, from a variety of loathsome smells, and brought on a sickness amongst the slaves, of which many died, thus falling victims to the improvident avarice, as I may call it, of their purchasers. This wretched situation was again aggravated by the galling of the chains, now become insupportable; and the filth of the necessary tubs, into which the children often fell, and were almost suffocated. The shrieks of the women and the groans of the dying, rendered the whole a scene of horror almost inconceivable. Happily perhaps for myself I was soon reduced so low here that it was thought necessary to keep me almost always on deck; and from my extreme youth I was not put in fetters. In this situation I expected every hour to share the fate of my companions, some of whom were almost daily brought on deck at the point of death, which I began to hope would soon put an end to my miseries. Often did I think many of the inhabitants of the deep much more happy than myself; I envied them the freedom they enjoyed, and as often wished I could change my condition for theirs. Every circumstance I met with served only to render my state more painful, and heightened my apprehensions and my opinion of the cruelty of the whites. One day they had taken a number of fishes, and when they had killed and satisfied themselves with as many as they thought fit, to our astonishment who were on the deck, rather than give any of them to us to eat, as we expected, they tossed the remaining fish into the sea again, although we begged and prayed for some as well as we could, but in vain; some of my countrymen, being possessed by hunger, took an opportunity, when they thought no one saw them of trying to get a little privately, but they were discovered, and the attempt procured them some very severe floggings.

One day, when we had a smooth sea, and moderate wind, two of my wearied countrymen, who were chained together (I was near them at the time), preferring death to such a life of misery, somehow made through the nettings, and jumped into the sea; immediately another quite dejected fellow, who, on account of his illness was suffered to be out of irons, also followed their example; and I believe many more would very soon have done the same, if they had not been prevented by the ship's crew who were instantly alarmed. Those of us that were the most active were in a minute put down under the deck; and there was such a noise and confusion amongst the people of the ship as I have never heard before, to stop her, and get the boat out to go after the slaves. However, two of the wretches were drowned, but they got the other, and afterwards flogged him unmercifully, for thus attempting to prefer death to slavery. In this manner we continued to undergo more hardships than I can now relate; hardships which are inseparable from this accursed trade.

A Reformed Slave Trader's Regrets, c. 1745–1754

JOHN NEWTON

I hope it will always be a subject of humiliating reflection to me, that I was once an active instrument in a business at which my heart now shudders. My headstrong passions and follies plunged me, in early life, into a succession of difficulties and hardships, which at length, reduced me to seek a refuge among the natives of Africa. There, for about the space of eighteen months, I was in effect, though without the name, a captive, and slave myself; and was depressed to the lowest degree of human wretchedness. Possibly I should not have been so completely miserable, had I lived among the natives only, but it was my lot to reside with white men; for at that time several persons of my own colour and language were settled upon that part of the Windward coast which lies between Sierra Leon and Cape Mount; for the purpose of purchasing and collecting slaves, to sell to the vessels that arrived from Europe.

This is a bourn from which few travellers return, who have once determined to venture upon a temporary residence there; but the good providence of God, without my expectation, and almost

Source: From *Thoughts upon the African Slave Trade*, pp. 98–107, by John Newton, London, 1788.

against my will, delivered me from those scenes of wickedness and woe; and I arrived at Liverpool, in May 1748. I soon revisited the place of my captivity, as mate of a ship, and, in the year 1750, I was appointed commander; in which capacity I made three voyages to the Windward coast for slaves.

I first saw the coast of Guinea, in the year 1745, and took my last leave of it in 1754. It was not, intentionally, a farewell; but, through the mercy of God, it proved so. I fitted out for a fourth voyage, and was upon the point of sailing, when I was arrested by a sudden illness, and I resigned the ship to another captain.

Thus I was unexpectedly freed from this disagreeable service. Disagreeable I had long found it; but I think I should have quitted it sooner, had I considered it as I now do, to be unlawful and wrong. But I never had a scruple upon this head at the time; nor was such a thought once suggested to me by any friend. What I did I did ignorantly; considering it as the line of life which Divine Providence had allotted me, and having no concern, in point of conscience, but to treat the slaves, while under my care, with as much humanity as a regard to my own safety would admit.

The experience and observation of nine years, would qualify me for being a competent witness upon this subject, could I safely trust to the report of memory, after an interval of more than thirty-three years. But, in the course of so long a period, the ideas of past scenes and transactions grow indistinct; and I am aware, that what I have seen, and what I have only heard related, may, by this time, have become so insensibly blended together, that, in some cases, it may be difficult for me, if not impossible, to distinguish them with absolute certainty. It is, however, my earnest desire, and will, therefore, engage my utmost care, that I may offer nothing in writing, as from my own knowledge, which I could not cheerfully, if requisite, confirm upon oath. . . .

For the sake of method, I could wish to consider the African trade,—first, with regard to the effect it has upon our own people; and secondly, as it concerns the blacks, or, as they are more contemptuously styled, the negro slaves, whom we purchase upon the coast. But these two topics are so interwoven together, that it will not be easy to keep them exactly separate.

1. The first point I shall mention is surely of political importance, if the lives of our fellow-subjects be so; and if a rapid loss of seamen deserves the attention of a maritime people. This loss, in the African

trade, is truly alarming. I admit, that many of them are cut off in their first voyage, and consequently, before they can properly rank as seamen; though they would have been seamen if they had lived. But the neighbourhood of our seaports is continually drained of men and boys to supply the places of those who die abroad; and if they are not all seamen, they are all our brethren and countrymen, subjects of the British government.

The people who remain on ship-board, upon the open coast, if not accustomed to the climate, are liable to the attack of an inflammatory fever, which is not often fatal, unless the occurrence of unfavorable circumstances makes it so. When this danger is over, I think they might probably be as healthy as in most other voyages, provided they could be kept from sleeping in the dews, from being much exposed to the rain, from the intemperate use of spirits, and especially from women.

But considering the general disposition of our sailors, and the nature of the slave trade, these provisoes are of little more significance than if I should say upon another occasion, that Great Britain would be a happy country, *provided* all the inhabitants were wise and good. The sailors *must be* much exposed to the weather; especially on the Windward coast, where a great part of the cargo is procured by boats, which are often sent to the distance of thirty or forty leagues, and are sometimes a month before they return. Many vessels arrive upon the coast before the rainy season, which continues from about May to October, is over; and if trade be scarce, the ships which arrive in the fair or dry season, often remain till the rains return, before they can complete their purchase. A proper shelter from the weather, in an open boat, when the rain is incessant, night and day, for weeks and months, is impracticable.

I have, myself, in such a boat, been, five or six days together, without, as we say, a dry thread about me, sleeping or waking. And, during the fair season, tornadoes, or violent storms of wind, thunder, and heavy rain, are very frequent, though they seldom last long. In fact, the boats seldom return, without bringing some of the people ill of dangerous fevers or fluxes, occasioned either by the weather, or by unwholesome diet, such as the crude fruits and palm wine, with which they are plentifully supplied by the natives.

Strong liquors, such as brandy, rum, or English spirits, the sailors cannot often procure, in such quantities as to hurt them; but they will if they can; and opportunities sometimes offer, especially to those who are in the boats: for strong liquor being an article much in demand, so that without it scarcely a single slave can be purchased, it is always at hand. And if what is taken from the casks or bottles that are for sale, be supplied with water, they are as full as they were before. The blacks who buy the liquor, are the losers by the adulteration; but often the people who cheat them are the greatest sufferers.

The article of women, likewise, contributes largely to the loss of our seamen. When they are on shore, they often, from their known thoughtless imprudence, involve themselves, on this account, in quarrels with the natives, and, if not killed upon the spot, are frequently poisoned. On shipboard they may be restrained, and in some ships they are; but such restraint is far from being general. It depends much upon the disposition and attention of the captain. When I was in the trade I knew several commanders of African ships who were prudent, respectable men, and who maintained a proper discipline and regularity in their vessels; but there were too many of a different character. In some ships, perhaps in the most, the licence allowed in this particular, was almost unlimited. Moral turpitude was seldom considered, but they who took care to do the ship's business, might, in other respects, do what they pleased. These excesses, if they do not induce fevers, at least render the constitution less able to support them; and lewdness, too frequently, terminates in death.

The risk of insurrections is to be added. These, I believe, are always meditated; for the men slaves are not easily reconciled to their confinement and treatment; and, if attempted, they are seldom suppressed without considerable loss; and sometimes they succeed, to the destruction of a whole ship's company at once. Seldom a year passes, but we hear of one or more such catastrophes; and we likewise hear, sometimes of Whites and Blacks involved, in one moment, in one common ruin, by the gunpowder taking fire, and blowing up the ship.

How far the several causes I have enumerated, may respectively operate, I cannot say; the fact, however, is sure, that a great number of our seamen perish in the slave trade. Few ships, comparatively, are either blown up, or totally cut off; but some are. Of the rest, I have known some that have lost half their people, and some a larger proportion. I am far from saying, that it is always, or even often, thus; but, I believe I shall state the matter sufficiently low, if I suppose, that at least one-fifth part of those who go from England to the coast of Africa, in ships which trade for slaves, never return from thence. I dare not depend too much upon my memory, as to the number of ships and men employed in the slave trade more than thirty years ago; nor do I know what has been the state of the trade since; therefore I shall not attempt to make calculations. But, as I cannot but form some opinion upon the subject, I judge it probable, that the collective sum of seamen, who go from all our ports to Africa within the course of a year (taking Guinea into the extensive sense, from Goree or Gambia, and including the coast of Angola), cannot be less than eight thousand; and if, upon an average of ships and seasons, a fifth part of these die, the annual loss is fifteen hundred. I believe those who have taken pains to make more exact inquiries, will deem my supposition to be very moderate.

Thus much concerning the first evil, the loss of seamen and subjects, which the nation sustains by the African slave trade.

2. There is a second, which either is, or ought to be, deemed of importance, considered in a political light: I mean, the dreadful effects of this trade upon the minds of those who are engaged in it. There are, doubtless, exceptions; and I would willingly except myself. But in general, I know of no method of getting money, not even that of robbing for it upon the highway, which has so direct a tendency to efface the moral sense, to rob the heart of every gentle and humane disposition, and to harden it, like steel, against all impressions of sensibility.

Usually, about two-thirds of a cargo of slaves are males. When a hundred and fifty or two hundred stout men, torn from their native land, many of whom never saw the sea, much less a ship, till a short space before they had embarked; who have, probably, the same natural prejudice against a white man, as we have against a black; and who often bring with them an apprehension they are bought to be eaten: I say, when thus circumstanced, it is not to be expected that they will tamely resign themselves to their situation. It is always taken for granted, that they will attempt to gain their liberty if possible. Accordingly, as we dare not trust them, we receive them on board, from the first as enemies; and, before their number exceeds, perhaps, ten or fifteen, they are all put in irons; in most ships, two and two together. And frequently, they are not thus confined, as they might most conveniently stand or move, the right hand and foot of one to the left of the other, but across; that is, the hand and foot of each on the same side, whether right or left, are fettered together: so that they cannot move either hand or foot, but with great caution, and with perfect consent. Thus they must sit, walk, and lie, for many months (sometimes for nine or ten), without any mitigation or relief, unless they are sick.

In the night, they are confined below; in the daytime (if the weather be fine) they are upon deck; and as they are brought by pairs, a chain is put through a ring upon their irons, and this likewise locked down to the ringbolts, which are fastened, at certain intervals, upon the deck. These, and other precautions, are no more than necessary; especially, as while the number of slaves increases, that of the people who are to guard them, is diminished, by sickness, or death, or by being absent in the boats: so that, sometimes, not ten men can be mustered, to watch, night and day, over two hundred, besides having all the other business of the ship to attend.

That these precautions are so often effectual, is much more to be wondered at, than that they sometimes fail. One unguarded hour, or minute, is sufficient to give the slaves the opportunity they are always waiting for. An attempt to rise upon the ship's company, brings on instantaneous and horrid war: for, when they are once in motion, they are desperate; and where they do not conquer, they are seldom quelled without much mischief and bloodshed on both sides.

Sometimes, when the slaves are ripe for an insurrection, one of them will impeach the affair; and then necessity, and the state policy, of these small but most absolute governments, enforce maxims directly contrary to the nature of things. The traitor to the cause of liberty is caressed, rewarded, and deemed an honest fellow. The patriots, who formed and animated the plan, if they can be found out, must be treated as villains, and punished, to intimidate the rest. These punishments, in their nature and degree, depend upon the sovereign will of the captain. Some are content with inflicting such moderate punishment as may suffice for an example. But unlimited power, instigated by revenge, and where the heart, by a long familiarity with the sufferings of slaves, is become callous, and insensible to the pleadings of humanity, is terrible!

I have seen them sentenced to unmerciful whippings, continued till the poor creatures have not had power to groan under their misery, and hardly a sign of life has remained. I have seen them agonizing for hours, I believe for days together, under the torture of the thumbscrews; a dreadful engine, which, if the screw be turned by an unrelenting hand, can give intolerable anguish. There have been instances in which cruelty has proceeded still further; but, as I hope they are few, and I can mention but one from my own knowledge, I shall but mention it.

I have often heard a captain, who has been long since been [*sic*] dead, boast of his conduct in a former voyage, when his slaves attempted to rise upon him. After he had suppressed the insurrection, he sat in judgment upon the insurgents; and not only, in cold blood, adjudged several of them, I know not how many, to die, but studied, with no small attention, how to make death as excruciating as possible. For my reader's sake, I suppress the recital of particulars.

Surely, it must be allowed, that they who are long conversant with such scenes as these, are liable to imbibe a spirit of ferociousness, and savage insensibility, of which human nature, depraved as it is, is not, ordinarily, capable. If these things be true, the reader will admit the possibility of a fact that was in current report when I was upon the coast, and the truth of which, though I cannot now authenticate it, I have no reason to doubt.

A mate of a ship in a long-boat, purchased a young woman, with a fine child, of about a year old, in her arms. In the night, the child cried much, and disturbed his sleep. He rose up in great anger, and swore, that if the child did not cease making such a noise, he would presently silence it. The child continued to cry. At length he rose up a second time, tore the child from the mother, and threw it into the sea. The child was soon silenced indeed, but it was not so easy to pacify the woman: she was too valuable to be thrown overboard, and he was obliged to bear the sound of her lamentations, till he could put her on board his ship.

I am persuaded that every tender mother, who feasts her eyes and her mind when she contemplates the infant in her arms, will commiserate the poor Africans. But why do I speak of one child, when we have heard and read a melancholy story, too notoriously true to admit of contradiction, of more than a hundred grown slaves, thrown into the sea, at one time, from on board a ship, when fresh water was scarce; to fix the loss upon the underwriters, which otherwise, had they died on board, must have fallen upon the owners of the vessel. These instances are specimens of the spirit produced, by the African trade, in men, who, once, were no more destitute of the milk of human kindness than ourselves.

Hitherto, I have considered the condition of the men slaves only. From the women, there is no danger of insurrection, and they are carefully kept from the men; I mean from the black men. But in what I have to offer, on this head, I am far from including every ship. I speak not of what is universally, but of what is too commonly, and I am afraid, too generally, prevalent.

I have already observed, that the captain of an African ship, while upon the coast, is absolute in his command; and if he be humane, vigilant, and determined, he has it in his power to protect the miserable; for scarcely any thing can be done on board the ship, without his permission or connivance. But this power is too seldom exerted in favour of the poor women slaves.

When we hear of a town taken by storm, and given up to the ravages of an enraged and licentious army, of wild and unprincipled Cossacks, perhaps no part of the distress affects a feeling mind more, than the treatment to which the women are exposed. But the enormities frequently committed in an African ship, though equally flagrant, are little known *here,* and are considered *there,* only as matters of course. When the women and girls are taken on board a ship, naked, trembling, terrified, perhaps almost exhausted with cold, fatigue, and hunger, they are often exposed to the wanton rudeness of white savages. The poor creatures cannot understand the language they hear, but the looks and manner of the speakers are sufficiently intelligible. In imagination, the prey is divided, upon the spot, and only reserved till opportunity offers. Where resistance or refusal, would be utterly in vain, even the solicitation of consent is seldom thought of. But I forbear.—This is not a subject for declamation. Facts like these, so certain and so numerous, speak for themselves. Surely, if the advocates for the Slave Trade attempt to plead for it, before the wives and daughters of our happy land, or before those who have wives or daughters of their own, they must lose their cause.

Perhaps some hard-hearted pleader may suggest, that such treatment would indeed be cruel, in Europe: but the African women are negroes, savages, who have no idea of the nicer sensations which obtain among civilized people. I dare contradict them in the strongest terms. I have lived long, and conversed much, amongst these supposed savages. I have often slept in their towns, in a house filled with goods for trade, with no person in the house but myself, and with no other door than a mat; in that security, which no man in his senses would expect in this civilized nation, especially in this metropolis, without the precaution of having strong doors, strongly locked and bolted. And with regard to the women, in Sherbro, where I was most acquainted, I have seen many instances of modesty, and even delicacy, which would not disgrace an English woman. Yet, such is the treatment which I have known permitted, if not encouraged, in many of our ships—they have been abandoned, without restraint, to the lawless will of the first comer.

Accustomed thus to despise, insult, and injure the slaves on board, it may be expected that the conduct of many of our people to the natives, with whom they trade, is, as far as circumstances admit, very similar; and it is so. They are considered as a people to be robbed and spoiled with impunity. Every art is employed to deceive and wrong them. And he who has most address in this way, has most to boast of.

Not an article that is capable of diminution or adulteration, is delivered genuine, or entire. The spirits are lowered by water. False heads are put into the kegs that contain the gunpowder; so that, though the keg appears large, there is no more powder in it, than in a much smaller. The linen and cotton cloths are opened, and two or three yards, according to the length of the piece, cut off, not from the end, but out of the middle, where it is not so readily noticed.

The natives are cheated, in the number, weight, measure, or quality of what they purchase, in every possible way: and, by habit and emulation, a marvellous dexterity is acquired in these practices. And thus the natives in their turn, in proportion to their commerce with the Europeans, and (I am sorry to add) particularly with the English, become jealous, insidious, and revengeful.

They know with whom they deal, and are accordingly prepared;—though they can trust some ships and boats, which have treated them with punctuality, and may be trusted by them. A quarrel, sometimes, furnishes pretext for detaining, and carrying away, one or more of the natives, which is retaliated, if practicable, upon the next boat that comes to the place, from the same port. For so far their vindictive temper is restrained by their ideas of justice, that they will not, often, revenge an injury received from a Liverpool ship, upon one belonging to Bristol or London.

They will usually wait with patience the arrival of one, which, they suppose, by her sailing from the same place, has some connection with that which used them ill; and they are so quick at distinguishing our little local differences of language and customs in a ship, that before they have been in a ship five minutes, and often before they come on board, they know, with certainty, whether she be from Bristol, Liverpool, or London.

Retaliation on their parts, furnishes a plea for reprisal on ours. Thus, in one place or another, trade is often suspended, all intercourse cut off, and things are in a state of war; till necessity, either on the ship's part or on theirs, produces overtures of peace, and dictates the price, which the offending party must pay for it. But it is a warlike peace. We trade under arms; and they are furnished with long knives.

For, with a few exceptions, the English and the Africans, reciprocally, consider each other as consummate villains, who are always watching opportunities to do mischief. In short, we have, I fear too deservedly, a very unfavourable character upon the coast. When I have charged a black with unfairness and dishonesty, he has answered, if able to clear himself, with an air of disdain, "What! do you think I am a white man?"

Kidnapping and Retaliation, 1767–1768

RICHARD STORY

On my first coming on the [Windward] Coast in the year 1767, I was put into a trading long boat, belonging to the ship in which I came from Whitehaven—at one time in particular there had been a marauding party in canoes that came from Grand Sesters, which landed in the night at Grand Cora, and carried off to the amount of from twelve to fourteen. A short time after that, we had a Native of Grand Sesters in our long boat (laying in the river Sesters)—it came to the knowledge of the people of Grand Cora that this man was in the long boat, and . . . they formed a plan to take him from us—in consequence of which they came over to the river Sesters, borrowed canoes at King's Town, and came to us, and informed the Mate, that they had a Slave to sell; upon which he went on shore with them to some distance from where the boat then laid, myself, one boy, and the Black men remaining in the boat. About four hours after the

---

Source: From *House of Commons Papers*, George III, 4281, Minutes of the evidence taken before a committee of the House of Commons, being a select committee, appointed to take the examination of witnesses respecting the African Slave Trade, minutes of 7 February 1791.

Canoe ferrying slaves to a Portuguese slaver anchored in the Bonny River, 1837. (Peabody Museum of Salem)

Mate was gone, a canoe with four men came on board our boat, the same men the Mate went away with. I asked them where the Mate was? Their answer was, pointing to a canoe at some distance, that he was in the canoe coming with a Slave. A little time afterwards, I not being on my guard, two of them seized me, and the other two got the black man [from Grand Sesters]; him they got overboard—I got clear of the two myself, though they had attempted to get me overboard also; as soon as I found myself to be at liberty, I immediately jumped down below and got arms, and came upon deck immediately, on which the two that had attempted to throw me overboard, jumped overboard themselves—by the time that I had got on deck again the black man had cleared himself, and was coming up the sides when I got on deck; on which we loaded muskets, and were going to fire at the people in the water, but they told us, if we killed or wounded one man, they would kill the Mate; on which the matter dropt—the Mate during all this time was confined, being tied neck and heels—as soon as they had got the Mate on shore, they told him that he must either deliver up the Native of Grand Sesters, or pay them a Slave's goods, that is, the price of a Slave in goods, which he refused—this was the reason of his confinement. . . .

Did he [the man from Grand Sesters] assign any reason for the expedition [that had taken the men from Grand Cora]?

The only reason that he did assign for it was, that his countrymen were poor. . . .

Did you ever know any instances of the Natives redeeming their countrymen from on board Slave ships?

Many. . . . They had been taken by the marauding parties, and after being sold, their countrymen got notice where they were, and came and redeemed them. I make no doubt but the Slaves, which they exchanged for their friends, had been also taken by them in the same manner.

It is your opinion, that the Natives are ever fraudulently or forcibly carried off by Europeans?

Often. . . . I have been told by the Natives, that they have lost their friends at different times, and supposed them to be taken by European ships going along the Coast—I have myself taken up canoes, which were afterwards challenged by the Natives, who supposed the men in them had been taken off the day before by a Dutchman. . . .

I once myself saved a Dutch longboat and crew, that the Natives meant to kill; this happened between the river Sesters and Setta Crue—laying to an anchor in my boat, a Dutch ship, running down the Coast, sent her longboat to where I was lying, to buy vegetables, fowls, &c.—as soon as he came to an anchor, there were a number of canoes came about the two boats. One of the head men of the place came to me, and desired that I would take my anchor up and go away—that they wanted to take the Dutch longboat, and kill the crew; but would not wish to do it, while I was there. On which I immediately hailed the Dutch longboat, and told him that he had better go away—that the Negroes wanted to take the boat, and kill the crew. The reason the Negroes assigned for this was, that a Dutch ship some few days before had taken four men belonging to that place. . . .

I once myself, in 1768, was going a passenger from Lagoo on the Gold Coast to the river Gabon, in one of the trading vessels belonging to the Coast, and meeting with contrary winds, we got into the river Angra or Danger; finding there was every probability of purchasing bees wax, ivory, and Slaves, we staid there. On the second day after our arrival two canoes with about twelve or fourteen men came on board with two men bound, which they wanted to sell. When the agreement was made, I went below to get a pair of irons and a hammer to put the one into irons that was agreed for. On coming up again, the master of the boat, myself, and another White man were all seized—the master's and the other man's throats were both cut immediately—I by some superior exertion got clear of them that had seized me, but standing below in the hatchway I made an attempt to get on deck, but I could not. Half an hour after, being covered with wounds, and finding myself very weak with the loss of blood, I told the natives on board, that if they would let me go to Gabon they might take the boat and cargo also, to which they consented. After they had got the major part of the goods out of the boat, they then assisted me to get on deck, and immediately stripped me naked, put me in a canoe, and took me on shore to their town. The reason they gave me of doing this was, that a ship from Liverpool (the Captain's name was Lambert, the ship's name I don't recollect) had taken sometime before a canoe full of their townsmen, and carried them away; as a corroboration of this, I was told of this same circumstance when I got to Gabon afterwards.

Views of the King of Asante, 1820

OSEI BONSU

"Now," said the king, after a pause, "I have another palaver, and you must help me to talk it. A long time ago the great king [of England] liked plenty of trade, more than now; then many ships came, and they bought ivory, gold, and slaves; but now he will not let the ships come as before, and the people buy gold and ivory only. This is what I have in my head, so now tell me truly, like a friend, why does the king do so?" "His majesty's question," I replied, "was connected with a great palaver, which my instructions did not authorise me to dis-

Source: From *Journal of a Residence in Asantee*, by Joseph Dupuis, pp. 162–164, London, 1824.

cuss. I had nothing to say regarding the slave trade." "I know that too," retorted the king; "because, if my master liked that trade, you would have told me so before. I only want to hear what you think as a friend: this is not like the other palavers." I was confessedly at a loss for an argument that might pass as a satisfactory reason, and the sequel proved that my doubts were not groundless. The king did not deem it plausible, that this obnoxious traffic should have been abolished from motives of humanity alone; neither would he admit that it lessened the number either of domestic or foreign wars.

Taking up one of my observations, he remarked, "the white men who go to council with your master, and pray to the great God for him, do not understand my country, or they would not say the slave trade was bad. But if they think it bad now, why did they think it good before. Is not your law an old law, the same as the Crammo [Muslim] law? Do you not both serve the same God, only you have different fashions and customs? Crammos are strong people in fetische, and they say the law is good, because the great God made the book; so they buy slaves, and teach them good things, which they knew not before. This makes every body love the Crammos, and they go every where up and down, and the people give them food when they want it. Then these men come all the way from the great water [the river Niger], and from Manding, and Dagomba, and Killinga; they stop and trade for slaves, and then go home. If the great king would like to restore this trade, it would be good for the white men and for me too, because Ashantee is a country for war, and the people are strong; so if you talk that palaver for me properly, in the white country, if you go there, I will give you plenty of gold, and I will make you richer than all the white men."

I urged the impossibility of the king's request, promising, however, to record his sentiments faithfully. "Well then," said the king, "you must put down in my master's book all I shall say, and then he will look to it, now he is my friend. And when he sees what is true, he will surely restore that trade. I cannot make war to catch slaves in the bush, like a thief. My ancestors never did so. But if I fight a king, and kill him when he is insolent, then certainly I must have his gold, and his slaves, and the people are mine too. Do not the white kings act like this? Because I hear the old men say, that before I conquered Fantee and killed the Braffoes and the kings, that white men came in great ships, and fought and killed many people; and then they took the gold and slaves to the white country: and sometimes they fought together. That is all the same as these black countries. The great God and the fetische made war for strong men every where, because then they can pay plenty of gold and proper sacrifice. When I fought Gaman, I did not make war for slaves, but because Dinkera (the king) sent me an arrogant message and killed my people, and refused to pay me gold as his father did. Then my fetische made me strong like my ancestors, and I killed Dinkera, and took his gold, and brought more than 20,000 slaves to Coomassy. Some of these people being bad men, I washed my stool in their blood for the fetische. But then some were good people, and these I sold or gave to my captains: many, moreover, died, because this country does not grow too much corn like Sarem, and what can I do? Unless I kill or sell them, they will grow strong and kill my people. Now you must tell my master that these slaves can work for him, and if he wants 10,000 he can have them. And if he wants fine handsome girls and women to give his captains, I can send him great numbers."

Views of a King at Old Calabar, 1850

EYO HONESTY II

The king maintained the utmost composure, paid respectful attention while we spoke, and then answered calmly in his own defence. He wished that he could do without slaves—it would be better for him; but, as the country stood, that was impossible. He did not employ men to steal slaves for him; nor would he knowingly buy those which were stolen. He bought them in the market, at market price, without being able to know how they were procured; and would let no man steal them from him. He admitted that they were obtained in various objectionable ways, and even expatiated on the subject. They came from different countries, and were sold for different reasons—some as prisoners of war, some for debt, some for breaking their country's laws, and some by great men, who hated them. The

---

Source: From *Twenty-Nine Years in the West Indies and Central Africa*, by Hope Masterton Waddell, London, 1863, excerpt from p. 429.

king of a town sells whom he dislikes or fears; his wives and children are sold in turn by his successor. A man inveigles his brother's children to his house, and sells them. The brother says nothing, but watches his opportunity, and sells the children of the other. He admitted that they were kidnapped also; but said that they came from different far countries, of which he knew nothing, and in which they had no other trade. Calabar people did not steal, but only bought, slaves. He concluded by saying, that he had so many, that his new people, if he did not protect them with a strong hand, would be constantly sold away again by the old ones, and reported to him as dead.

PART IV

Modern Views of Slaving and Slavers

VARIETY OF OPINION
---

*There were . . . the "loose-packers" and the "tight-packers."
. . . So great was the profit on each slave landed alive that
hardly a captain refrained from loading his vessel to its utmost capacity.*
MALCOLM COWLEY AND DANIEL P. MANNIX

*Thousands of ship crossings have now been statistically ana-
lyzed, and none show a correlation of any significance between either tonnage or space available and mortality.*
HERBERT S. KLEIN

*Of 100 people seized in Africa, 75 would have reached the
marketplaces in the interior; . . . 64 . . . would have arrived
at the coast; . . . 57 or so would have boarded the ships; . . .
and 48 or 49 would have lived to behold their first master
in the New World.*
JOSEPH C. MILLER

Written by noted literary critic Malcolm Cowley and amateur historian Daniel P. Mannix, the first selection in this part appeared in
the book *Black Cargoes: A History of the Atlantic Slave Trade
1518–1865* (1962), for many years one of the most widely read accounts of the Atlantic slave trade. Its great strength is its use of vivid

contemporary sources, especially those produced by the abolitionist campaigners. Its weakness from the perspective of more recent research lies in its failure to test that evidence and to place it in the larger context of the trade. Published only seven years later, Philip D. Curtin's study of the volume of slave trade (see Part II) belongs to a much more analytical tradition. It tries to capture the larger reality behind the vivid details and, as Curtin himself notes, puts aside the tone of moral outrage, characteristic of the abolitionist tradition, in the interests of dispassionate scholarship.

In the second selection a generation of scholarship on the slave trade since the publication of Curtin's landmark book is summarized by Herbert S. Klein, a Latin American historian at Columbia University who also has written an excellent summary of research on slavery throughout the Americas, *African Slavery in Latin America and the Caribbean* (1986). Owing a great deal to the issues raised by Eric Williams but very little to Cowley and Mannix's study, the historians cited by Klein have sought to measure and to place in context such aspects of the trade as its profitability, its importance to the larger Atlantic economy, and the reasons for the mortality rates in transit. In using statistical analysis and economic science to probe more important historical questions, these historians also have sacrificed the vividness and moralizing of the abolitionist tradition.

In his award-winning study, *Way of Death: Merchant Capitalism and the Angolan Slave Trade* (1988), from which the third selection is taken, Joseph C. Miller, a historian of Africa at the University of Virginia, tries to combine the newer scholarship with the vividness of the older historiography. Bringing together contemporary sources and the insights of modern studies, Miller reconstructs the experience of persons enslaved in the interior of Angola as they marched to the coast, waited in the slave pens of coastal ports, and were loaded on board slave ships for transport to Brazil. Some features of his account, such as the baptisms before departure, were unique to Angola, and the long distance to the coast and the high mortality would not have been as common in many other parts of Africa. Angola, however, was the single most important source of slaves throughout the long centuries of the Atlantic slave trade, so that the experiences that Miller re-creates would have been the sad reality for several million people. Can you detect a tone of moral outrage below the surface of his writing?

The Middle Passage

MALCOLM COWLEY AND DANIEL P. MANNIX

As soon as an assortment of naked slaves was carried aboard a Guineaman, the men were shackled two by two, the right wrist and ankle of one to the left wrist and ankle of another; then they were sent below. The women—usually regarded as fair prey for the sailors—were allowed to wander by day almost anywhere on the vessel, though they spent the night between decks, in a space partitioned off from that of the men. All the slaves were forced to sleep without covering on bare wooden floors, which were often constructed of unplaned boards. In a stormy passage the skin over their elbows might be worn away to the bare bones.

William [Willem] Bosman says, writing in 1701, "You would really wonder to see how these slaves live on board; for though their number sometimes amounts to six or seven hundred, yet by the careful management of our masters of ships"—the Dutch masters, in this case—"they are so regulated that it seems incredible: And in this particular our nation exceeds all other Europeans; for as the French, Portuguese and English slave-ships, are always foul and stinking; on the contrary ours are for the most part clean and neat."

Slavers of every nation insisted that their own vessels were the best in the trade. Thus, James Barbot, Jr., who sailed on an English ship to the Congo in 1700, was highly critical of the Portuguese. He admits that they made a great point of baptizing the slaves before taking them on board, but then, "It is pitiful," he says, "to see how they crowd those poor wretches, six hundred and fifty or seven hundred in a ship, the men standing in the hold ty'd to stakes, the women between decks and those that are with child in the great cabin and the children in the steeridge which in that hot climate occasions an intolerable stench." Barbot adds, however, that the Portuguese provided the slaves with coarse thick mats, which were

Source: From "Middle Passages" by Malcolm Cowley and Daniel P. Mannix, in *American Heritage* 13.2, February 1962. Copyright © 1962 by Daniel P. Mannix and Malcolm Cowley. Reprinted by permission of Harold Matson Company, Inc.

"softer for the poor wretches to lie upon than the bare decks . . . and it would be prudent to imitate the Portuguese in this point." The English, however, did not display that sort of prudence.

There were two schools of thought among the English slaving captains, the "loose-packers" and the "tight-packers." The former argued that by giving the slaves a little more room, better food, and a certain amount of liberty, they reduced the death rate and received a better price for each slave in the West Indies. The tight-packers answered that although the loss of life might be greater on each of their voyages, so too were the net receipts from a larger cargo. If many of the survivors were weak and emaciated, as was often the case, they could be fattened up in a West Indian slave yard before being offered for sale.

The argument between the two schools continued as long as the trade itself, but for many years after 1750 the tight-packers were in the ascendant. So great was the profit on each slave landed alive that hardly a captain refrained from loading his vessel to its utmost capacity. Says the Reverend John Newton, who was a slaving captain before he became a clergyman:

> The cargo of a vessel of a hundred tons or a little more is calculated to purchase from 220 to 250 slaves. Their lodging rooms below the deck which are three (for the men, the boys, and the women) besides a place for the sick, are sometimes more than five feet high and sometimes less; and this height is divided toward the middle for the slaves to lie in two rows, one above the other, on each side of the ship, close to each other like books upon a shelf. I have known them so close that the shelf would not easily contain one more.
>
> The poor creatures, thus cramped, are likewise in irons for the most part which makes it difficult for them to turn or move or attempt to rise or to lie down without hurting themselves or each other. Every morning, perhaps, more instances than one are found of the living and the dead fastened together.

Newton was writing in 1788, shortly before a famous parliamentary investigation of the slave trade that lasted four years. One among hundreds of witnesses was Dr. Alexander Falconbridge, who had made four slaving voyages as a surgeon. Falconbridge testified that "he made the most of the room," in stowing the slaves, "and wedged them in. They had not so much room as a man in his coffin either in length or breadth. When he had to enter the slave deck, he took off his shoes to avoid crushing the slaves as he was forced to crawl over them." Falconbridge "had the marks on his feet where the slaves bit and pinched him."

Captain Parrey of the Royal Navy was sent to measure the slave ships at Liverpool and make a report to the House of Commons. That was also in 1788. Parrey discovered that the captains of many slavers possessed a chart showing the dimensions of the half deck, lower deck, hold, platforms, gunroom, orlop, and great cabin, in fact of every crevice into which slaves might be wedged. Miniature black figures were drawn on some of the charts to illustrate the most effective method of packing in the cargo.

On the *Brookes*, which Parrey considered to be typical, every man was allowed a space six feet long by sixteen inches wide (and usually about two feet seven inches high); every woman, a space five feet ten inches long by sixteen inches wide; every boy, five feet by fourteen inches; every girl, four feet six inches by twelve inches. The *Brookes* was a vessel of 320 tons. By a new law passed in 1788 it was permitted to carry 454 slaves, and the chart, which later became famous, showed where 451 of them could be stowed away. Parrey failed to see how the captain could find room for three more. Nevertheless, Parliament was told by reliable witnesses, including Dr. Thomas Trotter, formerly surgeon of the *Brookes*, that before the new law she had carried 600 slaves on one voyage and 609 on another. . . .

Taking on slaves was a process that might be completed in a month or two by vessels trading in Lower Guinea, east and south of the Niger delta. In Upper Guinea, west and north of the delta, the process was longer. It might last from six months to a year or more on the Gold Coast, which supplied the slaves most in demand by the English colonies. Meanwhile the captain was buying Negroes, sometimes one or two a day, sometimes a hundred or more in a single lot, while haggling over each purchase.

Those months when a slaver lay at anchor off the malarial coastline were the most dangerous part of her voyage. Not only was her crew exposed to African fevers and the revenge of angry natives; not only was there the chance of her being taken by pirates or by a hostile man-of-war; but there was also the constant threat of a slave mutiny.

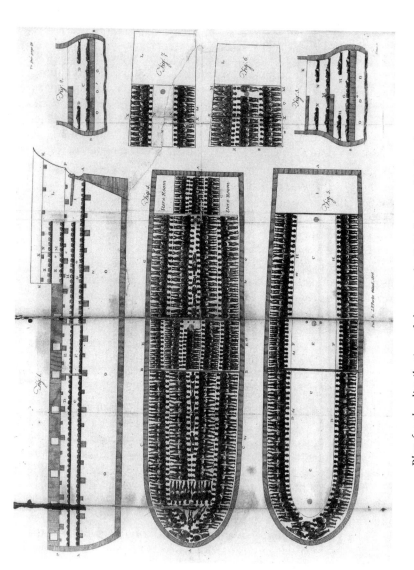

*Plan for the distribution of slaves in the British slave ship Brookes.
(Library of Congress)*

Captain Thomas Phillips says, in his account of a voyage made in 1693–94:

> When our slaves are aboard we shackle the men two and two, while we lie in port, and in sight of their own country, for 'tis then they attempt to make their escape, and mutiny; to prevent which we always keep centinels upon the hatchways, and have a chest full of small arms, ready loaden and prim'd, constantly lying at hand upon the quarter-deck, together with some granada shells; and two of our quarter-deck guns, pointing on the deck thence, and two more out of the steerage, the door of which is always kept shut, and well barr'd; they are fed twice a day, at 10 in the morning, and 4 in the evening, which is the time they are aptest to mutiny, being all upon the deck; therefore all that time, what of our men are not employ'd in distributing their victuals to them, and settling them, stand to their arms; and some with lighted matches at the great guns that yaun upon them, loaden with partridge, till they have done and gone down to their kennels between decks.

In spite of such precautions, mutinies were frequent on the Coast, and some of them were successful. Even a mutiny that failed might lead to heavy losses among the slaves and the sailors. Thus, we read in the Newport, Rhode Island, *Mercury* of November 18, 1765:

> By letters from Capt. Hopkins in a Brig belonging to Providence arrived here from Antigua from the Coast of Africa we learn That soon after he left the Coast, the number of his Men being reduced by Sickness, he was obliged to permit some of the Slaves to come upon Deck to assist the People: These Slaves contrived to release the others, and the whole rose upon the People, and endeavoured to get Possession of the Vessel; but was happily prevented by the Captain and his Men, who killed, wounded and forced overboard, Eighty of them, which obliged the rest to submit.

There are scores of similar items in the colonial newspapers.

William Richardson, a young sailor who shipped on an English Guineaman in 1790, tells of going to the help of a French vessel on which the slaves had risen while it was at anchor. The English seamen jumped into the boats and pulled hard for the Frenchman, but by the time they reached it there were "a hundred slaves in possession of the deck and others tumbling up from below." The slaves put up a desperate resistance. "I could not but admire," Richardson says, "the courage of a fine young black who, though his partner in irons lay dead at his feet, would not surrender but fought with his billet of wood until a ball finished his existence. The others fought as well as they could but what could they do against fire-arms?"

There are fairly detailed accounts of fifty-five mutinies on slavers from 1699 to 1845, not to mention passing references to more than a hundred others. The list of ships "cut off" by the natives—often in revenge for the kidnapping of free Africans—is almost as long. On the record it does not seem that Africans submitted tamely to being carried across the Atlantic like chained beasts. Edward Long, the Jamaica planter and historian, justified the cruel punishments inflicted on slaves by saying, "The many acts of violence they have committed by murdering whole crews and destroying ships when they had it in their power to do so have made these rigors wholly chargeable on their own bloody and malicious disposition which calls for the same confinement as if they were wolves or wild boars." For "wolves or wild boars" a modern reader might substitute "men who would rather die than be enslaved."

With the loading of the slaves, the captain, for his part, had finished what he regarded as the most difficult part of his voyage. Now he had to face only the ordinary perils of the sea, most of which were covered by his owners' insurance against fire, shipwreck, pirates and rovers, letters of mart and counter-mart, barratry, jettison, and foreign men-of-war. Among the risks not covered by insurance, the greatest was that of the cargo's being swept away by disease. The underwriters refused to issue such policies, arguing that they would expose the captain to an unholy temptation. If insured against disease among his slaves, he might take no precautions against it and might try to make his profit out of the insurance.

The more days at sea, the more deaths among his cargo, and so the captain tried to cut short the next leg of his voyage. If he had shipped his slaves at Bonny, Old Calabar, or any port to the southward, he might call at one of the Portuguese islands in the Gulf of Guinea for an additional supply of food and fresh water, usually enough, with what he had already, to last for three months. If he had traded to the northward, he made straight for the West Indies. Usually he had from four to five thousand nautical miles to sail—or even more, if the passage was from Angola to Virginia. The shortest passage—that from the Gambia River to Barbados—might be made in as little as three weeks, with favoring winds. If the course was much longer, and if the ship was becalmed in the doldrums or driven back by storms, it might take more than three months to cross the Atlantic, and slaves and sailors would be put on short rations long before the end of the Middle Passage. . . .

If the weather was clear, [the slaves] were brought on deck at eight o'clock in the morning. The men were attached by their leg irons to the great chain that ran along the bulwarks on both sides of the ship; the women and half-grown boys were allowed to wander at will. About nine o'clock the slaves were served their first meal of the day. If they were from the Windward Coast—roughly, the shoreline of present-day Liberia and Sierra Leone—the fare was boiled rice, millet, or corn meal, sometimes cooked with a few lumps of salt beef abstracted from the sailors' rations. If they were from the Bight of Biafra, at the east end of the Gulf of Guinea, they were fed stewed yams, but the Congos and the Angolas preferred manioc or plantains. With the food they were all given half a pint of water, served out in a pannikin.

After the morning meal came a joyless ceremony called "dancing the slaves." "Those who were in irons," says Dr. Thomas Trotter, surgeon of the *Brookes* in 1783, "were ordered to stand up and make what motions they could, leaving a passage for such as were out of irons to dance around the deck." Dancing was prescribed as a therapeutic measure, a specific against suicidal melancholy, and also against scurvy—although in the latter case it was a useless torture for men with swollen limbs. While sailors paraded the deck, each with a cat-o'-nine-tails in his right hand, the men slaves "jumped in their irons" until their ankles were bleeding flesh. Music was provided by a slave thumping on a broken drum or an upturned kettle, or by an African banjo, if there was one aboard, or perhaps by a sailor with a bagpipe or a fiddle. Slaving captains sometimes advertised for "A person that can play on the Bagpipes, for a Guinea ship." The slaves were also told to sing. Said Dr. Claxton after his voyage in the *Young Hero,* "They sing, but not for their amusement. The captain ordered them to sing, and they sang songs of sorrow. Their sickness, fear of being beaten, their hunger, and the memory of their country, etc., are the usual subjects."

While some of the sailors were dancing the slaves, others were sent below to scrape and swab out the sleeping rooms. It was a sickening task, and it was not well performed unless the captain imposed an iron discipline. James Barbot, Sr., was proud of the discipline maintained on the *Albion-Frigate.* "We were very nice," he says, "in keeping the places where the slaves lay clean and neat, appointing some of the ship's crew to do that office constantly and thrice a week we perfumed betwixt decks with a quantity of good vinegar in pails, and red-hot iron bullets in them, to expel the bad air, after the place had been well washed and scrubbed with brooms." Captain Hugh Crow, the last legal English slaver, was famous for his housekeeping. "I always took great pains," he says, "to promote the health and comfort of all on board, by proper diet, regularity, exercise, and cleanliness, for I considered that on keeping the ship clean and orderly, which was always my hobby, the success of our voyage mainly depended." Certainly he lost fewer slaves in the Middle Passage than the other captains, some of whom had the filth in the hold cleaned out only once a week.

At three or four in the afternoon the slaves were fed their second meal, often a repetition of the first. Sometimes, instead of African food, they were given horse beans, the cheapest provender from Europe. The beans were boiled to a pulp, then covered with a mixture of palm oil, flour, water, and red pepper, which the sailors called "slabber sauce." Most of the slaves detested horse beans, especially if they were used to eating yams or manioc. Instead of eating the pulp, they would, unless carefully watched, pick it up by handfuls and throw it in each other's faces.

That second meal was the end of their day. As soon as it was finished they were sent below, under the guard of sailors charged with stowing them away on their bare floors and platforms. The tallest men were placed amidships, where the vessel was widest; the shorter ones were tumbled into the stern. Usually there was only room for them to sleep on their sides, "spoon fashion." Captain William Littleton told Parliament that slaves in the ships on which he sailed might lie on their backs if they wished—"though perhaps," he conceded, "it might be difficult all at the same time."

After stowing their cargo, the sailors climbed out of the hatchway, each clutching his cat-o'-nine-tails; then the hatchway gratings were closed and barred. Sometimes in the night, as the sailors lay on deck and tried to sleep, they heard from below "an howling melancholy noise, expressive of extreme anguish." When Dr. Trotter told his interpreter, a slave woman, to inquire about the cause of the noise, "she discovered it to be owing to their having dreamt they were in their own country, and finding themselves when awake, in the hold of a slave ship."

More often the noise heard by the sailors was that of quarreling among the slaves. The usual occasion for quarrels was their problem of reaching the latrines. These were inadequate in size and number, and hard to find in the darkness of the crowded hold, especially by men who were ironed together in pairs.

In squalls or rainy weather, the slaves were never brought on deck. They were served their two meals in the hold, where the air became too thick and poisonous to breathe. Dr. Falconbridge writes:

> For the purpose of admitting fresh air, most of the ships in the slave-trade are provided, between the decks, with five or six air-ports on each side of the ship, of about six inches in length and four in breadth; in addition to which, some few ships, but not one in twenty, have what they denominate wind-sails [funnels made of canvas and so placed as to direct a current of air into the hold]. But whenever the sea is rough and the rain heavy, it becomes necessary to shut these and every other conveyance by which the air is admitted. . . . The negroes' rooms very soon become intolerably hot. The confined air, rendered noxious by the effluvia exhaled from their bodies and by being repeatedly breathed, soon produces fevers and fluxes which generally carry off great numbers of them.

Dr. Trotter says that when tarpaulins were thrown over the gratings, the slaves would cry, "Kickeraboo, kickeraboo, we are dying, we are dying." Falconbridge gives one instance of their sufferings:

> Some wet and blowing weather having occasioned the portholes to be shut and the grating to be covered, fluxes and fevers among the negroes ensued. While they were in this situation, I frequently went down among them till at length their rooms became so extremely hot as to be only bearable for a very short time. But the excessive heat was not the only thing that rendered their situation intolerable. The deck, that is, the floor of their rooms, was so covered with the blood and mucus which had proceeded from them in consequence of the flux, that it resembled a slaughter-house.

While the slaves were on deck they had to be watched at all times to keep them from committing suicide. Says Captain Phillips of the *Hannibal*, "We had about 12 negroes did wilfully drown themselves, and others starv'd themselves to death; for," he explained, "'tis their belief that when they die they return home to their own country and friends again."

This belief was reported from various regions, at various periods of the trade, but it seems to have been especially strong among the Ibos of eastern Nigeria. In 1788, nearly a hundred years after the *Hannibal's* voyage, Dr. Ecroide Claxton was the surgeon who attended a shipload of Ibos. Some, he testified,

> wished to die on an idea that they should then get back to their own country. The captain in order to obviate this idea, thought of an expedient viz. to cut off the heads of those who died intimating to them that if determined to go, they must return without heads. The slaves were accordingly brought up to witness the operation. One of them by a violent exertion got loose and flying to the place where the nettings had been unloosed in order to empty the tubs, he darted overboard. The ship brought to, a man was placed in the main chains to catch him which he perceiving, made signs which words cannot express expressive of his happiness in escaping. He then went down and was seen no more.

Dr. Isaac Wilson, a surgeon in the Royal Navy, made a Guinea voyage on the *Elizabeth,* [whose] captain [was] John Smith, [a man] who was said to be very humane. Nevertheless, Wilson was assigned the duty of flogging the slaves. "Even in the act of chastisement," Wilson says, "I have seen them look up at me with a smile, and, in their own language, say 'presently we shall be no more.'" One woman on the *Elizabeth* found some rope yarn, which she tied to the armorer's vise; she fastened the other end round her neck and was found dead in the morning.

On the *Brookes* when Thomas Trotter was her surgeon, there was a man who, after being accused of witchcraft, had been sold into slavery with all his family. During the first night on shipboard he tried to cut his throat. Dr. Trotter sewed up the wound, but on the following night the man not only tore out the stitches but tried to cut his throat on the other side. From the ragged edges of the wound and the blood on his fingers, he seemed to have used his nails as the only available instrument. His hands were tied together after the second wound, but he refused all food, and he died of hunger in eight or ten days.

Besides the propensity for suicide, another deadly scourge of the Guinea cargoes was a phenomenon called "fixed melancholy." Even slaves who were well fed, treated with kindness, and kept under relatively sanitary conditions would often die, one after another, for no apparent reason; they had simply lost the will to live. Dr. Wilson believed that fixed melancholy was responsible for the loss of two thirds of the slaves who died on the *Elizabeth*. "No one who had it was ever cured," he says, "whereas those who had it not and yet were ill, recovered. The symptoms are a lowness of spirits and despondency. Hence they refuse food. This only increases the symptoms. The stomach afterwards got weak. Hence the belly ached, fluxes ensued, and they were carried off." But in spite of the real losses from despair, the high death rate on Guineamen was due to somatic more than to psychic afflictions.

Along with their human cargoes, crowded, filthy, undernourished, and terrified out of the wish to live, the ships also carried an invisible cargo of microbes, bacilli, spirochetes, viruses, and intestinal worms from one continent to another; the Middle Passage was a crossroad and market place of diseases. From Europe came smallpox, measles (somewhat less deadly to Africans than to American Indians), gonorrhea, and syphilis (which last Columbus' sailors had carried from America to Europe). The African diseases were yellow fever (to which the natives were resistant), dengue, blackwater fever, and malaria (which was not specifically African, but which most of the slaves carried in their blood streams). If anopheles mosquitoes were present, malaria spread from the slaves through any new territories to which they were carried. Other African diseases were amoebic and bacillary dysentery (known as "the bloody flux"), Guinea worms, hookworm (possibly African in origin, but soon endemic in the warmer parts of the New World), yaws, elephantiasis, and leprosy. . . .

Smallpox was feared more than other diseases, since the surgeons had no way of curing it. One man with smallpox infected a whole vessel, unless—as sometimes happened—he was tossed overboard when the first scabs appeared. Captain Wilson of the *Briton* lost more than half his cargo of 375 slaves by not listening to his surgeon. It was the last slave on board who had the disease, says Henry Ellison, who made the voyage. "The doctor told Mr. Wilson it was the small-pox," Ellison continues. "He would not believe it, but said he would keep him, as he was a fine man. It soon broke out amongst the slaves. I have seen the platform one continued scab. We hauled up eight or ten slaves dead of a morning. The flesh and skin peeled off their wrists when taken hold of, being entirely mortified."

But dysentery, though not so much feared, probably caused more deaths in the aggregate. Ellison testified that he made two voyages on the *Nightingale*. On the first voyage the slaves were so crowded that thirty boys "messed and slept in the long boat all through the Middle Passage, there being no room below"; and still the vessel lost only five or six slaves in all, out of a cargo of 270. On the second voyage, however, the *Nightingale* buried "about 150, chiefly of fevers and flux. We had 250 when we left the coast."

The average mortality in the Middle Passage is impossible to state accurately from the surviving records. Some famous voyages were made without the loss of a single slave. On one group of nine voyages between 1766 and 1780, selected at random, the vessels carried 2,362 slaves and there were no epidemics of disease. The total loss of slaves was 154, or about six and one-half per cent. That figure is to be compared with the losses on a list of twenty voyages compiled by Thomas Clarkson, the abolitionist, in which the vessels carried 7,904 slaves with a mortality of 2,053, or twenty-six per cent. Balancing high and low figures together, the English Privy Council in 1789 arrived at an estimate of twelve and one-half per cent for the average mortality among slaves in the Middle Passage. To this figure it added four and one-half per cent for the deaths of slaves in harbors before they were sold, and thirty-three per cent for deaths in the so-called "seasoning" or acclimatizing process, making a total of fifty per cent. If these figures were correct, only one slave was added to the New World labor force for every two purchased on the Guinea Coast.

To keep the figures in perspective, it might be said that the mortality among slaves in the Middle Passage was possibly no greater than that of white indentured servants or even of free Irish, Scottish, and German immigrants in the North Atlantic crossing. On the better-commanded Guineamen it was probably less, and for a simple economic reason. There was no profit on a slaving voyage until the Negroes were landed alive and sold; therefore the better captains took care of their cargoes. It was different on the North Atlantic crossing, where even the hold and steerage passengers paid their fares before coming aboard, and where the captain cared little whether they lived or died.

After leaving the Portuguese island of São Tomé—if he had watered there—a slaving captain bore westward along the equator for a thousand miles, and then northwestward toward the Cape

Verde Islands. This was the tedious part of the Middle Passage. "On leaving the Gulf of Guinea," says the author of a *Universal Geography* published in the early nineteenth century, ". . . that part of the ocean must be traversed, so fatal to navigators, where long calms detain the ships under a sky charged with electric clouds, pouring down by torrents of rain and of fire. This *sea of thunder,* being a focus of mortal diseases, is avoided as much as possible, both in approaching the coasts of Africa and those of America." It was not until reaching the latitude of the Cape Verde Islands that the vessel fell in with the northeast trades and was able to make a swift passage to the West Indies.

Dr. Claxton's ship, the *Young Hero,* was one of those delayed for weeks before reaching the trade winds. "We were so streightened for provisions," he testified, "that if we had been ten more days at sea, we must either have eaten the slaves that died, or have made the living slaves *walk the plank,*" a term, he explained, that was widely used by Guinea captains. There are no authenticated records of cannibalism in the Middle Passage, but there are many accounts of slaves killed for various reasons. English captains believed that French vessels carried poison in their medicine chests, "with which they can destroy their negroes in a calm, contagious sickness, or short provisions." They told the story of a Frenchman from Brest who had a long passage and had to poison his slaves; only twenty of them reached Haiti out of five hundred. Even the cruelest English captains regarded this practice as Latin, depraved, and uncovered by their insurance policies. In an emergency they simply jettisoned part of their cargo.

Often a slave ship came to grief in the last few days of the Middle Passage. It might be taken by a French privateer out of Martinique, or it might disappear in a tropical hurricane, or it might be wrecked on a shoal almost in sight of its harbor. On a few ships there was an epidemic of suicide at the last moment.

These, however, were exceptional disasters, recounted as horror stories in the newspapers of the time. Usually the last two or three days of the passage were a comparatively happy period. All the slaves, or all but a few, might be released from their irons. When there was a remaining stock of provisions, the slaves were given bigger meals—to fatten them for market—and as much water as they could drink. Sometimes on the last day—if the ship was commanded by an easy-going captain—there was a sort of costume party on deck, with the women slaves dancing in the sailors' castoff clothing. Then the captain was rowed ashore, to arrange for the disposition of his cargo.

Profits and the Causes of Mortality

HERBERT S. KLEIN

In recent decades there has been a fundamental change in the study of the Atlantic slave trade. From almost total neglect, the trade has become an area of major concern to economists and historians who have dedicated themselves to analyzing the African experience in America. Especially since the publication by Philip Curtin of his masterly synthesis *The Atlantic Slave Trade: A Census* in 1969, a massive amount of archival research has resulted in publications both of collections of documents from all the major archives of Europe, America, and Africa and of major works of synthesis on the demography, politics, and economics of the slave trade. . . .

From the work of the European economic historians, it is now evident that slave trade profits were not extraordinary by European standards. The average 10 percent rate obtained in studies of the eighteenth-century French and English slave traders was considered a good profit rate at the time but not out of the range of other contemporary investments. From a recent detailed study of the nineteenth century, it would seem that profits doubled in the next century largely as a result of rising slave prices in America, which in turn were due to the increasing suppression of the trade by the British navy. On average (except for some extraordinary voyages to Cuba in the 1850s), the rate of profit for nineteenth-century slavers was just under 20 percent. Thus, while profits in the special period of suppression in the nineteenth century were quite high, even these profits were not astronomic.

Source: From "Economic Aspects of the Eighteenth-Century Atlantic Slave Trade" by Herbert S. Klein in *The Rise of the Merchant Empires* edited by James D. Tracy, 1990, excerpts from pp. 287, 299–308. Reprinted by permission of Cambridge University Press.

But if presuppression trading profits were not extraordinary, was the trade an open one or a restricted one that created concentrated oligopolistic profits that could then possibly serve as a fundamental source for capital investments in the European economy? It has been suggested that high initial costs of entrance plus the long time period needed to fully recover profits (up to five years on some slaving voyages) meant that only highly capitalized firms could enter the trade. Most merchants spread their costs around by offering stock in slaving voyages and otherwise trying to insure themselves from catastrophic loss on one or more lost voyages. But the costs of entrance, the experience of contacts, and the international nature of the complex negotiations suggest that there were limits on the number of merchants who could enter the trade. Although this specialization seems to have taken place (and there are cases of quite major houses operating in both England and France), it is also impressive just how many independent merchants participated in the trade and how many ships were outfitted for the trade in any given year.

This debate on the relative rates of merchant participation and control has generated a lively analytical literature. In this debate, however, no current scholars have been able to show that the gains from the trade were directly invested in the earliest industrial enterprises of Great Britain. All the studies of the sources of industrial capital in England suggest local origins from agriculture or European commerce or both. Nevertheless, the Williams thesis has come in for some support on the question of Africa as a market for European manufactures, especially of the more basic sort. It has been suggested that the French armaments industry was completely dependent on the African trade (which was paid for by slave exports) during times of European peace. Several other industries on the Continent and in England can also be shown to have been highly dependent on the African market. Because much of early industrial activity involved production of crude and popularly consumed products, it has been argued that the African market played a vital part in sustaining the growth of some of Europe's newest infant industries. This part of the trade has yet to be fully studied, but recent work does suggest a need to reevaluate the role of European exports to Africa in this crucial period of the early Industrial Revolution.

A subtheme of this debate about the use of slave trade profits has only just been suggested in the literature. This concerns the role of profit for American merchant participants in the trade: the West

Indians, the North Americans (above all, the New Englanders), and especially the Brazilians. In terms of volume and capital generated, there is little question that few regions compare to those of Bahia, Rio de Janeiro, and Rhode Island. The number of ships provisioned for the African trade in these areas suggests a major growth of local capital. Who these merchants were and what their relationship was to both the plantation economy and the new industrial mills are still to be determined.

In terms of the larger patterns of Europe's international trade, the role of the Atlantic slave trade can be analyzed with a bit more precision. In general, in terms of volume of shipping and relative exports, the trade absorbed at most a fifth of any major European nation's ships or resources. Among the French, for example, exports to Africa amounted to 25 percent of total exports to the colonies in the 1770s and 20 percent in the 1780s. They took up 15 percent of the ships and 13 percent of the tonnage devoted to these trades in 1788. If all foreign trade were included, the relative importance of the trade to Africa would drop by over half, though it would still represent a substantial 10 percent of the value of all French intracontinental and overseas foreign trade.

Among the British the same general pattern held true. We know, for example, that British exports and re-exports to Africa averaged around 4.5 percent of total British exports in the last quarter of the eighteenth century. In terms of the number of ships employed, the African trade was even more important. Thus at the height of its slave trade, Bristol slavers accounted for 14 percent of all ships cleared from that port, whereas a third of the Liverpool ships clearing port were slavers in the 1770s. Finally, from contemporary figures provided by Bryan Edwards it would appear that slaves represented just under a fourth of the value of all persons and goods imported into the British West Indies.

In the case of Brazil the value of slave imports did not differ that much from the British West Indies. In the period from 1796 to 1808 slaves represented between 23 and 33 percent of the value of all imports into the colony. Although the trade was a crucial component of Brazilian imports as it had been in the West Indies, it played a much lesser role in the trade accounts of Portugal itself because of the Brazilian control over a large percentage of the carrying trade.

To make a definitive judgment of the relative weight of the Atlantic slave trade in the total picture of Europe's overseas trade would require a full estimation of the value of slave imports, slave-produced colonial exports, and European consumption and re-exportation of these slave-generated products. This is a difficult set of calculations. The few attempts to undertake such an estimate have led to lively debate among scholars of the West Indian economy but have resulted in no definitive conclusions. Though there is considerable debate about the meaning of the numbers and which estimates to accept or reject, both major authors in this debate agree that the profits of the slave trade are rather a small part—less than 10 percent—of the entire wealth generated from Britain's possession of its American sugar colonies. Furthermore, a recent attempt to estimate the impact of Great Britain's relations with the non-European world and its influence on British capital formation has suggested (again, with some controversy) that only 15 percent of Britain's gross investment capital expenditures during its Industrial Revolution could have come from the profits on all Great Britain's overseas trades, including that of the Atlantic slave trade.

Though clearly the slave trade was in all respects a profitable and important trade, it evidently was not the single largest capital-generating trade of the Europeans even within the context of their American empires. Even if the part of the Asian trade that went to Africa is added to these calculations, along with the value from slave-produced American goods, the figures are still not a significant addition to potential European savings available for investment in the Industrial Revolution, nor do they match the figures for the most economically profitable of Europe's overseas trades, at least according to recent macroeconomic calculations of the New Economic Historians. If these estimations hold up under critical review, they will be a significant challenge to an important element in the Eric Williams thesis on the importance of the slave trade and American slavery in providing the capital savings for the Industrial Revolution in England.

The Atlantic slave trade was unique in the product it transported and in its impact on labor market conditions on several continents. In this last section of this essay, I would like to examine these two issues: the economics of shipping slaves and the impact that the demographic characteristics of the transported slaves had on the makeup of the American and African labor markets.

The conceptions prevalent in the popular literature about the relative costs of African slaves have their corollary hypotheses about the economics of their transportation. It was assumed that the low cost of the slaves made it profitable to pack in as many as the ship could hold without sinking and then accept high rates of mortality during the Atlantic crossing. If any slaves delivered alive were pure profit, then even the loss of several hundred would have made economic sense. But if the slaves were not a costless or cheap item to purchase, then the corresponding argument about "tight packing" also makes little sense. In fact, high losses on the crossing resulted in financial loss on the trip, as many ship accounts aptly prove.

Even more convincing than these theoretical arguments against reckless destruction of life is the fact that no study has yet shown a systematic correlation of any significance between the numbers of slaves carried and mortality at sea. Thousands of ship crossings have now been statistically analyzed, and none show a correlation of any significance between either tonnage or space available and mortality.

This does not mean that slaves were traveling in luxury. In fact, they had less room than did contemporary troops or convicts being transported. It simply means that after much experience and the exigencies of the trade, slavers only took on as many slaves as they could expect to cross the Atlantic safely. From scattered references in the pre-1700 period it seems that provisioning and carrying arrangements were initially deficient. But all post-1700 trade studies show that slavers carried water and provisions for double their expected voyage times and that in most trades they usually carried slightly fewer slaves than their legally permitted limits.

This increasing sophistication in the carrying of slaves was reflected in declining rates of mortality. In the pre-1700 trade, mean mortality rates over many voyages tended to hover around 20 percent. In turn this mean rate reflected quite wide variations, with many ships coming in with very low rates and an equally large number experiencing rates of double or more than double the mean figure. But in the post-1700 period the mean rates dropped, and the variation around the mean declined. By midcentury the mean stood at about 10 percent, and by the last quarter of the century all trades were averaging a rate of about 5 percent. Moreover the dispersion around these mean rates had declined, and two-thirds of the ships were experiencing no more than 5 percent variation above or below the mean rate.

These declines in mortality were due to the standardization increasingly adopted in the trade. First of all there developed a specialized and specifically constructed vessel used in the slave trade of most nations. By the second half of the eighteenth century slave ships were averaging two hundred tons among all European traders, a tonnage that seemed best to fit the successful carrying potential of the trade. Slave traders were also the first of the commercial traders to adopt copper sheathing for their ships, which was a costly new method to prolong the life of the vessels and guarantee greater speed. It should be stressed that these slave trade vessels were much smaller ships than Europeans used in either the West Indian or East Indian trades. This in turn goes a long way to explaining why the famous model of a triangular trade, long the staple of western textbooks, is largely a myth. This myth was based on the idea that the slave ships performed the multiple tasks of taking European goods to Africa, transporting slaves to America, and then bringing back the sugar or other slave-produced American staple for Europe all on the same voyage. In fact, the majority of American crops reached European markets in much larger and specially constructed West Indian vessels designed primarily for this shuttle trade; the majority of slavers returned to Europe with small cargoes or none at all; and in the largest slave trade of them all—that of Brazil—no slavers either departed from or returned to Europe.

All traders carried about two and a half slaves per ton, and although there was some variation in crew size and ratios, all slave trade ships carried at least twice the number of seamen needed to man the vessel, and thus double or more than that of any other long-distance oceanic trade. This very high ratio of sailors to tonnage was due to the security needs of controlling the slave prisoners. All the European slave traders were also using the same provisioning, health, and transportation procedures. They built temporary decks to house the slaves and divided them by age and sex. Almost all Europeans adopted smallpox vaccinations at about the same time, all carried large quantities of African provisions to feed the slaves, and all used the same methods for daily hygiene, care of the sick, and so on. This standardization explains the common experience of mortality decline, and it also goes a long way to rejecting contemporaneous assertions that any particular European trader was "better" or more efficient than any other.

Although these firmly grounded statistics on mortality certainly destroy many of the older beliefs about "astronomic" mortality and tight packing, there does remain the question of whether a 5 percent mortality rate for a thirty- to fifty-day voyage for a healthy young adult is high or low. If such a mortality rate had occurred among young adult peasants in eighteenth-century France, it would be considered an epidemic rate. Thus, although Europeans succeeded in reducing the rate to seemingly low percentages, these rates still represented extraordinary high death rate figures for such a specially selected population. Equally, although troop, immigrant, and convict mortality rates in the eighteenth century approached the slave death numbers, in the nineteenth century they consistently fell to below 1 percent for transatlantic voyages. For slaves, however, these rates never fell below 5 percent for any large group of vessels surveyed. There thus seems to have been a minimum death rate caused by the close quarters during transport, which the Europeans could never reduce.

Death in the crossing was due to a variety of causes. The biggest killers were gastrointestinal disorders, which were often related to the quality of food and water available on the trip, and fevers. Bouts of dysentery were common and the "bloody flux" as it was called could break out in epidemic proportions. The increasing exposure of the slaves to dysentery increased both the rates of contamination of supplies and the incidence of death. It was dysentery that accounted for the majority of deaths and was the most common disease experienced on all voyages. The astronomic rates of mortality reached on occasional voyages were due to outbreaks of smallpox, measles, or other highly communicable diseases that were not related to time at sea or the conditions of food and water supply, hygiene, and sanitation practices. It was this randomness of epidemic diseases that prevented even experienced and efficient captains from eliminating very high mortality rates on any given voyage.

Although time at sea was not usually correlated with mortality, there were some routes in which time was a factor. Simply because they were a third longer than any other routes, the East African slave trades that developed in the late eighteenth and nineteenth centuries were noted for overall higher mortality than the West African routes, even though mortality per day at sea was the same or lower than on the shorter routes. Also, just the transporting together of slaves from different epidemiological zones in Africa guaranteed the transmission of a host of local endemic diseases to all those who were aboard. In turn, this guaranteed the spread of all major African diseases to America.

Along with the impact of African diseases on the American populations, the biases in the age and sex of the migrating Africans also had a direct impact on the growth and decline of the American slave populations. The low ratio of women in each arriving ship, the fact that most of these slave women were mature adults who had already spent several of their fecund years in Africa, and the fact that few children were carried to America were of fundamental importance in the subsequent history of population growth. It meant that the African slaves who arrived in America could not reproduce themselves. The African women who did come to America had lost some potential reproductive years and were even less able to reproduce the total numbers of males and females in the original immigrant cohort, let alone create a generation greater than the total number who arrived from Africa. Even those American regions that experienced a heavy and constant stream of African slaves still had to rely on importation of more slaves to maintain their slave populations, let alone increase their size. Once that African migration stopped, however, it was possible for the slave populations to begin to increase through natural growth, so long as there was no heavy out-migration through emancipation.

It was this consistent negative growth of the first generation of African slaves which explains the growing intensity of the slave trade to America in the eighteenth and early nineteenth centuries. As the demand for American products grew in European markets because of the increasingly popular consumption of tobacco, cotton, coffee, and above all sugar, the need for workers increased and this could be met only by bringing in more Africans. It was only in the case of the United States that the growth of plantation crop exports to Europe did not lead to an increasing importation of African slaves. This was largely due to the very early North American experience of the local slave population achieving a positive growth rate and thus supplying its increasing labor needs from the positive growth of its native-born slave population. Although most demographic historians have shown that the creole slave populations had positive growth rates from the beginning and that it was the distortions of the African-born cohorts that explain overall decline, more traditional historians have tried to explain the increasing demand for slaves as due to the low life expectancy of the Afro-American slave population. Much cited is the contemporary belief found in the planter literature of most colonies that the Afro-American slave experienced an average working life of "seven years." This myth of a short-lived labor force was related to the observed reality of slave population decline under the impact of heavy immigration of African slaves. Observers did not recognize the age and sexual imbalance of these Africans as a causal factor for the negative population growth of the slave labor force. Rather, they saw this decline as related to a very high mortality and a low life expectancy. Yet all recent studies suggest both a positive rate of population growth among native-born slaves and a life expectancy well beyond the so-called average seven working years in all American societies.

The average life expectancy of slave males was in the upper twenties in Brazil, for example, and in the midthirties for the United States, which might suggest an average working life of at least twenty years in Brazil and twenty-five years in the United States. But this average figure, of course, takes into account the very high infant mortality rates. For those slaves who survived the first five years of life—and these are the only ones we are concerned with here—the comparable life expectancies was [*sic*] in the midthirties for the Brazilians and lower forties for the U.S. slaves. This suggests that the average working life was, at a minimum, twenty-five years for Brazilian slaves and thirty years for the U.S. ones—both figures far from the supposed seven-year average postulated in most histories.

Deaths Before the Middle Passage

JOSEPH C. MILLER

Initial Capture and Sale

... The background hunger and epidemics that sometimes forced patrons to give up clients and compelled parents to part with children set a tone of physical weakness and vulnerability behind slaving in the interior. Where warfare and violence stimulated the initial capture, the victims would have begun their odysseys in exhausted,

---

Source: From *The Way of Death* by Joseph C. Miller, 1988, excerpts from pp. 380–391, 398–405, 440–441. Reprinted by permission of The University of Wisconsin Press.

shaken, and perhaps wounded physical condition. Though the buyers preferred strong adult males, the people actually captured in warfare, even in pitched battles between formal armies, included disproportionately high numbers of less fit women and children, since the men could take flight and leave the less mobile retinue of young and female dependents to the pursuers. People sold for food, the last resort in time of famine, also started out physically ill-prepared for the rigors of the journey to come. In the commercialized areas, lords, creditors, and patrons, employing less dramatic methods to seize and sell the dependents who paid for imports or covered their debts, would have selected the least promising among their followings— young boys, older women, the sick, the indebted, the troublesome, and the lame. Populations raided consistently by stronger neighbors, harassed and driven from their homes and fields, and refugee populations hiding on infertile mountaintops could not have been as well-nourished as stronger groups who yielded fewer of their members to the slave trade.

The mixture of people swept off by thousands of isolated decisions and haphazard actions separated into two distinguishable drifts of people. One was a slow, favored one composed principally of the stronger and healthier women and younger children that dissipated into the communities of western central Africa, to remain there as wives and slaves for months or years, or perhaps for life. The debilitated residue became the faster-flowing and sharply defined main channel of people destined for immediate sale and export, victims of drought and raids at the source, joined by small feeder streams of older youths ejected from local communities along its banks as it flowed westward, along with a few women and older folk, and a variety of outcasts and criminals.

The flow headed for the Atlantic coast thus carried weakened individuals relatively vulnerable to disease and death, even by the low health standards of their time. These slaves were not necessarily constitutionally weaker than those left behind or kept but, rather, individuals taken at defenseless and enfeebled moments in their lives. Their temporarily reduced ability to withstand the stresses of enslavement, dislocation, and forced travel could not have failed to produce higher incidences of sickness and death among them than among the population of western central Africa as a whole, even without adding the physical traumas of violent seizure or the psychological shocks of nonviolent enslavement. . . .

Movement to the Coast

These slaves advanced from the hands of their captors, sometimes with periods of rest and partial recuperation in villages along the way, into the market centers where African sellers met European and Luso-African slave-buyers in the interior. People raised in small, dispersed settlements would have encountered the much more volatile disease environments among populations concentrated along the trails, at the staging posts, and finally in the marketplaces themselves. Those from more densely inhabited areas, and even captives who had lived along the roads, encountered new disease environments as they moved into terrain unlike that of their native lands and came into direct contact with foreigners. They would have suffered accordingly from pathogens against which they had no immunities.

The slaves' diets also deteriorated. Whatever plantains, sorghum, or millet they might have eaten at home, supplemented by a healthy variety of game, other crops, and wild plants, as they moved westward they depended increasingly on manioc—the dietary staple that was cheapest to grow, easiest to transport, and most resistant to spoilage—prepared poorly in one form or another. Fresh fruits and vegetables and meat virtually disappeared from their diet. Much of what they were given rotted or became vermin-infested. They were unlikely to have received foods of any sort in quantities sufficient to sustain them, particularly in their weakened conditions, and with vicious circularity they grew too weak to carry what little they were given as they moved. Those who stumbled from weakness were driven onward to keep the remainder moving, all bound together. They drank from inadequate water supplies along the way, sometimes streams, but often not, owing to the tendency of the trails to follow the elevated ridges along the watersheds and the caravan drivers' preference for travel in the dry months. Pools dug out at stopping places were often contaminated from the concentrations of slave caravans that built up around them.

Under such conditions, the slaves developed both dietary imbalances and sheer nutritional insufficiencies. Scurvy, so common among slaves who lived to cross the southern Atlantic that it was known as the *mal de Loanda* (or "Luanda sickness"), was the primary recognized form of undernourishment. The symptoms appeared on slave ships at sea long before they could have developed from shortages of rations on board except among slaves already debilitated by weeks or months of a diet restricted to low vitamin, low acetic acid starches like manioc. With innocent destructiveness some physicians prescribed more manioc as an anti-escorbutic. The slaves who died along the path must have suffered malnutrition to a degree approaching sheer starvation. Racialist Portuguese theories of tropical medicine at the time misdiagnosed the condition, holding that blacks needed to eat less than whites, since they could thrive for days at a time on nothing more than a few millet heads and a kola nut.

The alterations in diet and the amoeba in contaminated water supplies must also have caused the early spread of dysenteries and other intestinal disorders, the infamous "flux" that the British lamented among the slaves they carried across the Atlantic, known as *câmaras* among the Portuguese. Infected excreta left everywhere about water sources, in camp sites, and in the slave pens of the marketplaces assured that few individuals escaped debilitating and dehydrating epidemics of bloody bacillary dysenteries.

Exposure to the dry-season chill in the high elevations and to damp nights spent sitting in open pathside camps, utter lack of clothing and shelter, and increasingly weakened constitutions all contributed to the appearance of respiratory ailments vaguely described as *constipações*. As slaves neared the marketplaces and the main routes running from them down to the coast, they grew weaker and more susceptible to parasites and other diseases that swept in epidemic form through the coffles. The slave trade must have been a veritable incubator for typhus, typhoid, and other fevers or *carneiradas*, particularly smallpox, and other diseases that broke out in times of drought and famine from their usual confinement in the streams of slaves into the general rural population. The normal concentration of these diseases along the commercial routes may have contributed to the impression of overwhelming deadliness that Portuguese held of most of the central African interior, since every European who ventured there necessarily walked within these reservoirs of slave-borne infection on the pathways leading to the interior.

The inferable lethal consequences of malnutrition, disease, and other hardships along the path were death rates that rose at an increasing tempo as slaves flowed into the central channels of the slave trade, perhaps to catastrophic levels in the range of 400–600 per 1,000 per annum by the time slaves reached the coast. One experienced Luanda merchant reported that slavers toward the second half of the eighteenth century expected to lose about 40 percent of their captives to flight and death between the time they purchased them in the interior and the time they put them aboard the ships in Luanda. If the westward march averaged about six months from the central highlands or the Kwango valley, where most agents of the town merchants bought slaves at that time, and deaths in the seaport ran about 15 percent, that estimate would mean 25 percent of the slaves died en route to the coast. Such a figure would imply a mean death rate between time of purchase and time of arrival in the towns of 500 per 1,000 per year. In practice, lower death rates at the outset of the trek would have risen at an increasing rate to peak somewhere above that level at the coast, but averaging out to that overall percentage loss. A certain proportion of the losses would have been attributable to flight and to theft, leaving a bit less than the reported total owing to mortality.

Flight from the slave coffles heading toward the coast, though impossible to estimate precisely in terms of frequency, was not uncommon. Despite the nutritional and epidemiological odds against the slaves, some individuals somehow found the strength to flee their captors. Slaves fled from the marketplaces of the interior, taking refuge among the very people who had just sold them to the Europeans. As they neared the coast, they found willing, though often calculatingly self-interested, asylum among the independent Africans living on either side of Luanda, south of the Kwanza in Kisama, and north of the Dande among the southern Kongo of Musulu. Some fugitives established maroon colonies of their own within Portuguese territory, and there are hints that a major colony of renegades existed throughout the century virtually on the outskirts of Luanda. Some of these colonies had extensive fields and fortifications, including up to forty houses and populations of about 200 people, and lived by raiding Portuguese slave-run plantations in the river valleys.

The nearness of Kisama made it the favored destination for Luanda slaves seeking protection from independent Africans, and the willingness of chiefs there to welcome fugitives underlay the persistent enmity between the Portuguese and the Africans living south of the river. Kisama was in effect an enormous fugitive slave colony, or *quilombo*, as these were known in both Brazil and Angola. Kisama's role as a haven for fugitives probably declined at the end of the eighteenth century, since nineteenth-century references to the region no longer picked up the ancient refrain of hostility.

The fugitives generally hid out beyond rivers, in deep forests, and on inaccessible mountaintops, but individuals also found refuge in the churches of the town and on missionary-run estates in the vicinity, all of them ecclesiastical property exempt from intrusions by the civilian authorities. Slaves who fled the Portuguese after years of experience in Luanda found a particular welcome among the lords of Kisama, who used them as spies who could return undetected to the city, dressed like its other African residents, and report back on Portuguese military capacities and intentions. Other groups of fugitive slaves constantly assaulted the roads leading eastward from Luanda, particularly in the 1740s, 1750s, and 1760s to judge from the incidence of official government concern, mostly stealing trade goods from the caravans. The organization and tactics of these refugee communities seem to have differed hardly at all from maroon colonies elsewhere in Africa, Brazil, the Caribbean, and mainland North America.

The Barracoons of Luanda and Benguela

The slave population entering Luanda was heavily weighted toward younger males by the eighteenth century, reflecting the strain on western central African populations by that time and the widespread resort to debt as means of creating slaves. Older men (*barbados*) also passed through Luanda in significant numbers. Predominant among the women were young females, with a scattering of prime (nubile) women, mothers with infants, and girls, precisely the category of slave that African lords must have been least willing to give up and therefore a further indication of demographic and commercial pressures then bearing on the slave supply zones.

The ideal slave *peça*, or prime adult male, was in short supply, no longer available from the areas of commercialized slaving, and relatively few of the women taken in wars made it through the African transporters to arrive at the coast. The proportion of able-bodied adult males reaching the coast had declined to only one-eighth to one-sixth of the individuals offered for sale in the 1780s and 1790s. Scattered detailed breakdowns of prices received for mixed lots of captives show only a few individuals in the highest-priced, presumably *peça* category; none at all appeared in some groups changing hands in 1774 and 1799, and 10 percent (or perhaps 20 percent) showed up in others in the mid-1780s. An apparently prime shipment in 1809 still contained only one-third *peças*. A lot of 100 slave couples purchased for the Crown in 1819, and therefore presumably the very best to be found in Luanda, managed only just over half of the males in the top price category. This purchase indicated the absolute maximum proportion of prime slaves who could be assembled at that time. The usual coffle contained far fewer.

The terms employed to describe the slaves also reflected the decline in age and strength of the individuals being delivered by then. *Moleque*, a word that had referred to nearly adult youths a century or more before, became the general form of reference to ordinary slaves, but augmentative derivations, *molecão* or *molecote,* appeared to cover the mature young men left out as the original term was applied to the boys who constituted the majority of the captives.

Older people and small children appeared in relatively low numbers, and their absence probably reflected the high death rates along the trail that worked selectively against weaker individuals for months before the coffles reached the cities. These numbers also reflected Portuguese reluctance to buy the very old and the very young. In particular, slavers in Luanda avoided sending off young children, who, for all their usefulness for avoiding taxes and for tight-packing, were bad risks for shipment, since they were widely regarded as unlikely to survive the middle passage. In addition, infants imported to Brazil brought low prices. Their continued high death rates, their low productivity compared to new adult slaves, and the competition from American-born slave infants, who would grow up knowing Portuguese and were surely less costly to raise within the household or estate than paying out the cash necessary to buy new children from Angola, all made them bad investments. The *moleque* majority of the slaves shipped, on the other hand, who by this time included older children from eight to fifteen years of age, were regarded as trainable, capable of learning Portuguese, and less likely to flee or to die from shock and depression. The Portuguese reluctance to buy younger African children complemented the African desire to retain them and raise them for sale as young adults, with the result that few of them actually arrived at Luanda or Benguela for shipment or sale. . . .

All the slaves trembled in terror at meeting the white cannibals of the cities, the first Europeans whom many of the slaves would have seen. They feared the whites' intention of converting Africans' brains into cheese or rendering the fat of African bodies into cooking oil, as well as burning their bones into gunpowder. They clearly regarded the towns as places of certain death, as indeed they became for many, if not for the reasons slaves feared. . . .

The great majority of the slaves went directly to the slave pens of the city's large expatriate merchants. These barracoons—known as *quintais* (singular *quintal*), a word also applied to farmyards for keeping animals—were usually barren enclosures located immediately behind the large two-story residences in the lower town, but traders also constructed them around the edges of the city and on the beach. Large numbers of slaves accumulated within these pens, living for days and weeks surrounded by walls too high for a person to scale, squatting helplessly, naked, on the dirt and entirely exposed to the skies except for a few adjoining cells where they could be locked at night. They lived in a "wormy morass" (*ascaroz-issimo charco*) and slept in their own excrement, without even a bonfire for warmth. One observer described "two hundred, sometimes three and four hundred slaves in each *quintal*, and there they stayed, ate, slept, and satisfied every human necessity, and from there they infected the houses and the city with the most putrid miasmas; and because dried fish is their usual and preferred food, it was on the walls of these *quintais* and on the roofs of the straw dwellings that such preparation was done, with manifest damage to the public health." To the smell of rotting fish were added the foul odors of the slaves' dysenteries and the putrid fragrance of the bodies of those who died. The stench emanating from these squalid prisons overpowered visitors to the town.

At Benguela the slave pens were about 17 meters square, with walls 3 meters or more in height, and they sometimes contained as many as 150 to 200 slaves, intermixed with pigs and goats also kept in them. That left about two square meters per individual, or barely enough to lie down and to move about a bit. In some instances, at least, the walls had openings cut in them, through which guards outside could thrust musket barrels to fire on slaves within who grew unruly.

The merchants' casual disrespect for the mortal remains of the thousands of slaves dying in and around the city created a grisly hazard to public health. Few aspects of the trade expressed the valuelessness of dead slaves more clearly than the merchants' habit of dumping the bodies in a heap in a small cemetery adjacent to the

Nazareth chapel near Luanda's commercial district, or depositing them in shallow graves in numbers far greater than the ground could cover decently. They preferred to leave them for the hyenas (*lobos*) to pick over during the night rather than pay the fees the vicar of the chapel charged for proper burials. The poor cleric was left to try to support his place of worship by accepting far more remains of the wealthy for interment than his crypt could hold. The sharp distinctions of wealth among the living at Luanda thus carried through to the disposal of the dead.

At Benguela, widely regarded as even more mortiferous than Luanda, traders simply threw out the bodies of the slaves on the beach along with sewage until the very end of the eighteenth century. They then laid out a special cemetery for slaves dying on the ships and for other unbaptized Africans, but the new policy seems merely to have led to the corpses being partially burnt and left there for scavenging birds and animals. Even later in the nineteenth century, the "great number of cadavers" buried each year was covered with only a few inches of earth, again excepting the rich, for the hyenas to dig up and eat what they liked, and then strew the residue about. . . .

The slaves' wait in the barracoons, filthy and unhealthful as it was, leaves the impression of food and water adequate to begin the long process of recuperation from the greater hardships of enslavement and the westward trail. Daily visits to the bay to bathe afforded some slaves an opportunity for limited personal hygiene even amidst the squalor of the slave pens, though they received little that would require cash expenditures by their managers: no clothing, and food barely adequate to sustain them until they would be sold or handed on to the care of the ships' captains waiting to transport them to Brazil. Living conditions for slaves at Benguela would have been worse, owing to the greater shortages of food and water there than in Luanda. But in both ports the sheer opportunity for rest after the rigors of the march from the interior and the availability of salt, iodine, and protein from fish probably allowed the strongest of the young male slaves to recover some of the strength drained from them on their way to the coast. The most penurious merchant could have honestly prided himself on restoring the captives he received toward health, in conformity with his responsibilities to their owners. There may even have been some modest substance to merchants' exaggerated claims that they were doing so. . . .

... A general estimate on the order of 10 to 15 percent ought not to be far out of line for mid- to late-eighteenth-century mortality among the slaves held at Angolan ports. It is probable, though undocumented, that rates had been higher in the past and declined through the 1700s, except in periods of drought and famine. The damages wrought by famine in the town, too, were lessened after the 1760s by the operation of the *terreiro público* public granary. . . .

The annualized mortality rate for the slaves' stay on the coast . . . would have averaged twice the mean for the preceding months on the trails of the interior, mostly as an extension of the highest rates attained toward the end of their march to the sea into their first few days or weeks in the city. Slaves from higher elevations in the interior would have succumbed to unfamiliar diseases endemic along the coast soon after their arrival. Death rates probably declined perceptibly thereafter, and many slaves boarded the ships in physical condition marginally stronger than the near-delirium in which they had stumbled into the city.

Embarkation Procedures

When the day of the slaves' departure finally dawned, they and their owners and managers set out along yet another tortuous course leading from the slave pens through the long chain of government officials charged with enforcing the maze of rules intended to protect the slaves' bodies and souls and the revenues of the king, though in fact often to the enhancement of none of these. The procedures had been relatively simple earlier in the eighteenth century, but later efforts to curtail tight-packing and smuggling and to improve supplies of food and water aboard the slave ships gradually lengthened the gantlet through which they passed.

In broad terms, all embarking slaves had to be certified as Christian, which implied instruction in the Catholic faith followed by baptism, certified as to their taxable status (adult *cabeça,* child, or infant), and then formally dispatched in conformity with loading limits on the ships and counted to document the contractor's or government's claims to export duties from their owners. Two underlying conflicts came to a head in the course of these formalities. The first concerned the amounts of the fees, duties, and other charges owners owed on each slave. The other, and probably the more vital of the two, focused on the speed with which the slaves could be processed.

Since owners desired to avoid every possible expense on slaves, particularly weakened and dying ones who might bring no return on further investments, they delayed religious instruction, baptism, and payment of taxes until the last possible moment. The missions, the church, and the government, on the other hand, wished to save as many souls and to collect as many fees and duties as they could, and they therefore attempted to advance the processing of the slaves as early as possible in their stay in the city. The difference in revenues was potentially significant, equal in theory to deaths that reduced taxable bodies and redeemable souls entering the city by as much as 40 percent before the survivors left it. The counterpoint to this rhythm of rush and delay was generated by petty officials who, paid only the most derisory of official salaries, stalled deliberately to collect bribes from owners desperate to get their slaves on board the ships before they died.

Slaves on their way to the port, dressed in loincloths (*tangas*) or crude camisoles made, as often as not, of burlap wrappings recovered from the bundles and bales of imported goods, were initially assembled before customs officials competent to mark their progress. Holders of the official position of catechist for slaves (*catequizador dos negros/dos escravos,* and other variant titles), normally clerics, were responsible for their religious instruction. None could be processed through the customs house without a *bilhete* (chit or pass) certifying their knowledge of the Catholic faith and their baptism. The catechists gradually acquired other responsibilities in the course of the eighteenth century, including defense of the minimal rights conceded to the unfortunate individuals brought as captives to Luanda. In particular, these priests acted as official interpreters between the captives and officials of the colony, directed by increasingly enlightened governments in Lisbon to free slaves captured unjustly in the interior upon their arrival in Luanda. The catechists were eventually recognized officially . . . and may in fact have represented occasional cases of unjust capture to the governors, some of whom claimed regularly to free the victims of such misfortunes.

The official government catechist, usually a local appointed to the position as a sinecure, did not personally supervise instruction and baptism of each of the 8,000–10,000 slaves passing through the city each year, but rather, employed slaves who spoke Kimbundu, the *lingua franca* of the town, and taught the written Kimbundu catechism in use by the end of the eighteenth century. How much of this instruction the thousands of captives from Kikongo, Ruund, Ovimbundu, and other distant African language areas might have understood is an open question. . . .

Though publication of a late-eighteenth-century Kimbundu catechism indicated at least a minimal seriousness of purpose, ecclesiastics' protests of sincerity, thoroughness, and care showed mostly their obvious pecuniary interest in observing at least the formalities. The instruction given most slaves and the baptism itself were in fact little more than caricatures. Cynical and careless priests fulfilled their duties by last-minute sprinklings from a hog trough filled with holy water rigged hastily aboard ships ready to leave. Such callousness obviously stemmed from the owners' desires not to waste the cost of saving souls that death would release before government certification or retard the movement of dying slaves from their pens to the ships and on to Brazil.

The principal memory that most slaves retained of their encounter with imperial bureaucracy was probably the repeated applications of hot irons to their chests and upper arms. The Portuguese branded slaves as evidence of ownership, exactly as they branded cattle or horses, and also to certify various aspects of the captives' legal status, like customs inspectors burning marks on bales of goods as they dispatched them through the customs shed. To judge from the tatooing ubiquitous on many of the people taken as slaves, such marking not only inflicted pain but also in a profound sense humiliated and disfigured people who expressed their status by designs on their skins. The brands applied in Angola seared their new identities as capitalist property into their very flesh.

All parties with an interest in the slave, through ownership or through rights to fees levied on his or her passage through Luanda, registered their claims by the application of hot metal to the slaves. The first Luso-Africans to own the slaves applied their personal brands to the captives' arms upon purchase, to identify and to certify their possession of specific individuals as they continued on their way under the supervision of subsequent agents and shippers. Early in the eighteenth century, contractors added a further mark of fiscal identity to slaves whose owners had paid export duties on them. At least since the late seventeenth century, the government appointed an official slave brander, the *marcador dos escravos,* charged with burning the royal arms onto the right breast of slaves, signifying their vassalage to the Crown. Efforts to enforce the provisions for baptism led to addition of a cross brand overlaying the royal mark. The only slaves excepted from enduring the brands of baptism, ownership, and export duty necessary to clear customs were mulattoes born and raised in the town of Luanda and taken with their masters (and fathers?) when they retired to Brazil. . . .

Conclusion: Mortality in Comparison

. . . Of 100 people seized in Africa, 75 would have reached the marketplaces in the interior; 85 percent of them, or about 64 of the original 100, would have arrived at the coast; after losses of 11 percent in the barracoons, 57 or so would have boarded the ships; of those 57, 51 would have stepped onto Brazilian soil, and 48 or 49 would have lived to behold their first master in the New World. The full "seasoning" period of 3–4 years would leave only 28 or 30 of the original 100 alive and working. A total "wastage" factor of about two-thirds may thus be estimated for the late-eighteenth-century Angolan trade, higher earlier in the trade, probably a bit lower by the 1820s, with slaves from the wetter equatorial latitudes always showing a lower mortality rate than those from Luanda and Benguela. As such, even at that late date it was a number amply large to rivet the fatalistic attention of the slavers in the Angolan trade and the merchants supporting them, to force all involved to stress speed, and to prompt the wealthy and powerful to organize its financial structures so as to avoid, where they could, the risks and costs resulting from mortality they could not control. It was literally, and sadly, true that "if few die the profit is certain, but if many are lost so also is their owner."

PART V

Effects in Africa

The truth is that a developing Africa went into slave trading and European commercial relations as into a gale-force wind, which shipwrecked a few societies, set many others off course, and generally slowed down the rate of advance.

WALTER RODNEY

The coastal exports of young adult slaves, twice as many men as women, tended to transform the structure of the population and the organization of society.

PATRICK MANNING

It was only in the slave trade era that African Atlantic trade kept pace with the growth of world trade. . . . Despite the relative strength of the slave trade, the economy of western Africa remained little affected.

DAVID ELTIS

The effects of the Atlantic slave trade varied widely in Africa. They depended on how long and how much a society was involved, on whether its people were the slave traders or the slaves traded, and on how well a society managed the strains introduced by the trade. Case studies of a large number of individual African societies have been written, many of which are listed in the Suggestions for Further Reading at the end of this book. Rather than examine a few individual cases, the readings in this part concentrate on the broad effects of the slave trade on Africa generally, though they often refer to the more specialized studies.

In the first reading the late West Indian historian Walter Rodney argues that participation in the Atlantic slave trade affected Africa negatively by causing population loss, by deflecting Africans' energies away from productive activities, by undercutting African manufacturing with cheap consumer goods and "assorted rubbish," but most of all by tying Africans to an inferior relationship with the European capitalist economy that blocked their economic and technological progress. Yet Rodney also argues that many parts of Africa that participated in the Atlantic slave trade did progress during this period, and he insists that this progress occurred despite the slave trade, not because of it. A historian of West Africa and the Caribbean, Rodney is the author of *A History of the Upper Guinea Coast, 1545–1800* (1970) and a *History of the Guyanese Working People, 1881–1905* (1981).

Historian Patrick Manning of Northeastern University places his interpretation of the slave trade's impact in the context of schools of historical interpretation about Africa that go back more than two centuries. He contrasts older views of African societies as static with modern historians' presumption of an "African dynamism," while further distinguishing between those who see Africa's history as controlled from within ("emergent Africa") and those who see it as externally dominated ("Afrique engagée"). He places Rodney in the latter school, but he criticizes Rodney's view that Africa was simultaneously being stifled by its relationship with capitalism while some parts of the continent were experiencing positive development despite the trade. In effect, Manning faults Rodney for trying to have one foot in each camp. Manning then goes on to support the interpretation of "Afrique engagée," stressing that the demographic and social effects of the slave trade were interconnected with the economic effects, a point that he subsequently has developed in his book *Slavery and African Life: Occidental, Oriental and African Slave Trades* (1990).

David Eltis, an economic historian at Queens University, Ontario, takes a different approach, looking at the items and value of trade between Europe and Africa at different points before, during, and after the Atlantic slave trade was at its peak. He declines to debate Manning on the demographic and social impacts of the trade, agreeing with David Henige (earlier, in Part II) that Manning's arguments may be plausible but not provable. However, he directly challenges Rodney's view of the economic effects of the trade, disputing Rodney's charge that the goods Africans received in exchange for slaves were worthless and harmful. Eltis cites evidence that these goods did not differ significantly from those that other parts of the world imported, and that African imports during the slave-trade era included less alcohol and tobacco and fewer textiles that could undermine local industry than were imported after the Atlantic slave trade ended. Finally, he argues that the Atlantic exchanges in which Africans participated before 1870 were too small to have created the dependency on the external economy that Rodney claims. David Eltis has written many articles on the volume and economics of the Atlantic slave trade as well as the book *Economic Growth and the Ending of the Transatlantic Slave Trade* (1987).

The Unequal Partnership Between Africans and Europeans

WALTER RODNEY

The European Slave Trade as a Basic Factor in African Underdevelopment

. . . Undoubtedly, with few exceptions such as Hawkins,* European buyers purchased African captives on the coasts of Africa and the transaction between themselves and Africans was a form of trade. It is also true that very often a captive was sold and resold as he made his way from the interior to the port of embarkation—and that too was a form of trade. However, on the whole, the process by which captives were obtained on African soil was not trade at all. It was through warfare, trickery, banditry, and kidnaping. When one tries to measure the effect of European slave trading on the African con-

Source: From *How Europe Underdeveloped Africa* by Walter Rodney, excerpts from pp. 95–6, 98–100, 101–109, 113–15, 134–35. Copyright © 1972 by Walter Rodney. Reprinted by permission of Howard University Press.

*See John Hawkins, "An Alliance to Raid for Slaves, 1568" in Part III of this book.

tinent, it is essential to realize that one is measuring the effect of social violence rather than trade in any normal sense of the word.

Many things remain uncertain about the slave trade and its consequences for Africa, but the general picture of destructiveness is clear, and that destructiveness can be shown to be the logical consequence of the manner of recruitment of captives in Africa. One of the uncertainties concerns the basic question of how many Africans were imported. This has long been an object of speculation, with estimates ranging from a few millions to over one hundred million. A recent study has suggested a figure of about ten million Africans landed alive in the Americas, the Atlantic islands, and Europe. Because it is a low figure, it is already being used by European scholars who are apologists for the capitalist system and its long record of brutality in Europe and abroad. In order to whitewash the European slave trade, they find it convenient to start by minimizing the numbers concerned. The truth is that any figure of Africans imported into the Americas which is narrowly based on the surviving records is bound to be low, because there were so many people at the time who had a vested interest in smuggling slaves (and withholding data). Nevertheless, if the low figure of ten million was accepted as a basis for evaluating the impact of slaving on Africa as a whole, the conclusions that could legitimately be drawn would confound those who attempt to make light of the experience of the rape of Africans from 1445 to 1870.

On any basic figure of Africans landed alive in the Americas, one would have to make several extensions—starting with a calculation to cover mortality in transshipment. The Atlantic crossing, or "Middle Passage," as it was called by European slavers, was notorious for the number of deaths incurred, averaging in the vicinity of 15 to 20 per cent. There were also numerous deaths in Africa between time of capture and time of embarkation, especially in cases where captives had to travel hundreds of miles to the coast. Most important of all (given that warfare was the principal means of obtaining captives) it is necessary to make some estimate as to the number of people killed and injured so as to extract the millions who were taken alive and sound. The resultant figure would be many times the millions landed alive outside of Africa, and it is that figure which represents the number of Africans directly removed from the population and labor force of Africa because of the establishment of slave production by Europeans.

The massive loss to the African labor force was made more critical because it was composed of able-bodied young men and young women. Slave buyers preferred their victims between the ages of fifteen and thirty-five, and preferably in the early twenties; the sex ratio being about two men to one woman. Europeans often accepted younger African children, but rarely any older person. They shipped the most healthy wherever possible, taking the trouble to get those who had already survived an attack of smallpox, and who were therefore immune from further attacks of that disease, which was then one of the world's great killer diseases. . . .

So long as the population density was low, then human beings viewed as units of labor were far more important than other factors of production such as land. From one end of the continent to the other, it is easy to find examples showing that African people were conscious that population was in their circumstances the most important factor of production. Among the Bemba, for instance, numbers of subjects were held to be more important than land. Among the Shambala of Tanzania, the same feeling was expressed in the saying "A king is people." Among the Balanta of Guinea-Bissau, the family's strength is represented by the number of hands there are to cultivate the land. Certainly, many African rulers acquiesced in the European slave trade for what they considered to be reasons of self-interest, but on no scale of rationality could the outflow of population be measured as being anything but disastrous for African societies.

African economic activity was affected both directly and indirectly by population loss. For instance, when the inhabitants of a given area were reduced below a certain number in an environment where the tsetse fly was present, the remaining few had to abandon the area. In effect, enslavement was causing these people to lose their battle to tame and harness nature—a battle which is at the basis of development. Violence almost meant insecurity. The opportunity presented by European slave dealers became the major (though not the only) stimulus for a great deal of social violence between different African communities and within any given community. It took the form more of raiding and kidnaping than of regular warfare, and that fact increased the element of fear and uncertainty.

Both openly and by implication, all the European powers in the nineteenth century indicated their awareness of the fact that the activities connected with producing captives were inconsistent with

other economic pursuits. That was the time when Britain in particular wanted Africans to collect palm produce and rubber and to
grow agricultural crops for export in place of slaves; and it was clear
that slave raiding was violently conflicting with that objective in
Western, Eastern, and Central Africa. Long before that date, Europeans accepted that fact when their self-interest was involved. For
example, in the seventeenth century, the Portuguese and Dutch actually discouraged slave trade on the Gold Coast, for they recognized
that it would be incompatible with gold trade. However, by the end
of that century, gold had been discovered in Brazil, and the importance of gold supplies from Africa was lessened. Within the total
Atlantic pattern, African slaves became more important than gold,
and Brazilian gold was offered for African captives at Whydah (Dahomey) and Accra. At that point, slaving began undermining the
Gold Coast economy and destroying the gold trade. Slave raiding
and kidnaping made it unsafe to mine and to travel with gold; and
raiding for captives proved more profitable than gold mining. One
European on the scene noted that "as one fortunate marauding
makes a native rich in a day, they therefore exert themselves rather
in war, robbery and plunder than in their old business of digging and
collecting gold."

The above changeover from gold mining to slave raiding took
place within a period of a few years between 1700 and 1710, when
the Gold Coast came to supply about five thousand to six thousand
captives per year. By the end of the eighteenth century, a much
smaller number of captives were exported from the Gold Coast, but
the damage had already been done. It is worth noting that Europeans
sought out different parts of West and Central Africa at different
times to play the role of major suppliers of slaves to the Americas.
This meant that virtually every section of the long western coastline
between the Senegal and Cunene rivers had at least a few years' experience of intensive trade in slaves—with all its consequences. Besides, in the history of eastern Nigeria, the Congo, northern Angola,
and Dahomey, there were periods extending over decades when exports remained at an average of many thousands per year. Most of
those areas were also relatively highly developed within the African
context. They were leading forces inside Africa, whose energies
would otherwise have gone towards their own self-improvement and
the betterment of the continent as a whole.

The changeover to warlike activities and kidnaping must have affected all branches of economic activity, and agriculture in particular. Occasionally, in certain localities food production was increased to provide supplies for slave ships, but the overall consequences of slaving on agricultural activities in Western, Eastern, and Central Africa were negative. Labor was drawn off from agriculture and conditions became unsettled. Dahomey, which in the sixteenth century was known for exporting food to parts of what is now Togo, was suffering from famines in the nineteenth century. The present generation of Africans will readily recall that in the colonial period when able-bodied men left their homes as migrant laborers, that upset the farming routine in the home districts and often caused famines. Slave trading after all meant migration of labor in a manner one hundred times more brutal and disruptive.

To achieve economic development, one essential condition is to make the maximum use of the country's labor and natural resources. Usually, that demands peaceful conditions, but there have been times in history when social groups have grown stronger by raiding their neighbors for women, cattle, and goods, because they then used the "booty" from the raids for the benefit of their own community. Slaving in Africa did not even have that redeeming value. Captives were shipped outside instead of being utilized within any given African community for creating wealth from nature. It was only as an accidental by-product that in some areas Africans who recruited captives for Europeans realized that they were better off keeping some captives for themselves. In any case, slaving prevented the remaining population from effectively engaging in agriculture and industry, and it employed professional slave-hunters and warriors to destroy rather than build. Quite apart from the moral aspect and the immense suffering that it caused, the European slave trade was economically totally irrational from the viewpoint of African development.

For certain purposes, it is necessary to be more specific and to speak of the trade in slaves not in general continent-wide terms but rather with reference to the varying impact on several regions. The relative intensity of slave-raiding in different areas is fairly well known. Some South African peoples were enslaved by the Boers and some North African Moslems by Christian Europeans, but those were minor episodes. The zones most notorious for human exports were, firstly, West Africa from Senegal to Angola along a belt extending about two hundred miles inland and, secondly, that part of East-Central Africa which today covers Tanzania, Mozambique, Malawi, northern Zambia, and eastern Congo. Furthermore, within each of those broad areas, finer distinctions can be drawn.

It might therefore appear that slave trade did not adversely affect the development of some parts of Africa, simply because exports were non-existent or at a low level. However, the contention that European slave trade was an underdeveloping factor for the continent as a whole must be upheld, because it does not follow that an African district which did not trade with Europe was entirely free from whatever influences were exerted by Europe. European trade goods percolated into the deepest interior, and (more significantly) the orientation of large areas of the continent towards human exports meant that other positive interactions were thereby ruled out. . . .

One tactic that is now being employed by certain European (including American) scholars is to say that the European slave trade was undoubtedly *a moral evil,* but it was *economically good* for Africa. Here attention will be drawn only very briefly to a few of those arguments to indicate how ridiculous they can be. One that receives much emphasis is that African rulers and other persons obtained European commodities in exchange for their captives, and this was how Africans gained "wealth." This suggestion fails to take into account the fact that several European imports were competing with and strangling African products; it fails to take into account the fact that none of the long list of European articles were of the type which entered into the productive process, but were rather items to be rapidly consumed or stowed away uselessly; and it incredibly overlooks the fact that the majority of the imports were of the worst quality even as consumer goods—cheap gin, cheap gunpowder, pots and kettles full of holes, beads, and other assorted rubbish.

Following from the above, it is suggested that certain African kingdoms grew strong economically and politically as a consequence of the trade with Europeans. The greatest of the West African kingdoms, such as Oyo, Benin, Dahomey, and Asante are cited as examples. Oyo and Benin were great long before making contact with Europeans, and while both Dahomey and Asante grew stronger during the period of the European slave trade, the roots of their achievements went back to much earlier years. Furthermore—and this is a major fallacy in the argument of the slave-trade apologists—the fact that a given African state grew politically more powerful at the same time as it engaged in selling captives to Europeans is not automatically to be attributed to the credit of the trade in slaves. A cholera epidemic may kill thousands in a country and yet the population increases. The increase obviously came about *in spite of* and not because of the cholera. This simple logic escapes those who speak about the European slave trade benefiting Africa. The destructive tendency of slave trading can be clearly established; and, wherever a state seemingly progressed in the epoch of slave trading, the conclusion is simply that it did so in spite of the adverse effects of a process that was more damaging than cholera. This is the picture that emerges from a detailed study of Dahomey, for instance, and in the final analysis although Dahomey did its best to expand politically and militarily while still tied to slave trade, that form of economic activity seriously undermined its economic base and left it much worse off.

A few of the arguments about the economic benefits of the European slave trade for Africa amount to nothing more than saying that exporting millions of captives was a way of avoiding starvation in Africa! To attempt to reply to that would be painful and time-wasting. But, perhaps a slightly more subtle version of the same argument requires a reply: namely, the argument that Africa gained because in the process of slave trading new food crops were acquired from the American continent and these became staples in Africa. The crops in question are maize and cassava, which became staples in Africa late in the nineteenth century and in the present century. But the spread of food crops is one of the most common phenomena in human history. . . .

All of the above points are taken from books and articles published recently, as the fruit of research in major British and American universities. They are probably not the commonest views even among European bourgeois scholars, but they are representative of a growing trend that seems likely to become the new accepted orthodoxy in metropolitan capitalist countries; and this significantly coincides with Europe's struggle against the further decolonization of Africa economically and mentally. In one sense, it is preferable to ignore such rubbish and isolate our youth from its insults; but unfortunately one of the aspects of current African underdevelopment is that the capitalist publishers and bourgeois scholars dominate the scene and help mold opinions the world over. It is for that reason that writing of the type which justifies the trade in slaves has to be exposed as racist bourgeois propaganda, having no connection with reality or logic. It is a question not merely of history but of present-day liberation struggle in Africa.

Technical Stagnation and Distortion of the African Economy in the Pre-Colonial Epoch

It has already been indicated that in the fifteenth century European technology was not totally superior to that of other parts of the world. There were certain specific features which were highly advantageous to Europe—such as shipping and (to a lesser extent) guns. Europeans trading to Africa had to make use of Asian and African consumer goods, showing that their system of production was not absolutely superior. It is particularly striking that in the early centuries of trade, Europeans relied heavily on Indian cloths for resale in Africa, and they also purchased cloths on several parts of the West African coast for resale elsewhere. Morocco, Mauritania, Senegambia, Ivory Coast, Benin, Yorubaland, and Loango were all exporters to other parts of Africa—through European middlemen. . . .

African demand for cloth was increasing rapidly in the fifteenth, sixteenth, and seventeenth centuries, so that there was a market for all cloth produced locally as well as room for imports from Europe and Asia. But, directed by an acquisitive capitalist class, European industry increased its capacity to produce on a large scale by harnessing the energy of wind, water, and coal. European cloth industry was able to copy fashionable Indian and African patterns, and eventually to replace them. Partly by establishing a stranglehold on the distribution of cloth around the shores of Africa, and partly by swamping African products by importing cloth in bulk, European traders eventually succeeded in putting an end to the expansion of African cloth manufacture.

. . . When European cloth became dominant on the African market, it meant that African producers were cut off from the increasing demand. The craft producers either abandoned their tasks in the face of cheap available European cloth, or they continued on the same small hand-worked instruments to create styles and pieces for localized markets. Therefore, there was what can be called "technological arrest" or stagnation, and in some instances actual regression, since people forgot even the simple techniques of their forefathers. The abandonment of traditional iron smelting in most parts of Africa is probably the most important instance of technological regression.

Development means a capacity for self-sustaining growth. It means that an economy must register advances which in turn will promote further progress. The loss of industry and skill in Africa was extremely small, if we measure it from the viewpoint of modern scientific achievements or even by standards of England in the late eighteenth century. However, it must be borne in mind that to be held back at one stage means that it is impossible to go on to a further stage. When a person was forced to leave school after only two years of primary school education, it is no reflection on him that he is academically and intellectually less developed than someone who had the opportunity to be schooled right through to university level. What Africa experienced in the early centuries of trade was precisely a loss of development *opportunity,* and this is of the greatest importance. . . .

The European slave trade was a direct block, in removing millions of youth and young adults who are the human agents from whom inventiveness springs. Those who remained in areas badly hit by slave capturing were preoccupied about their freedom rather than with improvements in production. Besides, even the busiest African in West, Central, or East Africa was concerned more with trade than with production, because of the nature of the contacts with Europe; and that situation was not conducive to the introduction of technological advances. The most dynamic groups over a great area of Africa became associated with foreign trade—notably, the Afro-Portuguese middlemen of Upper Guinea, the Akan market women, the Aro traders of Mozambique, and the Swahili and Wanyamwezi of East Africa. The trade which they carried on was in export items like captives and ivory which did not require the invention of machinery. Apart from that, they were agents for distributing European imports. . . .

Apart from inventiveness, we must also consider the borrowing of technology. When a society for whatever reason finds itself technologically trailing behind others, it catches up not so much by independent inventions but by borrowing. Indeed, very few of man's major scientific discoveries have been separately discovered in different places by different people. Once a principle or a tool is known, it spreads or diffuses to other peoples. Why then did European technology fail to make its way into Africa during the many centuries of contact between the two continents? The basic reason is that the very nature of Afro-European trade was highly unfavorable to the movement of positive ideas and techniques from the European capitalist system to the African pre-capitalist (communal, feudal, and pre-feudal) system of production.

. . . The lines of economic activity attached to foreign trade were either destructive, as slavery was, or at best purely extractive, like ivory hunting and cutting camwood trees. Therefore, there was no reason for wanting to call upon European skills. The African economies would have had little room for such skills unless negative types of exports were completely stopped. A remarkable fact that is seldom brought to light is that several African rulers in different parts of the continent saw the situation clearly, and sought European technology for internal development, which was meant to replace the trade in slaves.

Europeans deliberately ignored those African requests that Europe should place certain skills and techniques at their disposal. . . . When Agaja Trudo of Dahomey sought to stop the trade in captives, he made an appeal to European craftsmen, and he sent an ambassador to London for that purpose. One European who stayed at the court of Dahomey in the late 1720s told his countrymen that "if any tailor, carpenter, smith or any other sort of white man that is free be willing to come here, he will find very good encouragement." The Asantehene Opoku Ware (1720–50) also asked Europeans to set up factories and distilleries in Asante, but he got no response. . . .

Well into the nineteenth century, Europe displayed the same indifference to requests for practical assistance from Africa, although by that period both African rulers and European capitalists were talking about replacing slave trade. In the early nineteenth century, one king of Calabar (in eastern Nigeria) wrote the British asking for a sugar refinery; while around 1804 King Adandozan of Dahomey was bold enough to ask for a firearms factory! By that date, many parts of West Africa were going to war with European firearms and gunpowder. There grew up a saying in Dahomey that "He who makes the powder wins the war," which was a far-sighted recognition that Africans were bound to fall before the superiority of Europeans in the field of arms technology. Of course, Europeans were also fully aware that their arms technology was decisive, and there was not the slightest chance that they would have agreed to teach Africans to make firearms and ammunition.

The circumstances of African trade with Europe were unfavorable to creating a consistent African demand for technology relevant to development; and when that demand was raised it was ignored or rejected by the capitalists. After all, it would not have been in the interests of capitalism to develop Africa. . . . Placing the whole question in historical perspective allows us to see that capitalism has always discouraged technological evolution in Africa, and blocks Africa's access to its own technology. As will be seen in a subsequent section, capitalism introduced into Africa only such limited aspects of its material culture as were essential to more efficient exploitation, but the general tendency has been for capitalism to underdevelop Africa in technology.

The European slave trade and overseas trade in general had what are known as "multiplier effects" on Europe's development in a very positive sense. This means that the benefits of foreign contacts extended to many areas of European life not directly connected with foreign trade, and the whole society was better equipped for its own internal development. The opposite was true of Africa not only in the crucial sphere of technology but also with regard to the size and purpose of each economy in Africa. Under the normal processes of evolution, an economy grows steadily larger so that after a while two neighboring economies merge into one. That was precisely how national economies were created in the states of Western Europe through the gradual combination of what were once separate provincial economies. Trade with Africa actually helped Europe to weld together more closely the different national economies, but in Africa there was disruption and disintegration at the local level. At the same time, each local economy ceased to be directed exclusively or even primarily towards the satisfaction of the wants of its inhabitants; and (whether or not the particular Africans recognized it) their economic effort served external interests and made them dependent on those external forces based in Western Europe. In this way, the African economy taken as a whole was diverted away from its previous line of development and became distorted. . . .

Continuing Politico-Military Developments in Africa—1500 to 1885

Modern African nationalist historians correctly stress that Africa had a meaningful past long before the coming of Europeans. They also stress that Africans made their own history long after coming into contact with Europe, and indeed right up to the period of colonization. That African-centered approach to the continent's past is quite compatible with one which equally emphasizes the transformatory role of external forces, such as overseas trade in slaves, gold, ivory. . . .

Developments continued in certain areas such as south Central Africa, because the population there was free to pursue a path dictated by the interplay between African people and the African environment in the particular localities. Besides, there were achievements even in those societies under the heaviest bombardment of slaving. Slave trading led to the commercial domination of Africa by Europe, within the context of international trade. In very few instances did Europeans manage to displace African political authorities in the various social systems. So African states in close contact with Europe in the pre-colonial era nevertheless had scope for political maneuver, and their evolution could and did continue.

Military conquest of Africa awaited the years of the imperialist Scramble. In pre-colonial centuries of contact with Europe, African armies were in existence, with all the socio-political implications which attach to an armed sector in society. Equally important was the fact that direct imports from Europe in the cultural and ideological spheres were virtually nil. Christianity tried sporadically and ambivalently to make an impact on some parts of the continent. But most of the few missionaries in places like the Congo, Angola, and Upper Guinea concentrated on blessing Africans as they were about to be launched across the Atlantic into slavery. As it was, Christianity continued only in Ethiopia, where it had indigenous roots. Elsewhere, there flourished Islam and other religions which had nothing to do with European trade. As before, religion continued to act as an element of the superstructure, which was crucial in the development of the state.

So long as there is political power, so long as a people can be mobilized to use weapons, and so long as a society has the opportunity to define its own ideology and culture, then the people of that society have some control over their own destinies, in spite of constraints such as those imposed as the African continent slipped into orbit as a satellite of capitalist Europe. After all, although historical development is inseparable from material conditions and the state of technology, it is also partially controlled by a people's consciousness at various stages. That is part of the interdependence of base and superstructure alluded to at the outset. . . .

Politico-military development in Africa from 1500 to 1885 meant that African social collectives had become more capable of defending the interests of their members, as opposed to the interests of people outside the given community. It also meant that the individual in a politically mature and militarily strong state would be free from external threat of physical removal. He would have more opportunities to apply his own skill in fields as diversified as minstrelsy and bronze-working, under the protection of the state. He could also use his creativity and inventiveness to refine the religion of his people, or to work out a more manageable constitution, or to contribute to new techniques of war, or to advance agriculture and trade. Of course, it is also true that the benefits of all such contributions went mainly to a small section of African society, both within and without the zone of slaving; for, as communalism receded, the principle of egalitarian distribution was disregarded. . . .

At the beginning of this section, attention was drawn to the necessity for reconciling a recognition of African development up to 1885 with an awareness of the losses simultaneously incurred by the continent in that epoch, due to the nature of the contact with capitalist Europe. That issue must also be explicitly alluded to at this point. It is clearly ridiculous to assert that contacts with Europe built or benefited Africa in the pre-colonial period. Nor does it represent reality to suggest (as President Leopold Senghor once did) that the slave trade swept Africa like a bush fire, leaving nothing standing. The truth is that a developing Africa went into slave trading and European commercial relations as into a gale-force wind, which shipwrecked a few societies, set many others off course, and generally slowed down the rate of advance. However, (pursuing the metaphor further) it must be noted that African captains were still making decisions before 1885, though already forces were at work which caused European capitalists to insist on, and succeed in taking over, command.

Social and Demographic Transformations

PATRICK MANNING

The old interpretations and the old disputes on Africa and the slave trade have left their mark. The vision of eternal Africa allowed room for disagreement about the impact of the slave trade, and these disagreements have found their way into the current literature. The contrasting interpretations separated those who contended that the transatlantic commerce in slaves brought major changes to African societies from those who denied that trade in slaves disturbed the African social order. Archibald Dalzel, the eighteenth-century English slave trader and propagandist, argued that African society remained unaffected, and he quoted King Kpengla of Danhomè* in support of his position. David Livingstone, the mid-nineteenth-century explorer and missionary, argued forcefully that, to the contrary, slavery and the slave trade were devastating to African society. At the turn of the twentieth century Sir Harry Hamilton Johnston, an imperial man-on-the-spot and amateur scholar, attempted to synthesize these conflicting positions in an interpretation that is in some ways more optimistic than either: "Abominable as the slave trade has been in filling Tropical Africa with incessant warfare and rapine . . . , its ravages will soon be repaired by a few decades of peace and security during which this prolific, unextinguishable negro race will rapidly increase its numbers."

Both the similarities and the differences among these arguments are instructive. Dalzel and Johnston saw African societies as robust and able to withstand the pressures of the slave trade, while Livingstone viewed African societies as fragile and easily shattered. All three, however, shared the view of African societies as static. Although it had survived the slave trade intact, the "prolific, unextinguishable negro race," in Johnston's words, had not progressed—had not gained the ability "to start the children from a higher level than

Source: From "Contours of Slavery and Social Change in Africa" by Patrick Manning in *American Historical Review* vol. 88, no. 4 (Oct. 1983), excerpts from pp. 836–39, 844–51, 853, 856–57. Reprinted by permission of the American Historical Association.

*Also spelled "Dahomey" (Ed.).

the parents." This vision of eternal Africa, emphasizing stagnation and resistance to change, took root and survived in the minds of observers largely because of the difficulty of knowing what changes had taken place. This difficulty, in turn, stemmed not only from the scarcity and dispersal of documentation on precolonial Africa but also from the blurring of perception brought about by cultural differences between African and European observers.

Contemporary Africanist historians have shown remarkable success in bridging the gaps within the documentary record and between cultures, not least because of the growing number of African contributors to the literature. Yet the rise of the Africanist tradition has not been sufficient to resolve the role of the slave trade in precolonial Africa. Instead, the earlier contending views—whether trade in slaves exerted great or small influence on African historical development—have aligned themselves with two interpretive tendencies that have grown up within the Africanist literature. For instance, Basil Davidson, writing in the early 1960s when many African countries were regaining their independence, argued, "Viewed as a factor in African history, the precolonial connection with Europe—essentially, the slave trade—had powerfully degrading consequences for the structure of society." Some years later John D. Fage brought to the debate the revised figures on the magnitude of the slave trade; he concluded that the eighteenth-century loss of four million persons from West Africa did not reduce its population, and he later added that the region's social institutions similarly remained unaffected. Considering many of the same data but also taking underdevelopment into account, Walter Rodney reasoned that, on the contrary, the trade in slaves had brought great harm to African economic and political structures. A decade later Joseph C. Miller argued, with reference to West Central Africa, that a domestically generated cycle of drought, disease, and famine did more to limit population and provoke social change than did the impact of slave exports.

All of the participants in this recent discussion of the impact of the slave trade on Africa have assumed an African dynamism. The differences among them are in the relative emphases they have given to external forces of change. Can the external forces be safely minimized and treated as boundary conditions for a situation in which the major forces for change were domestic, as Fage and Miller have argued? Such an analytical approach may be termed the vision of "emergent Africa": as the historical reconstruction of African social change has become increasingly detailed, this approach has become widely influential in the thinking of Africanist historians. Or must external factors be drawn fully into the analysis of precolonial forces for change, as Davidson and Rodney have contended? This is the vision of "Afrique engagée," which focuses on such interactions as much as on domestic evolution. The choice between the two is determined by ascertaining which leads to the most detailed and yet elegant interpretation of the historical record.

John Fage's view of the role of the slave trade in precolonial Africa dominated the opinions of historians during the 1970s. For West Africa, Fage compared eighteenth-century slave exports that averaged forty thousand per year with a population he estimated at twenty-five million and a growth rate he estimated at 1.5 per thousand—or, some thirty-eight thousand—per year. Hence, "the effect of the export slave trade in the eighteenth century may have been more or less to check population growth," and its impact was in consequence minimal even at the height of slave exports. Fage continued, "The conclusion to which one is led, therefore, is that whereas in East and Central Africa the slave trade, sometimes conducted in the interior by raiding and warring strangers, could be extremely destructive of economic, political and social life, in West Africa it was part of a sustained process of economic and political development." West Africa's domestic processes of evolution were potent enough, in Fage's view, to absorb, neutralize, and, conceivably, even benefit from the effects of participation in slave exports. Although he admitted that the negative effects of slave trade might have been greater outside of West Africa, other scholars have claimed that, particularly for Central Africa, the population and social institutions successfully withstood the pressures of the slave trade. This is the vision of emergent Africa, as applied to the impact of the trade in slaves.

Basil Davidson and Walter Rodney, while basing their views on the assumption of an evolving, developing African society, nevertheless asserted that the slave trade had a significantly detrimental effect on African society. Theirs was a vision of a precolonial Afrique engagée and of a continent that suffered from the engagement. The details of their arguments, however, rely not so much on demographic reasoning (both assumed that the African population did not decline) as on the interruption of African institutional and social progress. "The years of trial," as Davidson called the precolonial era, "were years of isolation and paralysis wherever the trade with Europe, essentially a trade in slaves, could plant its sterilizing hand." Although Davidson, with his slaves-for-guns thesis, and Rodney, with his underdevelopment thesis, listed striking examples to support this view, neither was able to develop a sustained and detailed analysis. Moreover, their image of the meeting of European and African influences depicted not so much a true interaction of the two as the truncation of the latter by the former. Their interpretation thus veers back toward Harry Johnston's image of eternal Africa, except that Davidson and Rodney emphasized the negative, rather than the positive, contributions of European contact to African development.

With a reformulation of the argument, however, the vision of Afrique engagée has gained validity as the relevant framework for interpreting the role of the slave trade in precolonial African history. The limits of Fage's interpretation are centered in his aggregative approach: he did not give much attention to the breakdown of slave exports by sex or age or to the impact of changes in quantities and prices of slave exports over time. Disaggregation of the data, when combined with analysis based on demographic principles and price theory, leads to results that are different from, and in some cases contradictory to, those previously accepted. The interactions of the New World demand for slaves with domestic conditions in Africa brought about—long before the late nineteenth century Scramble for Africa—pervasive social change. Such social changes included the expansion and subsequent transformation of polygyny, the development of two different types of African slavery, the creation and subsequent impoverishment of a class of African merchants, and a final expansion of slavery in the decades before the Scramble. Although the most profound changes from the interaction of the slave trade and African conditions occurred along the western coast of Africa, almost all regions of Africa were touched by the influence of the export trade at one time or another. . . .

The Atlantic slave trade before 1650 rarely carried more than ten thousand slaves per year. Its aggregate impact on the continent was, therefore, small, although the experiences of certain regions prefigured the sharp pressures that were subsequently felt on a broader scale. The Kongo kingdom, for instance, became the main source of slaves for the sugar plantations of São Thomé in the sixteenth century, and numerous sources confirm the corrosive effect of slave exports on Kongo political structure and on the spread of Christianity there. The Upper Guinea Coast supplied large numbers of slaves (predominantly male) as New World laborers in the early seventeenth century, and accounts of contemporary observers give strong support to the image of a predominantly female society left behind, in which women took over agricultural and fishing tasks to assure sufficient production. Although only these two regions, Senegambia, and perhaps the kingdom of Benin exported enough slaves in these early days to influence population size and composition, virtually every region on the western coast of Africa provided some slaves to European purchasers in the years before 1650. But slaves had not yet become Africa's dominant export: gold exports, especially from the Gold Coast, exceeded the value of African slave exports until the end of the seventeenth century.

A qualitative change in the slave trade took form at the turn of the eighteenth century; a four-fold increase in slave prices occurred within thirty years. From the late sixteenth century to the mid-eighteenth century, the quantity of slaves shipped across the Atlantic grew at an average rate of 2 percent per year. Driving this growing demand was the sugar plantation system, as Brazil came to be joined by Barbados, Jamaica, Martinique, and other colonies. By 1650 the New World had displaced the Middle East as the dominant destination of African slaves. During the final years of price stability in the seventeenth century, African suppliers developed efficient methods for delivering more slaves with no increase in cost. But, by the opening of the eighteenth century, the limits on the ability of Africans to provide cheap slaves had been reached, and prices rose dramatically. The cost of obtaining slaves rose as prospective captives learned to defend themselves better and as middlemen and toll collectors interposed themselves into the process of delivery. For these reasons as well as actual population decline, slaves became scarce relative to the level of demand. The price increases in this period led to the establishment of something resembling a world market for slave labor, in which New World demand and prices for slaves were so high that both slave prices and the quantity of slaves moved were affected not only along the western coast but in many regions of the African continent as well.

Two African regions bore the brunt of the expansion in exports at the turn of the eighteenth century: the Bight of Benin and the Gold Coast. Both of these regions experienced numerous wars among small states near the coast, from which captives were sold to the Europeans. For the Gold Coast, it meant the eclipse of gold as the main regional export for a time; for the Bight of Benin it brought entry into large-scale Atlantic trade. In both cases, the volume of slave exports rose within three decades to a level that reduced the region's population, after which slave exports declined slowly. Similar patterns of export increase to the limits of population tolerance, with a subsequent slow decline in exports, can be traced for other regions at other times. For Upper Guinea, the most substantial export of slaves occurred between 1600 and 1630. For the Senegambia, after a spurt of exports in the sixteenth century, exports rose again to a peak in the late seventeenth century. For the Bight of Biafra, slave exports shot up from the 1740s to the 1760s and remained at a high level through the 1820s. The Loango coast experienced a sharp increase in export volume in the years from 1720 to 1740 and another increase to a still higher volume from 1780 to 1800. Angola also experienced two great spurts in exports: one in the mid-seventeenth century, after which slave exports declined, and one during the 1720s to 1740s, after which exports remained at a high level into the nineteenth century.

Each of these sudden regional expansions in the slave trade caused—and reflected—changes in the methods and the morality of obtaining slaves. War, judicial procedures, and kidnapping were the main processes by which slaves were obtained—war predominated in most of West Africa, kidnapping predominated in the Bight of Biafra, and judicial procedures played a leading role in Central Africa. For the Gold Coast, Ray Kea has documented changes in the technology and social organization of war that preceded the expansion of slave exports there. As war was transformed from the combat of elites, with minimal and defensive war aims, to combat based on musketry, on the *levée en masse,* and on objectives of territorial conquest, a seemingly endless stream of conflicts and captives was unleashed. A similar transformation accompanied the rise of slave exports from the Bight of Benin.

Were the wars provoked by the desire to sell slaves, or were the captives simply a by-product of wars fought for other reasons? Observers of the slave trade have debated the question inconclusively ever since the Atlantic trade began. Philip Curtin posed this choice with an eye to sustaining the vision of emergent Africa: he contrasted a political model and an economic model for enslavement in the

Senegambia and concluded that the evidence best supported the political model. E. Phillip LeVeen offered the economist's response. The decision to export slaves captured according to the political model depended on the level of prices, and thus slave exporting, as opposed to capturing, fits the economic model. The test of the issue is the responsiveness of slave export quantities to price changes. Even for small and well-defined areas, the elasticity of slave supply fluctuated sharply with the passage of time. Much of the apparent disorder, however, can be resolved by distinguishing periods when the system of supply was stable and positive price-responsiveness was clear (1730 to 1800 in the Bight of Benin) from periods when the ability of merchants to supply slaves was either improving sharply (1740 to 1780 in the Bight of Biafra) or declining (1690 to 1730 in the Bight of Benin). These three examples can be set within the vision of Afrique engagée. In the Bight of Benin in the eighteenth century, domestic and external forces were locked in an equilibrium of sorts; in the Bight of Biafra in the mid-eighteenth century, domestic conditions changed more rapidly than can be explained by the influence of external forces alone; and in the Bight of Benin from the late seventeenth through the early eighteenth century external influences were the main source of African sociodemographic change.

As the demand for slaves continued to grow, opportunities for restrictive and monopolistic practices arose. Richard Nelson Bean, who has collected the best data on prices, joined with Robert Paul Thomas to argue that the Atlantic slave market was competitive and did not allow for monopoly profits, since European shippers could escape price gouging in one African port by going to another. The contrary position is based on the argument that, since European shippers required a speedy turn-around and good relations with their African suppliers, they were tied to a single port. Even without monopoly profits, however, some African slave exporters may have collected high rates of profit through economic rent—that is, those merchants who were able to obtain slaves at unusually low cost still sold them at the prevailing market price. The African revenues from slave exports, which rose along with prices at the turn of the eighteenth century, were almost all turned into expenditures on imported goods: the value and volume of these imports thus increased dramatically at the same time that export prices rose.

The sudden increases in mercantile profit and in the volume of imported goods simultaneously began to restrict African population size. The technique of using New World inventories of slaves to project the ethnic origins of slave exports has established that, for the Bight of Benin, slaves came almost entirely from the Aja-speaking peoples in and around the kingdom of Danhomè, near the coast. The full demographic drain on the Bight of Benin was concentrated on this group, which experienced a loss estimated at over 3 percent of the population each year for over forty consecutive years. This loss was sufficient to reduce the Aja population substantially over the course of a century, both in absolute terms and in relation to the surrounding ethnic groups, notably the Yoruba. . . .

The coastal exports of young adult slaves, twice as many men as women, tended to transform the structure of the population and the organization of society. A surplus of women developed, so that polygyny was reinforced, and work done by women in some places replaced that done by men. African traditions of family structure and division of labor, no matter how deeply instilled, could not but bend before these demographic pressures. The tradition of female agricultural labor in the matrilineal belt of Zaire and Angola may have been strengthened as an accommodation to the shortage of men for production. Similarly, although the institution of polygyny preceded the slave trade, its extent was reinforced by the surplus of women. In addition, a surplus of women meant that men did not need to wait until their late twenties and thirties to marry their first and second wives. Indeed, the fear of enslavement may have encouraged men to marry at a young age. . . .

The demand for slaves affected African polities by causing them not only to participate in slave exports but also to attempt to end it. The kingdom of Benin successfully withdrew from supplying slaves early in the sixteenth century. The Oyo Empire, though by reputation long tied to the slave trade, probably contributed only minimally to the export of slaves from Africa until late in the eighteenth century. And Boubacar Barry has interpreted the political events of the late seventeenth century in the Waalo kingdom of Senegal as an abortive attempt to withdraw from the slave trade. It is for the kingdom of Danhomè that the issue of attempted withdrawal from the slave trade has caused the most controversy. There is a certain plausibility to the notion that, in an area that was ravaged by trade in slaves and that experienced depopulation along with internecine wars, one state should attempt to conquer the whole region to end such conflicts and prevent social collapse. The question remains whether King Agaja's wars of the 1770s were an attempt to do so. But Danhomè's invasion and subjugation by the distant yet powerful Oyo made any such expanded Aja state impossible, and from 1730 to 1830 Danhomè faced a ring of weakened but by no means vanquished enemies; the internecine wars provided the New World with an inordinately large proportion of its slave laborers.

The case of Asante, to the west, represents a slightly different resolution of the same problem. Asante rose in the late seventeenth century to challenge Denkyira, the Gold Coast's dominant power, and eventually succeeded in incorporating virtually all the Twi-speaking peoples. As a result, the export of the people of Asante declined after about 1730, and the large number of slaves exported from the Gold Coast in succeeding years came increasingly from the interior Voltaic peoples. In Oyo, only with the constitutional crisis and a series of factional disputes that began in the 1770s did that kingdom's export slave trade become significant, and the magnitude of slave exports grew with the decay of the state. Thus, although the slave trade certainly affected politics, the nature of the trade's impact varied sharply from polity to polity; sometimes, as in the case of Oyo, politics influenced the trade in slaves more than the trade influenced internal affairs.

The aggregate demographic impact of the slave trade on Africa reached a peak in the late eighteenth century, when slave exports averaged some one hundred thousand per year, and this high level of export continued into the early nineteenth century. During this period, the foci of enslavement tended to move from west to east and from coast to interior. For this period, then, it is most appropriate to assert that slave exports diminished the African population.

One method of assessing the population drain on individual ethnic groups entails, as mentioned above, making a New World inventory of slaves' ethnic origins. A second approach focuses on whole regions, assessing the ability of regional populations to reproduce themselves in the face of the population drain resulting from slave exports. Roger Anstey, David Northrup, and, most effectively, John Thornton have used this procedure to good effect. Thornton's results indicate a decline in the population of the whole Congo-Angola region during the eighteenth century, and his analysis further suggests that, during the height of the export trade, most of the regions of the

West African coast could have withstood the pressure from the trade in slaves only with difficulty. A third approach, continental in scope, has been adopted by Joseph Inikori. His method focuses not so much on the actual reduction in population as on the difference between the actual population of Africa and the counterfactual population that might have existed in the absence of slave exports.

Yet another approach involves the estimation of the impact of the slave trade through computer simulation. In this case, a model African population is postulated, divided into raiding and raided groups, and assigned a series of demographic and slave-trade rates: fertility, mortality, age-sex composition of the captured population, division of the captives between domestic and exported slaves, and so forth. Preliminary projections of the model's results suggest that the slave trade caused losses that, if not devastating to the continent, were certainly severe. For the western coast, a region with an estimated population of twenty-five million in 1700, some six million slaves left in the course of the eighteenth century. The total number enslaved is projected at some twelve million, with four million retained in domestic slavery and over two million lost to death in the course of enslavement. Under these conditions, the African population in 1800 was substantially less than it would have been in the absence of the trade in slaves. For the northern savanna and Horn, whose exports rarely exceeded twenty thousand per year, losses in slave exports were felt more acutely than the numbers alone suggest, because of the predominance of women exported. As a result, the northern savanna and the Horn were probably unable to experience any increase in population during the seventeenth and eighteenth centuries.

The demographic drain of the slave trade interacted with Africa's periodic droughts and famines. As the experience of the nineteenth century suggests, the incidence of drought and famine served at once to increase and to decrease slave exports. The onset of bad times caused the destitute to sell themselves or their children into slavery; but the decline in population resulting from famine tended to reduce the number of slaves. Stephen Baier and Paul E. Lovejoy have documented the great drought of the northern savanna in the mid-eighteenth century, which caused hardship, migration, and economic decline. Climatic recovery in the following decades led to economic growth, which was reflected both in the increase in slave exports and in the rise of the

Sokoto Caliphate. Jill Dias and Joseph C. Miller have documented a cycle of drought, famine, and epidemic in Angola that severely limited population growth. These Malthusian checks on population provide the primary evidence for revising downward Inikori's estimates of the counterfactual African population: Africa's population would surely have been substantially greater without the slave trade, but to know how much so requires a better knowledge of the effects of famine and disease than we now have. Miller may, however, have gone too far in arguing that the limits imposed by disease and drought were so great that these factors, rather than the slave trade, provided the fundamental limits on Angola's population.

The selective export of women from the coastal regions had its greatest impact in the late eighteenth century. The results of the simulation model suggests [sic] that, while the sex ratio among those populations that lost slaves remained roughly equal, the proportion of adult women to men rose substantially for the western coast as a whole: the estimated ratio of adult women to men rose to roughly six to five among the raiding populations. But in those areas with the heaviest participation in slave exporting, the disparity in the sex ratio became greater. John Thornton's analysis of the Portuguese censuses for Angola indicates that the ratio of adult women to men was as much as two to one. On the one hand, this sex ratio shows how African societies could attempt to cope with an enormous drain on the population with losing their ability to reproduce; the people of Angola virtually became a livestock herd to be harvested. On the other, one woman was exported for every two to three men, and the loss of the women's reproductive potential made it all the more difficult for the population to maintain itself. The bulk of the agricultural labor fell on the women who remained in Angola, and the incidence of polygyny remained high. . . .

By the mid-nineteenth century, a dramatic reversal in the character of the Atlantic slave trade had taken place. Most New World areas had dropped out of the slave trade, and slave imports were illegal in the remaining areas of demand—Cuba and Brazil. As a result, although the prices of slaves in the New World rose because of the scarcity of new imports, the export demand for slaves at any given price on the African coast had fallen significantly, and the price of slaves in Africa fell almost as significantly. The relatively scarce price data available for the early nineteenth century are somewhat contradictory, so the precise timing of the price decline remains to be confirmed. But it is clear that, sometime between 1780 and 1850, the price of slaves on the African coast fell, in real terms, by one-half. The mechanisms of slave supply remained in place, however, so that a glut on the slave market became evident. This nineteenth-century glut brought a pervasive change in the character of African slavery: as slaves, particularly male slaves, came within the purchasing power of African buyers, the scope of African slavery expanded greatly in the mid-nineteenth century, although the total number of people captured may not have changed greatly.

As more women remained in Africa, the number of births dramatically increased; and, as more men stayed, the previous drain on the adult male population ended, although the process of enslavement for the African market still implied a significant mortality. These changes resulted in rapid population growth. In addition, the large number of cheap male slaves now made the situation on the coast much more like that in the savanna, where male slaves were used for agricultural labor. Thus the coastal areas now developed slave plantations that produced for palace populations, for the African market, and for export. The mid-nineteenth-century growth in the export of palm oil, coffee, and peanuts thus reflected not only the rise in European demand for these products but also a significant decline in the cost of production because of the fall in slave prices. . . .

Ethnographers of the early twentieth century, writing in the last days of [African] slavery, described the institution as relatively benign, emphasizing the legal and societal protections available to slaves as well as their potential for upward mobility. These reports— written after slave raiding and the trade in slaves had ceased and after slaveholders had lost the support of the state—stand in sharp contrast to the travelers' reports of the late nineteenth century, which tell of brutal raids, immense loss of life, and massive exploitation of slaves by masters. Each of these views of African slavery was appropriate to the precise time at which it was written. Both views, but particularly the former, have in turn been taken by subsequent scholars as appropriate characterizations of African slavery across the centuries.

The vision of emergent Africa, based on the assumed existence of continuous pressures for change within African societies, tends to suggest that both of these static views of servile institutions were invalid, without posing an alternative. The vision of Afrique engagée, by explicitly reintroducing external forces of causation into a framework that assumes an African dynamism not only confirms that suggestion but indicates the nature and timing of some important African social changes. In so doing, this historiographical approach must admit to a range in the type of interactions. In some cases, domestic forces dominated the interactions; the expansion and transformation of polygyny under the influence of the slave trade, for example, took place in the context of a previous African attachment to multiple marriage. In other cases, external forces dominated the interaction; both depopulation and the impact of imported goods, for instance, represent the domination of outside influences. And the precise combination of domestic and external forces provided the key impetus to certain changes, notably in the rise of Asante and Danhomè, the collapse of Kongo, and the mutual reinforcement of the slave trade, famine, and epidemic.

The return on this increased complexity in analytical framework is a clearer time-perspective on African society. African slavery, along with a range of associated institutions, underwent successive transformations in the seventeenth, eighteenth, and nineteenth centuries under the impact of changing economic, demographic, and political conditions. Suzanne Miers and Igor Kopytoff, in an essay that sits firmly within the emergent Africa tradition of analysis, have gone so far as to criticize the use of the term "slavery" in Africa on the grounds that it implies a greater uniformity in African institutions of servitude than is warranted. Their emphasis on the specificity, in sociological cross-section, of African systems of slavery is valid in principle if somewhat exaggerated in practice. To their sociological specificity must be added, however, the specificity of African societies in historical time-perspective, as they changed through the action of the diverse creative powers within them and the varying external pressures upon them. In the era of the slave trade, the external influences were so powerful as to set in motion comparable trends in social change in many parts of the African continent two centuries before the colonial conquest did in a vastly different fashion.

The Economics of African
Participation in the Slave Trade

DAVID ELTIS

Scholars researching the origins and development of the Atlantic economy tend to be more interested in the contribution of precolonial Africa to the Atlantic economy than in the importance of that economy to Africa. The vital role occupied by Africa in the development of the Americas is beyond question, yet that contribution cannot be understood fully without an awareness of the significance of transatlantic trade to Africans. Most scholars with an "Atlantic" orientation would probably argue that transatlantic trade ties affected Africa as profoundly as they affected the Americas, though in obviously different ways. The shift in the 1970s toward a new focus on that part of the historical African economy producing for domestic consumption, as represented by Curtin's work on Senegambia and Peukert's on Dahomey, seems to have halted. Recently, both detailed regional studies and continentwide syntheses have returned to an older concern with the effects on Africa of the slave trade, its abolition, and the subsequent rapid increase in transatlantic produce exports.

This more recent concern with external trade is firmly rooted in the quantitative work of the last two decades. Few scholars have failed to take advantage of numerous new estimates of volume and prices in both the slave and commodity trades. But despite this interest, most researchers have not aggregated the different data sources to arrive at estimates for particular African regions (as opposed to countries in Europe and the Americas). More important, they have not given center stage to the implications of these new data for the importance of the overseas economy to Africans. . . . Except for the issue of the demographic impact of the slave trade on Africa,

Source: From "Precolonial Western Africa and the Atlantic Economy" by David Eltis, in *Slavery and the Rise of the Atlantic System* edited by Barbara Solow, 1991, excerpts from pp. 97–99, 102–110, 112–119. Reprinted by permission of Cambridge University Press.

where ironically the data are weak, recent economic historians have assumed a strong impact from the external sector rather than attempted to assess how great that impact was. The mechanism through which the Atlantic affected Africa has received rather more attention than the strength of that effect. But even here the plausibility of competing hypotheses has tended to rest on qualitative evidence.

A quick review of these hypotheses from an economist's standpoint might go as follows. For the traffic in people, the older literature often depicted slaves as having been stolen from Africa. At the very least, Europeans sold merchandise to Africans for extortionate prices. This can be represented as very unfavorable terms of trade for Africans. A second and more recent view is the opposite of the first. According to it, the influx of trade goods at low prices was so great that domestic production was seriously impaired and an African dependency on foreign producers developed. In a sense, leaving aside for the moment the issue of private versus social costs, the first argument suggests that the slave traders paid too little, whereas the second suggests that they paid too much. The third broad interpretation focuses on the social dislocation that the slave trade caused within Africa. From this standpoint, the slave trade was responsible for spreading the institution of slavery, encouraging social stratification in African societies, and altering relations between African states. For economists, a variant of this view is that the negative externalities (or social costs not covered by slave prices) of selling an African into the Atlantic traffic were considerable. These would include the disruptions of slave raiding and the effects of population decline or slower population growth.

The first two of these broad interpretations, as well as the broader issue of the relative importance of domestic and external sectors within the economies of most West African societies, are, in fact, amenable to quantitative evaluation. New data on prices, volumes, and the composition of trade between Africa and the Atlantic world make possible the reconstitution of decadal "snapshots" of aggregate trading activity from an African perspective over nearly two centuries of the prepartition era. These new aggregations, used in conjunction with backward population projections and inferences about African living standards, permit some new insights on the scale and nature of the impact of the Atlantic world on western Africa.

We turn first to the data. It is now possible to estimate the value of total trade between the Atlantic world and western Africa from Senegambia to Angola for five widely separated decades between the seventeenth and nineteenth centuries. They are the 1680s, the 1730s, the 1780s, the 1820s, and the 1860s. . . . For four of these decades, estimates of the regional and compositional distributions are also possible—in the latter case, on the basis of physical volumes as well as values. . . .

The total trade series of [Figure 1], which combines the slave and commodity trades, indicates two cycles of growth in Africa's Atlantic trade. The first, based on the slave trade, and the second, on commodities supplied to an industrializing Europe, were interrupted by a marked decline corresponding to the partial closing of markets for slaves in the Americas. Given the trends in prices of African exports and imports discussed previously, however, there can be little doubt that the volume of total trade increased much more rapidly after 1780 than before, and much more rapidly than the current value

Figure 1. *Estimated value of total trade (imports and exports combined)*
between Africa and the Atlantic world in selected decades,
1680s–1860s, in millions of pounds sterling.

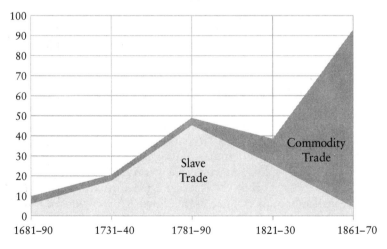

Source: David Eltis, Table 1.

totals for the 1780s, 1820s, and 1860s suggest. The volume of goods imported into Africa in the 1820s was certainly no less than it had been in the 1780s. The volume of British exports to Africa increased ten times between 1817–20 and 1846–9, and there was a fivefold increase in the volume of British imports. If the British data are any guide, it follows that trade volumes between Africa and the Atlantic world may well have increased five times between the 1820s and 1860s rather than more than doubling, as suggested by the current value figures. What also follows from the previous discussion is that except for a short reversal during the Napoleonic wars, the terms of trade moved steadily in favor of Africa from the end of the seventeenth century. Probably no other major area trading with Europe in the two centuries before 1870 experienced as continuous and massive a shift. Thus an average slave or a hundredweight of ivory sold on the African coast in the 1860s could command fifteen times the textiles and six or seven times the muskets of their counterparts in the 1680s.

These figures are dramatic, though the scale of the trade expansion and the apparently much greater price elasticity of supply that existed for produce than for slaves probably conform to what most scholars would expect. However, these findings are likely to mislead if we concern ourselves purely with African Atlantic trade. A broader perspective suggests two less obvious and more controversial themes. First, despite the rapid growth of the trade in African produce after 1800, it was only in the slave trade era that African Atlantic trade kept pace with the growth of world trade. Second, despite the relative strength of the slave trade, the economy of western Africa remained little affected by trade with the Atlantic in the period covered here—measured at least with the statistics currently available to us.

The first of these two propositions can be dealt with quickly. Between the 1680s and the 1780s, the growth rate in the volume of African trade with the Atlantic was probably about the same as that between Britain and the Americas. This is hardly surprising in view of the interconnection of the slave and plantation produce trades. But the important point to note is that English trade with both Africa and the Americas increased much faster in these years than did English trade with the rest of the world. A different picture emerges after the 1780s, however. In that decade the Atlantic slave trade peaked in volume, and once this peak had passed, African trade with the Atlantic fell behind in relative terms. Between 1800 and 1860, world trade increased nearly fivefold measured in current values and perhaps tenfold in quantity. Whether we look at current values or physical volumes, the changes in African trade between the 1780s and the 1860s look less impressive by comparison. The traffic in slaves continued to be of major importance in the nineteenth century, but once it stopped expanding in the 1780s, the growth of commodity trade was not enough to sustain Africa's relative position in world trade. In this sense, Africa differed from other less developed regions, most of which participated fully in the nineteenth-century expansion of world trade. Indeed, it is probable that Africa's share of world trade continued to shrink into the twentieth century and has never approached the levels attained when the slave trade was at its height.

Yet the question of the importance of overseas trade to Africa cannot be addressed without reference to the African domestic economy. There are four ways of approaching this crucial issue in the premodern African context. One is to examine the types of goods imported into and exported from western Africa. Products with a pronounced antisocial impact could have had an effect beyond what the data might at first suggest. The second is to estimate the approximate physical quantities of major products imported on a per capita basis. The third is to compare the levels of per capita trade in Africa with those of Africa's main trading partners. The fourth is to sample the evidence on African domestic product in light of the trade figures discussed previously. Three of these approaches require some reference to population estimates of Africa. Patrick Manning has developed estimates for those parts of sub-Saharan Africa that were affected by the slave trade. On the whole, they posit a severe demographic impact by the slave trade, though the series used here actually lies midway between the upper and lower limits of the range of estimates that Manning develops. Specifically, a population of 20.6 million is projected for 1860, 20.3 for 1820, 22.5 for 1780, and 23.0 for 1680. A lower assessment of the demographic impact of the slave trade would generate larger populations than these and smaller per capita trade figures than appear subsequently.

The first of the preceding approaches examin[es] the composition of trade with Africa. . . . On the export side, the rise and fall of the slave trade is summarized in [Figure 1], and little need be added to the debate on the socially disruptive impact of that trade. We should at least note that there is no consensus on the extent of that disruption. On the produce component of exports, it has been argued that the produce exports that superseded the slave trade actually maintained rates of enslavement (and therefore the extent of social disruption) at levels that existed prior to suppression of the traffic. However, the prices of slaves declined sharply in Africa subsequent to suppression, which suggests that domestic demand did not fully take the place of declining demand from overseas markets.

On the import side, [Figure 2] presents estimates of the types of goods imported into Africa for four widely separated decades. Although capital goods appear to have been scarce, and although the disruptive impact of firearms, alcohol, and perhaps tobacco needs to be acknowledged, there is actually little in [Figure 2] to separate out Africa from other importers of the pre- and early industrializing

Figure 2. *Estimated relative value of imports into western Africa in selected decades, 1680s–1860s.*

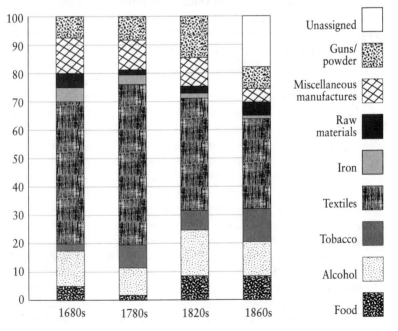

Source: David Eltis, Table 2, with corrections kindly supplied by the author.

worlds. Consumer goods may be divided into those that satisfy the basic requirements of nutrition, clothing, and shelter and those that satisfy psychological needs. In the preindustrial context the latter included sugar, tobacco, and alcohol, along with a host of purely decorative items, some textiles, and most luxury goods. Such "psychic" goods formed no greater share of African imports than of the imports of most other parts of the world. It is likely, in fact, that luxurious textiles and other expensive gifts made up a considerably smaller share of Africa's overseas imports than elsewhere. If the composition of trade magnified the impact of the Atlantic on Africa, it was more likely because of the nature of African exports than imports. The evidence of the composition of trade on the issue of Atlantic impact is thus mixed, with much hinging on the contentious questions of what proportion of the captives were the product of war and the demographic implications of the trade.

The physical quantities of four products imported into sub-Saharan Africa over the two centuries preceding partition may be inferred from the customs data used earlier. These, combined with Manning's population estimates, yield crude per capita import figures that form the second of the four approaches to assessing the domestic importance of overseas trade. The four products are textiles, guns, alcohol, and tobacco, which together accounted for well over half of all imports. We begin with textiles. During each year of the 1860s the British and French exported on average about 45 million yards of cotton textiles to Africa. A rough allowance for exports by other nations, and a further adjustment for textiles other than cottons—a very small category at this time—suggests that about 57 million yards of imported textiles of all kinds were traded annually in the decade 1861–70. Using the preceding population estimate, this amounts to nearly three yards per person; and as a two-yard "wrapper" is sufficient to clothe one person, it would seem that overseas imports supplied up to half (depending on one's estimates of per capita consumption) of the region's textile consumption. The point to note, however, is that per capita textile imports were far below what they were shortly to become. In Dahomey between 1890 and 1914, imported cloth provided no less than fifteen yards per person each year, and there was still a vibrant domestic industry in existence, exporting some of its output to Brazil.

. . . It might be concluded that imported cloths reached a wider African market in the eighteenth century but began to impinge on the domestic textile industry only as the slave trade was replaced by the traffic in commodities in the mid-nineteenth century. This increase in imported textile use was a function of the dramatic decline in the price of English fabrics in the nineteenth century, but the domestic industry remained competitive.

The population estimates permit a new perspective on gun imports. Per capita gun imports were likely greater in the 1860s than in any of the major slave-exporting decades. Combined values of African imports of guns and gunpowder are estimated here at £0.008 per person for each year in the 1780s, or one gun per 118 persons; £0.009 in the 1820s, or one gun per 145 persons; and £0.016 in the 1860s, or one gun per 103 persons, all values measured f.o.b. in the source countries. One further relative perspective might be considered. Census data for the United States make possible a transatlantic comparison of guns and gunpowder. In 1820 a lower bound estimate of the value of these items produced in the United States implies a ratio of £0.013, larger than the African ratio for the 1820s though somewhat below the 1860 figure. By 1860 in the United States, however, Americans were producing £0.037 arms per person, more than double the contemporary African import ratio. As net exports of guns and gunpowder from the United States were very small before the Civil War, and domestic production of armaments in Africa was negligible at this time, we can conclude that more guns and gunpowder were used in the United States, and probably by other societies in the Americas, than in that part of Africa affected by the slave trade. Similar comparisons are not possible for the eighteenth century, but the 1780s African ratio of £0.008 worth of guns and gunpowder per person in Africa was lower than any of the previously given nineteenth-century ratios. The discussion suggests that those claiming a major impact from arms have to build their arguments on some basis other than just the volume of imports. The supply of arms obviously facilitated slave raids, and guns may have been concentrated geographically, so that local effects may have been considerable. If this was the case, then it is also clear that over large geographic areas their impact must have been small.

The other two imported products examined here were less important. Tobacco, in semiprocessed form, averaged 12.8 million pounds per year in the 1860s, or about half a pound per person—not a large amount by modern standards. It was, nevertheless, more than double the per capita consumption of the 1820s or the 1780s, though exact comparisons are complicated by the switch from roll to leaf tobacco. Alcoholic beverages averaged 0.75 million gallons in the 1780s, 1.0 million gallons in the 1820s, and 6.1 million gallons in the 1860s, again on a per year basis. The annual per capita consumption is calculated at 0.033, 0.05, and 0.3 gallon for the 1780s, 1820s, and 1860s, respectively. For the 1680s, consumption of both products by Africans must have been infinitesimally small. Again, perspective is provided by consumption ratios for the late nineteenth and early twentieth centuries. In this period, Dahomey was importing four or five times the amount of both tobacco and alcohol per person that western Africa had imported in the 1860s. The scale of precolonial imports of these products signals something less than a revolution in consumer behavior—even in the 1860s. Just as clearly, however, rapid growth did occur in the mid-nineteenth century. These figures suggest that merchandise distributed from the Atlantic was of small importance relative to what it was shortly to become. Furthermore, if elite groups took a disproportionate share of these goods, many, perhaps most, living within reach of the Atlantic would have had little experience of imports. . . .

[Another] approach to assessing the importance of the Atlantic to the African domestic economy is to look at export income relative to possible ranges of African domestic income. Evidence concerning African income levels in the precolonial era is thin but not nonexistent. There can be little doubt that early-nineteenth-century nutritional intakes, and probably living standards, as the twentieth century would conceive the term, were lower in Africa than in the Americas. Yet there also seems little doubt that per capita income was high in Africa relative to most parts of the world outside the Americas and that, at the very least, assessments that place Africa at the bottom of the preindustrial continental income tables need to be revised.

This last statement can be supported in three ways. First, land/labor ratios in Africa were high. Africa was under- rather than overpopulated. Moreover, as Boserup has pointed out, the technology used by Africans ensured a high marginal physical product. The question of why Africans were forcibly removed from one area of high marginal physical product (Africa) to another (the Americas) is an intriguing one when we consider the large transatlantic transportation costs. The explanation no doubt has something to do with the epidemiological environment and African military pressures that prevented the establishment of European plantations in Africa before the late nineteenth century. Second, of the approximately 911,000 intercontinental indentured migrants who came to the Americas after the end of slavery, only 57,900, or 6%, came from Africa. To the flow of laborers to other recruiting regions such as Malaya, Fiji, Australia, and, more surprisingly, Natal and the Mascarene Islands, Africans contributed nothing. The great bulk of the indentured laborers recruited between 1826 and 1939 came from Asia, and in particular India—areas with much lower land/labor ratios, and presumably per capita incomes, than Africa. . . .

As already noted, there remains the possibility that the income generated by overseas commerce was concentrated either geographically or among classes in such a way as to guarantee it an impact beyond what the aggregate figures here would suggest as likely. There is also the very real possibility that the social costs of the slave trade were of a different order of magnitude to the essentially private returns estimated here. These are issues largely beyond the scope of the present chapter. It is, however, possible to make a tentative distribution of trade from the 1730s to the 1860s.

. . . With the exception of west-central Africa in the 1730s, no region ever accounted for as much as one-third of total western African Atlantic trade—and west-central Africa, it might be noted, is easily the biggest in terms of coastline, hinterland and perhaps, too, population, of all the regions represented. . . . The Bight of Benin and the Gold Coast, regions with a high profile in the historiography, were not the highest revenue earners, and . . . only two areas—the Bight of Biafra and Senegambia—weathered suppression of the slave trade without a drop in trade revenues. The Bight of Biafra had consistently the greatest trade contact with the Atlantic—probably from the 1740s. This was also the region with the highest population density. . . . Per capita calculations of regional trade might be stretching the data too far. But the order of magnitude of the figures . . . suggests that in no region could the revenue per person of ocean-going trade have been significant. To put the same point differently, African populations would have had to have been extremely small for Atlantic trade to have been important—so small, in fact, that transatlantic traffic on the scale and duration of the latest estimates of the slave trade would have been impossible.

This assessment requires at least two qualifications. First, ocean-going trade was only one of the long-distance trading outlets. For some west African and west-central African societies, trans-Saharan and Indian Ocean trade provided an alternative outlet, and for most Africans the long-distance intra–sub-Saharan African traffic had at least potential importance. Thus, for example, the large drop in Gold Coast revenues between the 1780s and the 1820s may be more apparent than real. The Asante state developed a strong land-based trade in cola nuts in the early nineteenth century, the scale of which is beyond assessment but which might have more than offset the decline in revenues from the Atlantic. The second qualification is that revenues within a region may have been severely skewed in favor of one or more states. It is highly likely that two-thirds or more of all slaves entering the Atlantic traffic left from no more than a dozen ports. The "coasting" trade was mainly an Upper Guinea phenomenon, induced probably by the lack of a major river between the Senegal and the Volta. Communities within or adjacent to the estuaries of the Senegal, Niger, and Zaire rivers, as well as those located at strategic points on the lagoon systems of the Slave and Loango coasts, obviously depended heavily on trade with the Atlantic. The pleading for the return of the slave trade in the early nineteenth century on the part of the Loango Mafouks was a result of this dependence. The greatest geographic concentration of trade within any region during the precolonial decades surveyed here was probably in the nineteenth-century Niger Delta communities. Brass, New Calabar, Old Calabar, and Bonny together must have received close to £0.5 million . . . worth of merchandise a year in the 1820s and probably over £0.5 million in the 1860s (in current values). But these were essentially trading rather than producing states, and the further away from these points the analysis is carried, the more dispersed would be the impact of the Atlantic. There is surely no realistic estimate of population and/or income for the region stretching from the Niger Delta east to the Cameroon mountains and north to Hausaland, which would make £0.5 million of goods per year significant.

The hinterlands of other regions were less densely populated than this, but trading entrepots were also generally more widely scattered than in the Bight of Biafra, and few regions had annual Atlantic trade as high as £0.5 million before the 1860s. In the Bight of Benin, the eighteenth-century slave trade did tend to be more geographically concentrated than the later produce traffic. Whydah, the main outlet for Dahomey, dominated Atlantic trade in the Bight of Benin in the 1730s and 1780s, and probably during the years in between. Indeed, although the Bight of Benin permanently lost its position as the major Atlantic trading region of Africa after the 1730s, the popular impression of Dahomey as the African state most involved in Atlantic trade is probably supported by this analysis. If there is a possible exception to the generally small quantitative impact of the Atlantic on western Africa argued for in the present chapter, Dahomey would come closest to qualifying. . . .

We can now return to the broad historiographical themes discussed at the beginning of this chapter. Clearly, the slave trade engulfed Africa's Atlantic commerce in the eighteenth century and in much of the nineteenth too. But it is equally clear that any plausible numerical assessment indicates a similarly massive dominance of the domestic sector over the external *within* most African societies. This assessment obviously ignores the social costs of the external slave trade, but to this we will return. At the very least, the ratio of overseas trade to domestic economic activity was far lower for the majority of Africans than for the typical inhabitant of Europe or the Americas.

As for the three possible mechanisms in the historiography through which Atlantic trade might have manifested itself in Africa, severely unfavorable terms of trade, creation of a dependency, or heavy negative externalities, only the third is not called into question by the data assembled here. The first, positing strongly negative terms of trade for Africa, is highly unlikely. As the Royal African Company's records testify, significant volumes of merchandise were exchanged for slaves in the 1680s, and for most of the nearly two succeeding centuries the terms of trade shifted in favor of Africa. The second, positing a volume of merchandise imports high enough to create an African dependency on overseas producers, seems equally unlikely. The value of Atlantic trade relative to possible African income and population levels, and relative, too, to what it was to become in the early twentieth century, makes a dependency effect before 1870 improbable. We are left with the negative externalities or socially dislocative effects of the slave trade. The data developed here shed little light on this approach, except to imply that the disruption did not undermine the predominance of domestic economic activity. It would seem, nevertheless, to be the most promising route to evaluating the effect of the slave trade on Africa.

Some might see the later part of this analysis as tending to minimize the significance of the transatlantic slave trade, at least as far as Africa is concerned. This would be unfortunate. It is highly likely that what the British extracted from their North American mainland colonies represented a tiny fraction of North American income, and that the drain from India to Britain in the late eighteenth century was an insignificant share of Indian domestic product. But these facts in no way reduced the significance of British imperialism to contemporaries, nor will it reduce it for modern historians of the United States and India. The same point may be made about the present analysis of the forced removal of Africans from Africa. The intention here is merely to focus the search for the effects of the slave trade on Africa and to nudge scholars into giving more attention to trends within Africa in understanding precolonial African history. Like the peoples of the Americas, and more than most populations in the nineteenth-century world, Africans were feeding, clothing, and sheltering themselves, as well as developing the full panoply of a multi-faceted cultural existence, without overseas economic exchange.

The opening sentence to the published proceedings of a recent symposium on Africa's long distance trade reads "[T]he period 1800–1914 was one of deep structural change in economic organization in many parts of Africa" and goes on to link this with growing external trade. The evidence examined here suggests that this is misleading for the years before 1870—at least as far as the Atlantic is concerned. Except for some coastal regions, it is hard to believe that any significant domestic industry was threatened by overseas imports until well past midcentury. Nor, with the exception of new food crops and possibly firearms—easily the largest precolonial capital good imports—is it easy to see a large impact from any imported technology. West Africans had iron, sophisticated textiles, a range of indigenous metalwares, and, outside the tsetse zone, draught animals. Despite a prolonged shift in the terms of trade in favor of Africa, European products could not penetrate the African market until the second half of the nineteenth century. The same products made greater inroads into other parts of the Atlantic world at much earlier dates. George Brooks has commented that Africans were remarkably self-sufficient in 1800 after three centuries of Atlantic trade. The same may be said of 1870.

PART VI

Abolition

The other chief traders on the river . . . are strong in professions of having altogether abandoned the [slave] trade, . . . and they speak in high terms of the tranquillity that they enjoy in being released from apprehension of the cruisers.

BRITISH COMMISSIONERS, SIERRA LEONE, 1822

The capitalists had first encouraged West Indian slavery and then helped to destroy it.

ERIC WILLIAMS

Any general account which attributes the rise of the anti-slavery movement to considerations of economic necessity is open to serious objections.

HOWARD TEMPERLEY

The resistance of the slaves unequivocally contributed . . . to the fact that the slave system was increasingly seen in Britain to be not only morally wrong and economically inefficient, but also politically unwise.

MICHAEL CRATON

Once Parliament had outlawed participation in the slave trade, the British government used diplomatic pressure and financial incentives to persuade other nations to end the trade and sent Royal Navy patrols to intercept ships trading illegally along the African and American coasts. According to calculations by David Eltis, during the half-century after 1815, Britain spent some £12 million in trying to end the slave trade, ironically about as much profit as British traders had made in the previous half-century. More than 160,000 Africans were freed from the 1,635 slave ships captured by Britain's antislavery squadron.

Most captured ships ("prizes") were taken to the small colony of Sierra Leone, where the slavers were tried and the slaves freed. The following report by two British commissioners shows that by 1822 the British squadron had made considerable progress in halting the slave trade in the vicinity of Sierra Leone. However, the slave trade increased in more distant ports in the Gulf of Guinea, Angola, and southeastern Africa during the next decade. As long as owning slaves remained legal, some individuals were willing to traffic in them. Not until 1867, when slavery itself had been abolished in most of the Americas, did the Atlantic slave trade end.

Why did Britain, the greatest slave-trading nation at the beginning of the century, devote such resources to destroying this profitable trade? At the time and long after, the principal explanation focused on the profound change in moral sensibilities associated with the philosophical Enlightenment and with the religious consciences of English Quakers, Methodists, and Evangelicals, who played a major part in the campaigns against the slave trade and slavery. As we have seen, this explanation was incomprehensible to King Osei Bonsu, and in 1944 Eric Williams championed a different explanation. While acknowledging the importance of the moral supporters of abolition, he proposed that it was the additional support of new economic interests associated with the growth of industrialization that gave success to the long abolitionist campaign. Although subsequent researchers have challenged nearly every part of Williams's argument, his overall thesis still has many supporters.

Howard Temperley of the University of East Anglia (United Kingdom) assesses how far the debate has come, evaluating the strengths and weaknesses of each side. He suggests that neither school—nor any blending of them—offers a satisfactory explanation of abolitionism. Instead, he looks at the prevailing mind-sets or social "ideologies" of British and American abolitionists, arguing that sustained economic growth without slavery had fostered a belief in the possibility of moral progress as well. David Brion Davis has greatly expanded upon this argument in *Slavery and Human Progress* (1986), a section of which appears in Part I.

However, an end to slavery (and thus to the slave trade) came first in the largest plantation colony of the West Indies, France's Saint Domingue (modern Haiti), as the result of a massive slave revolt in which neither moral crusaders nor industrialization played any major role. Michael Craton of the University of Waterloo (Ontario) follows up on this point, arguing that slave revolts in the British Caribbean also contributed decisively to slavery's end, another point raised by Eric Williams.

The British Antislavery Squadron in 1822

E. GREGORY AND EDWARD FITZGERALD

Messrs. Gregory and Fitzgerald to the Marquess of Londonderry.— (Received February 14, 1823)

MY LORD,   *Sierra Leone, September 20, 1822.*

In obedience to the instructions conveyed in your Lordship's letter, dated March the 10th, that we should continue to transmit to your Lordship, from time to time, Reports of the state of the Slave Trade, founded upon the most authentick intelligence that our situation enables us to collect; we have the honour to submit the substance of the information obtained by us on that subject, subsequent to our despatch of the 30th of April.

Considering the coast in three divisions, as before, we have no information of any Slave Trade in the division to the northward of this Colony, further than that we understand that Lieutenant Hagan, in a visit to Bissao and Cacheo about the middle of September, was informed that the Apollo, already noticed in our communications, and especially in our Report of the 30th of April, carried off a full cargo of Slaves as then mentioned; and that another vessel carried off a full cargo since that.

From the Rio Pongos our information is positive and certain. No Slave ship has been in that river since the capture of the Rosalia, on

Source: From Great Britain, *Parliamentary Papers,* 1823 volume XIX, Correspondence. Class B. Correspondence with the British commissioners at Sierra Leone . . . relating to the Slave Trade 1822, 1823.

the 11th of January last, by His Majesty's brig Thistle, Lieutenant Hagan. Francisco Freire, the Pilot of that vessel, to whom the command of the vessel and the management of the trade devolved on the death of the original Master, is still in the river, residing at the factory of John Ormond, of Bangaben, not having yet found an opportunity to depart. If the opportunity of a Slave-trading vessel should present itself, there cannot be a doubt that the Slaves retained of those collected for the Rosalia would be shipped off on board of her, for only a certain number of these Slaves, (sixty,) and these of inferior class, were delivered up to Lieutenant Hagan. There is as little doubt that Ormond would readily supply as many others as might be wanted to complete a cargo; for he avows his present abstinence from the trade to be the consequence merely of want of opportunity to dispose of Slaves.

The other chief traders on the river, more particularly William Lawrence and Lightburn, are strong in professions of having altogether abandoned the trade, with a determination not to return to it under any circumstances, but to pursue the fair course of legitimate industry and commerce as planters and general merchants. They declare further, that they find their profits in this course satisfactory and encouraging; and they speak in high terms of the tranquillity that they enjoy in being released from apprehension of the cruizers, and in the consideration of being assured of the protection of the British arms.

These converts from the Slave Trade are, however, but newly entered on this virtuous course, and no secure reliance can be placed on their professions unless they are guarded from relapse, and from the temptations of opportunity for Slave Trade, by frequent returns of British cruizers to the river.

William Lawrence, who resides at Dominge, at the entrance of the river, has been recently at Sierra Leone.

The objects of William Lawrence's visit to Sierra Leone were to recommend himself to British protection, and to make arrangements for a regular commercial intercourse with the Colony. He succeeded in both objects, which necessarily implies a full assurance of his abandonment of the Slave Trade.

William Lawrence left Sierra Leone to return to his residence at Dominge towards the end of August; he carried with him a large stock of coffee plants supplied from the Chief Justice's farm, near Free Town, at the request of Mr. Macaulay. These plants were intended not for the use of Lawrence alone, but also for distribution to Lightburn and others, among whom Irving and Sterne, of the Kissing branch of the river, were particularly named.

We have been induced to be minute and particular in our account of the circumstances connected with the trade of the Rio Pongos, because the vicinity of that river to the Colony of Sierra Leone, and the commercial intercourse already established, give fair hopes of the speedy and complete eradication of the Slave Trade from its banks.

A commencement would thus be made in the abolition of the Slave Trade in the countries of the native Africans, which we regard as the only perfect abolition. . . .

In the country between Sierra Leone and the Rio Pongos, dissentions and disturbances have arisen from opposite pretensions to the succession to the late King Mungo Demba. The Chief of Foricaria has extended the confusion by insisting, that all trade from the Foulah country shall pass through that place. The people of this Chief hold one of the principal towns on the path of Port Logo, by which a direct intercourse between the Foulah country and Sierra Leone was lately established. That path is now stopped.

In the middle division of the coast, between Sierra Leone and Cape Coast Castle, much Slave Trade has been carried on. The principal resort of these traders is the Rio Gallinas. The vessels employed in this trade have been chiefly French; but some of all the countries concerned in the trade have been occasionally seen there. We have been informed that Krause, the Master and part owner of the schooner Joseph, lately condemned in the British and Spanish Court of Mixed Commission, has a factory at the Gallinas, and has been for some years a constant Slave trader there.

According to the information which we have received at various times from individuals who had opportunity of personal observation, or of communicating with those who had such opportunities, the station of the Gallinas has scarcely at any time been free from Slave traders, and generally from three to five vessels may be found there in search of Slaves.

In the range of coast southward from Cape Coast Castle to the Equator, which is the third division in the apportionment made in our former reports, a remarkable change has taken place by the transfer of the Portuguese Slave Trade from its recent favourite haunts in the Bight of Biafra to the Bight of Benin.

Crowded slave deck, 1860. From an actual photograph of the bark Wildfire, *captured and brought into Key West, Florida. (Schomberg Center for Research in Black Culture)*

After the capture of the French and Spanish Slave ships in the river Bonny, on the 7th of April, by the boats of His Majesty's ships Iphigenia and Myrmidon, under the command of Lieutenant Mildmay, Captain Leeke proceeded in the Myrmidon to examine the Calabar.

The Calabar was examined on the 27th and 28th of April by the boats of the Myrmidon and Iphigenia, under the command of Lieutenant Elliot. The Portuguese schooner Defensora da Patria, having one hundred Slaves on board, bound to Prince's Island and Bahia, was taken by Lieutenant Elliot. The vessel being found not seaworthy was destroyed: the Slaves were brought to Sierra Leone, and emancipated by the British and Portuguese Mixed Court. A French vessel called La Tamise, of Marseilles, belonging to Rougemont and Co. was in the river at the time, and had come for a cargo of four hundred Slaves. She was boarded by Lieutenant Elliot, who ascertained these facts from her papers.

No other Slave-ships had been in the Calabar during the four months preceding. This information Lieutenant Elliot received from the Masters of the English vessels trading for palm oil. A tender belonging to one of those vessels arrived from the Cameroons a short time before Lieutenant Elliot visited the Calabar: the information derived from the crew of the tender was that no Slave-trading vessel had been in the Cameroons during the last five or six months. In consequence of this information, Lieutenant Elliot did not proceed to the Cameroons. That river was formerly a station of great resort for the Slave Trade.

Lieutenant Hagan visited the Calabar in the end of the month of June, and learned that no Slave Trade had taken place in the interval since the visit of the boats of the Iphigenia and Myrmidon, with the exception of, a shipment of thirty slaves on board of a very small vessel called the San José Xalaca. This vessel put to sea with a short supply of provisions and water, in the expectation of arriving speedily at Prince's Island. The number of Slaves was in the same expectation greatly overproportioned to her means of accommodation. Contrary winds drove her unfortunately out of her course, and, after extreme suffering, she returned to Duke Ephraim's Town at Calabar. Ten of the negroes died of their sufferings, either on board or after the return to the Calabar. The others were delivered up to Lieutenant Hagan and brought to Sierra Leone, with the exception of three, whose exhausted state surpassed the humane efforts of Lieutenant Hagan for their recovery. For the further details of this shocking case, we refer to the particular despatch respecting it.

In the river Bonny no Slave-trading vessel had arrived since the capture of the Vecua and Icanam by the boats of the Iphigenia and Myrmidon. The Captain of the Vecua, and her crew, as well as the crews of the French vessels taken at the same time, were still at King Peppel's Town at Bonny, no opportunity for their departure thence having occurred.

Lieutenant Hagan noticed as a happy result of the check given to the Slave Trade in the rivers Bonny, Calabar, and Cameroons, the improved state of the legitimate commerce. The George Canning, a ship of seven hundred tons, from Liverpool, come for palm oil, had completed her cargo in four months. While the Slave Trade was in full vigour, this would have been a business of nearly twelve months.

In the Bight of Benin, Lieutenant Hagan took the Portuguese brig Estrella, having on board a cargo of Slaves. For the details of that case, we beg leave to refer to the particular statement respecting it. We have only to add here, that the letter of instructions from the owner indicates an intention of taking a number of Slaves beyond the regular proportion to the tonnage of the vessel, for each of which extraordinary slaves, an additional freight was to be charged.

Lieutenant Hagan could have taken another vessel with a cargo of Slaves, if the strength of his crew had been sufficient to allow him to man two prizes with due regard to their security and that of the Thistle. He saw no less than nine vessels, under the Portuguese flag, all come for Slaves. He considered the Portuguese Slave-traders to have transferred themselves entirely to the Bight of Benin from their former haunts in the Bight of Biafra. Lieutenant Hagan conceived that the motives of this change were, the depth of water along the shore in the Bight of Benin and the vicinity of the Slave-trading stations to the sea, by means of which the Slave-trading vessels are enabled to get away rapidly on the approach of a ship of war, and to attain a safe distance in a short time, after they have taken advantage of a favourable opportunity to embark their slaves.

In the rivers of the Bight of Biafra, they had hoped that they would be inaccessible to attack, or capable of resisting with success the attacks of boats. But events have proved that they are accessible, and that the attacks by boats are not to be successfully resisted by them, while they are disabled from escape by flight, being so completely land-locked.

We have had occasion to notice, particularly in our reports of many of the cases brought before the British and Portuguese Courts of Mixed Commission, the undue facilities given to the illegal traffick by those in authority at Prince's Island, and the perversion of the liberty to call at that Island, and at Saint Thomas's, in voyages from Brazil, to the purposes of Slave Trade in the stations North of the Line. In the cases of the Defensora da Patria, of the Nymfa del Mar, and some others, the collusion to this illegal purpose was most foul and glaring, as the particular reports of those cases, and the parts of the evidence especially noticed in those reports, will shew in a more decisive manner.

The papers of all vessels cleared out from the ports of Brazil for the coast of Africa are perfectly regular. If the destination be avowedly for the Coast, North of the Equator, the objects of the voyage are distinctly limited to legal commerce, with an express prohibition against meddling in any way with Slave Trade. In the case of the Des de Fevreiro, these documents were coupled with private letters of the same tenor, so numerous, so uniform, and so strong, that nothing short of the positive proofs found, of her being actually engaged in obtaining a cargo of Slaves, could efface the impression of innocent and laudable commerce, made by the contents of these papers. Subsequent cases of the same description, although without the same combination of private as well as public papers, have shewn that papers of that description are used as common means of deception.

The vessels that clear out avowedly for the Slave Trade have papers of express destination to Molembo or Cabinda, South of the Line, sometimes with liberty adjoined to call at Prince's Island, or at the Island of Saint Thomas, the uniform abuse of which permission, for the purpose of inlet to the Slave-trading stations North of the Line, has already been noticed.

The general practice of keeping the slaves on shore until the whole cargo is collected in readiness for embarkation, causes many vessels so engaged to be left unmolested, and in the cases in which vessels found in such circumstances have been detained, on the ground of having had one slave, or more, actually on board, for the purposes of the traffick, the proofs have been found in some instances deficient, as in the case of the Rosalia, Spanish schooner, taken in the Rio Pongos, in January last, by His Majesty's brig Thistle; in some imperfect, as in the case of the Estrella, Spanish schooner, prize to His Majesty's ship Morgiana, Captain Knight, taken in the month of March off Trade Town; in others very difficult, as in the Joseph, Spanish schooner, prize to the detachment from the Iphigenia, placed under Lieutenant Clarkson, on board of the American schooner Augusta; the Des de Fevreiro, Portuguese brig, prize to His Majesty's ship Iphigenia, Commodore Sir Robert Mends; and the Nymfa del Mar also prize to the Iphigenia.

If we may presume to recommend to Your Lordship the amendment of any particular deficiency in the existing Treaties, otherwise than in our usual manner of presenting to your Lordship's notice the circumstances that furnish the suggestion, we would entreat that, if vessels having Slave-trading outfit cannot,—at least, this crying abuse of having cargoes of Slaves collected on shore should, be made equivalent to having them on board, and that vessels in such circumstances should be made liable to detention and condemnation.

With respect to the state of foreign co-operation, since the date of our last report, we have to mention merely the appearance of the French corvette La Diane off this harbour, on Sunday the 17th of May. She cruized off and on during the whole of the day, but did not come in, nor communicate with any of the small vessels or boats in the offing; and when the harbour-master approached her in his boat, for the purpose of offering his services to bring her in, she made all sail from him. No account has been received of her proceedings on the coast.

No vessel of force belonging to the United States of America has appeared on the coast.

We have the honour to be, &c.
(Signed)   E. Gregory.
                Edward Fitzgerald.

Capitalism and Abolitionism

ERIC WILLIAMS

In June, 1783, the Prime Minister, Lord North, complimented the Quaker opponents of the slave trade on their humanity, but regretted that its abolition was an impossibility, as the trade had become necessary to almost every nation in Europe. Slave traders and sugar planters rubbed their hands in glee. The West Indian colonies were still the darlings of the empire, the most precious jewels in the British diadem.

Source: Excerpted from *Capitalism and Slavery,* by Eric Williams, pp. 126–127, 135–136, 169–173, 178–181, 189–190, 192. Copyright © 1944 by the University of North Carolina Press. Reprinted by permission of the University of North Carolina Press.

But the rumblings of the inevitable storm were audible for those who had ears to hear. The year of Yorktown was the year of Watt's second patent, that for the rotary motion, which converted the steam engine into a source of motive power and made industrial England, in Matthew Boulton's phrase, "steam-mill mad." Rodney's victory over the French, which saved the sugar colonies, coincided with Watt's utilization of the expansive power of steam to obtain the double stroke for his pistons. The peace treaty of 1783 was being signed while Henry Cort was working on his puddling process which revolutionized the iron industry. The stage was set for that gigantic development of British capitalism which upset the political structure of the country in 1832 and thereby made possible the attack on monopoly in general and West Indian monopoly in particular. . . .

The attack on the West Indians was more than an attack on slavery. It was an attack on monopoly. Their opponents were not only the humanitarians but the capitalists. The reason for the attack was not only that the West Indian economic system was vicious but that it was also so unprofitable that for this reason alone its destruction was inevitable. The agent for Jamaica complained in 1827 that "the cause of the colonies altogether, but more especially that part of it which touches upon property in slaves, is so unattractive to florid orators and so unpopular with the public, that we have and must have very little protection from Parliamentary speaking." Hibbert was only half right. If West Indian slavery was detestable, West Indian monopoly was unpopular, and the united odium of both was more than the colonies could bear.

The attack falls into three phases: the attack on the slave trade, the attack on slavery, the attack on the preferential sugar duties. The slave trade was abolished in 1807, slavery in 1833, the sugar preference in 1846. The three events are inseparable. The very vested interests which had been built up by the slave system now turned and destroyed that system. The humanitarians, in attacking the system in its weakest and most indefensible spot, spoke a language that the masses could understand. They could never have succeeded a hundred years before when every important capitalist interest was on the side of the colonial system. "It was an arduous hill to climb," sang Wordsworth in praise of Clarkson. The top would never have been reached but for the defection of the capitalists from the ranks of the slave-owners and slave traders. The West Indians, pampered and petted and spoiled for a century and a half, made the mistake of elevating into a law of nature what was actually only a law of mercantilism. They thought themselves indispensable and carried over to an age of anti-imperialism the lessons they had been taught in an age of commercial imperialism. When, to their surprise, the "invisible hand" of Adam Smith turned against them, they could turn only to the invisible hand of God. The rise and fall of mercantilism is the rise and fall of slavery. . . .

The capitalists had first encouraged West Indian slavery and then helped to destroy it. When British capitalism depended on the West Indies, they ignored slavery or defended it. When British capitalism found the West Indian monopoly a nuisance, they destroyed West Indian slavery as the first step in the destruction of West Indian monopoly. That slavery to them was relative not absolute, and depended on latitude and longitude, is proved after 1833 by their attitude to slavery in Cuba, Brazil and the United States. They taunted their opponents with seeing slavery only where they saw sugar and limiting their observation to the circumference of a hogshead. They refused to frame their tariff on grounds of morality, erect a pulpit in every custom house, and make their landing-waiters enforce antislavery doctrines.

Before and after 1815 the British government tried to bribe the Spanish and Portuguese governments into abolition of the slave trade—in 1818 Spain was given £400,000 in return for a promise to do so. All to no avail. The treaties were treated as scraps of paper, as abolition would have ruined Cuba and Brazil. The British government, therefore, urged on by the West Indians, decided to adopt more drastic measures. Wellington was sent to the international conference at Verona to propose that the Continental Powers boycott the produce of countries still engaged in the slave trade. If he were met with the inquiry, whether Britain was similarly prepared to exclude the produce of slave-trading countries imported not for consumption but in transit, he was to express his readiness to refer that proposition for immediate consideration to his government. These instructions did little justice to the perspicacity of the Continental statesmen. Wellington's proposal was received in silence, and he observed "those symptoms of disapprobation and dissent which convince me not only that it will not be adopted, but that the suggestion of it is attributed to interested motives not connected with the humane desire of abolishing the slave trade!" As Canning reported to his cabinet: "The proposed refusal to admit Brazilian sugar into the dominions of the Emperors [of Russia and Austria-Hungary] and the King of Prussia was met (as might be expected) with a smile; which indicated on the part of the continental statesmen a suspicion that there might be something of self-interest in our suggestion for excluding the produce of rival colonies from competition with our own, and their surprise that we should consent to be the carriers of the produce which we would fain dissuade them from consuming."

It was clearly what a member of Parliament was later to call "lucrative humanity." The independence of Brazil gave Canning a better opportunity. Recognition in return for abolition. But there was a danger that France would recognize Brazil on condition that the slave trade be continued. What then of the British carrying trade and British exports? "There are immense British interests engaged in the trade with Brazil," Canning reminded Wilberforce, "and we must proceed with caution and good heed; and take the commercial as well as moral feelings of the country with us." Morality or profit? Britain had to choose. "You argue," wrote Canning candidly to Wilberforce, "against the acknowledgment of Brazil unpurged of Slave Trade . . . you are surprised that the Duke of Wellington has not been instructed to say that he will give up the trade with Brazil, (for that is, I am afraid, the amount of giving up the import and re-export of the sugar and cotton), if Austria, Russia and Prussia will prohibit her produce. In fair reasoning, you have a right to be surprised, for we ought to be ready to make sacrifices when we ask them, and I am for making them; but who would dare to promise such a one as this without a full knowledge of the opinions of the commercial part of the nation?"

The commercial part of the nation did not leave Canning long in doubt. A bill had already been presented in Parliament in 1815 to proscribe the slave trade as an investment for British capital. Baring, of the great banking house which was to have such intimate relations with independent Spanish America, issued a solemn warning that every commercial organization in Britain would petition against it, and the House of Lords threw it out. In 1824 one hundred and seventeen merchants of London petitioned for the recognition of the independence of South America—the petitioners were, in a word, the city of London. The President, Vice-President and members of the Chamber of Commerce of Manchester declared that the opening of the South American market to British industry would be an event which must produce the most beneficial results to British commerce. British capitalism could no longer be content with smuggling.

This South American market, Brazil in particular, was based on slave labor and required the slave trade. The British capitalists, therefore, began a vigorous campaign against their government's policy of forcible suppression of the slave trade by stationing warships on the African coast. The policy was expensive, exceeding the annual value of the total trade with Africa. African exports were £154,000 in 1824; imports £118,000 in British goods and £119,000 in foreign. This was the great extent of commerce, said Hume, for which the country was to make such a vast sacrifice of human life on the deadly slave coast. Humanity for English sailors demanded its abandonment. If some abolitionists were suffering from a humane delusion, why should they be allowed to delude the English Parliament? The British people could not afford to become purchasers on such extravagant terms of indulgences for Africa.

All this was before 1833, contemporaneous with the capitalist attacks on West Indian slavery. After 1833 the capitalists were still involved in the slave trade itself. British goods, from Manchester and Liverpool, cottons, fetters and shackles, were sent direct to the coast of Africa or indirectly to Rio de Janeiro and Havana, where they were used by their Cuban and Brazilian consignees for the purpose of purchasing slaves. It was said that seven-tenths of the goods used by Brazil for slave purchases were British manufactures, and it was whispered that the British were reluctant to destroy the barracoons on the coast because they would thereby destroy British calicoes. In 1845 Peel refused to deny the fact that British subjects were engaged in the slave trade. The Liverpool representative in Parliament, questioned point blank, was not prepared to contradict that Liverpool exports to Africa or elsewhere were appropriated to "some improper purpose." British banking firms in Brazil financed the slave traders and insured their cargoes, thereby earning the goodwill of their hosts. British mining companies owned and purchased slaves whose labor they employed in their enterprises. "We must needs adopt the painful conclusion," said Brougham with reference to Cuban and Brazilian development, "that in great part at least such an ample amount of capital as was required, must have belonged to the rich men of this country." John Bright was well aware of the interests of his Lancashire constituents when he argued eloquently in 1843 against a bill prohibiting the employment of British capital, however indirectly, in the slave trade on the ground that it would be a dead letter, and that the matter should be left to the honorable and moral feelings of individuals. In that very year, British firms handled three-eighths of the sugar, one-half of the coffee, five-eighths of the cotton exported from Pernambuco, Rio de Janeiro and Bahia.

The capitalists had had enough of Britain's "noble experiment." Commerce was the great emancipator. The only way to put down slavery was to trust to the eternal and just principles of free trade. Leave the slave trade alone, it would commit suicide. If the miscreants of any nation chose to engage in it, their guilt be upon their own heads; leave to a higher tribunal the moral government of the world. The money expended in fruitless efforts to suppress the slave trade could be more beneficially and philosophically employed at home. . . .

This study has deliberately subordinated the inhumanity of the slave system and the humanitarianism which destroyed that system. To disregard it completely, however, would be to commit a grave historical error and to ignore one of the greatest propaganda movements of all time. The humanitarians were the spearhead of the onslaught which destroyed the West Indian system and freed the Negro. But their importance has been seriously misunderstood and grossly exaggerated by men who have sacrificed scholarship to sentimentality and, like the scholastics of old, placed faith before reason and evidence. Professor Coupland, in an imaginary interview with Wilberforce, asks him: "What do you think, sir, is the primary significance of your work, the lesson of the abolition of the slave system?" The instant answer is: "It was God's work. It signifies the triumph of His will over human selfishness. It teaches that no obstacle of interest or prejudice is irremovable by faith and prayer."

This misunderstanding springs, in part, from a deliberate attempt by contemporaries to present a distorted view of the abolitionist movement. When the slave trade was abolished in 1807, the bill included a phrase to the effect that the trade was "contrary to the principles of justice, humanity and sound policy." Lord Hawkesbury objected; in his opinion the words "justice and humanity" reflected on the slave traders. He therefore moved an amendment excluding those words. In so doing he confined the necessity of abolition solely to expediency. The Lord Chancellor protested. The amendment would take away the only ground on which the other powers could be asked to co-operate in abolition. The Earl of Lauderdale declared that the words omitted were the most essential in the bill. The omission would lend color to the suspicion in France that British abolition was dictated by the selfish motive that her colonies were well-stocked with Negroes. "How, in thus being supposed to make no sacrifice ourselves, could we call with any effect upon foreign powers to co-operate in the abolition?" The Lords voted for the original version.

The British humanitarians were a brilliant band. Clarkson personifies all the best in the humanitarianism of the age. One can appreciate even today his feelings when, in ruminating upon the subject of his prize-winning essay, he first awoke to the realization of the enormous injustice of slavery. Clarkson was an indefatigable worker, who conducted endless and dangerous researches into the conditions and consequences of the slave trade, a prolific pamphleteer whose history of the abolition movement is still a classic. His labors in the cause of justice to Africa were accomplished only at the cost of much personal discomfort, and imposed a severe strain on his scanty resources. In 1793 he wrote a letter to Josiah Wedgwood which contains some of the finest sentiments that motivated the humanitarians. He needed money and wished to sell two of his shares in the Sierra Leone Company, founded in 1791 to promote legitimate commerce with Africa. "But," he pointed out, "I should not chuse to permit anyone to become a purchaser, who would not be better pleased with the good resulting to Africa than from great commercial profits to himself; not that the latter may not be expected, but in case of a disappointment, I should wish his mind to be made easy by the assurance that he has been instrumental in introducing light and happiness into a country, where the mind was kept in darkness and the body nourished only for European chains." Too impetuous and enthusiastic for some of his colleagues, Clarkson was one of those friends of whom the Negro race has had unfortunately only too few. . . .

The abolitionists were not radicals. In their attitude to domestic problems they were reactionary. The Methodists offered the English worker Bibles instead of bread and Wesleyan capitalists exhibited open contempt for the working class. Wilberforce was familiar with all that went on in the hold of a slave ship but ignored what went on at the bottom of a mineshaft. He supported the Corn Laws, was a member of the secret committee which investigated and repressed working class discontent in 1817, opposed feminine anti-slavery associations, and thought the First Reform Bill too radical. . . .

The abolitionists at first had not confined their attention to the British slave trade. They had dreamed of nothing short of the total and universal abolition of the slave trade. They took advantage of the return of peace in 1815 and the international conferences then in vogue to disseminate their views. They sent whole "loads of humbug" to Parliament; in thirty-four days in 1814, they sent 772 petitions with a million signatures. They denounced the paper declaration of the Congress of Vienna against the slave trade, where they had won over Britain's plenipotentiary, Wellington, and were even prepared to go to war for abolition. They gained the support of the Tsar of Russia. They sent a special observer, Clarkson, to the Congress of Aix-la-Chapelle. They were ready to fight France all over again to prevent French reconquest of Saint Domingue, and were unwilling to recognize the independence of Brazil from Portugal without an explicit promise to renounce the slave trade. They forced the British government, by their "friendly violence," to station a squadron on the African coast to suppress the slave trade by force.

The pressure on the government was terrific. The government pleaded for time, for caution. "Morals," said Castlereagh, "were never well taught by the sword." He begged the humanitarians to "moderate their virtuous feelings, and put their solicitude for Africa under the dominion of reason." But the abolitionists gave the government no peace. As Liverpool confessed on one occasion to Wilberforce: "If I were not anxious for the abolition of the slave trade on principle, I must be aware of the embarrassment to which any government must be exposed from the present state of that question in this country." The government was considerably hampered in its foreign relations for they knew that all negotiations were futile. But they never dared to say so openly. "We shall never succeed," wrote Wellington to Aberdeen, "in abolishing the foreign slave trade. But we must take care to avoid to take any steps which may induce the people of England to believe that we do not do everything in our power to discourage and put it down as soon as possible."

In an unforgettable general election in 1831, in which candidates were quizzed on their views on slavery, the abolitionists dragged Negroes to election with golden chains, and, where they could find no Negroes, chimney sweeps. They placarded the hustings all over the kingdom with full-length pictures of white planters flogging Negro women. In their campaigns they appealed to the hearts and consciences of British women, and even approached children. Leeds published an anti-slavery series for juvenile readers. An anti-slavery dial was manufactured, so that benevolent people, enjoying the domestic comforts of an evening fireside in England, would know that the Negroes were toiling on the plantations under the oppressive heat of a tropical sun. This was in the years before 1833. Bliss was in that dawn. . . .

The barbarous removal of the Negroes from Africa continued for at least twenty-five years after 1833, to the sugar plantations of Brazil and Cuba. Brazilian and Cuban economy depended on the slave trade. Consistency alone demanded that the British abolitionists oppose this trade. But that would retard Brazilian and Cuban development and consequently hamper British trade. The desire for cheap sugar after 1833 overcame all abhorrence of slavery. Gone was the horror which once was excited at the idea of a British West Indian slave-driver armed with a whip; the Cuban slave-driver, armed with whip, cutlass, dagger and pistols, and followed by bloodhounds, aroused not even comment from the abolitionists. Exeter Hall, the center of British humanitarianism, yielded to the Manchester School, the spearhead of British free trade.

The Idea of Progress

HOWARD TEMPERLEY

The problem is easily stated: What was it, in the late eighteenth and early nineteenth centuries, that made men turn against an institution which, in one form or another, had existed since time immemorial? Why was slavery attacked *then?* Why not in the seventeenth century, or the sixteenth? Why, indeed, was it attacked at all?

Traditionally, the answers given to this question have taken two forms.

One is to describe how ideas, initially expressed by a handful of

Source: From Howard Temperley, "The Ideology of Antislavery" in David Eltis and James Walvin, ed., *The Abolition of the Atlantic Slave Trade,* 1981, pp. 21–30. Reprinted by permission of The University of Wisconsin Press.

AM I NOT A SISTER?

(Left) "Am I Not a Man and a Brother?" Medallion of the London Abolition Society.
(Right) "Am I Not a Sister?" From the cover of The Liberty Almanac for 1851, *published by the American and Foreign Anti-Slavery Society.*
(Library Company of Philadelphia)

thinkers, were taken up, elaborated, added to, and ultimately incorporated into the beliefs of the population at large. This was essentially the approach of Thomas Clarkson, whose *History of Abolition* (1808) is notable both as the first attempt to provide a comprehensive account of the origins of the antislavery movement and as a model for later writers. In a foldout map which appears at the end of the introductory section of his work he shows how, beginning far back in the sixteenth century as tiny springs and rivulets, each marked with the name of some prominent thinker or statesman, the waters converge to become rivers, eventually "swelling the torrent which swept away the slave-trade." As Clarkson saw it, the victory of the abolitionists represented the triumph of right thinking over error, of the forces of light over the forces of darkness. It had been a long struggle, extending over centuries, but in the end truth had prevailed.

Until a generation ago few historians felt disposed to dissent from this view. Although less overtly Manichean in their approach, they were prepared to accept Clarkson's analysis, at least to the extent that they saw the ideas which eventually came together and energized the antislavery crusade as having originated in the distant past, in most cases with identifiable individuals or groups. Few later commentators would have chosen, as Clarkson did, to include Pope Leo X or Queen Elizabeth in their list of precursors, nor would they have cared to invoke, as Clarkson also did, the hand of Providence as a guiding force; but at bottom the processes they described were much the same. This, for example, is the approach adopted in the early chapters of Frank Klingberg's *The Anti-Slavery Movement in England* (1926), and in one form or another it informs the work of most early twentieth century writers and many later writers, a notable recent example being David Brion Davis's *The Problem of Slavery in Western Culture* (1966).

The principle challenge to this view has come from those historians who have seen the abolition of the slave trade and slavery as having been the result, not of moral, but of economic pressures. The classic statement of this case was Eric Williams's *Capitalism and Slavery* (1944). Williams, it is true, did not entirely discount the influence of moral teaching, to the extent that he saw the abolitionists as a "spearhead." They spoke "a language the masses could understand" and thereby "were successful in raising anti-slavery sentiments almost to the status of a religion in England." In this sense they helped the process along. But at bottom it was the forces of economic rather than moral change that mattered. It was "mercantilism" that created the slave system and "mature capitalism" that destroyed it. He states his case forcefully: "The attack falls into three phases: the attack on the slave trade, the attack on slavery, the attack on the preferential sugar duties. The slave trade was abolished in 1807, slavery in 1833, the sugar preference in 1846. These three events are inseparable."

Leaving aside for the moment the question of whether the evidence will actually support this view, we may simply note that what we have here are two fundamentally contradictory explanations as to why abolition occurred at the time it did. In the one case it is seen as the product of a long process of intellectual inquiry. The antislavery argument that was presented to Parliament and the British public in the 1780s and 1790s was not, and given its complexity could not conceivably have been, the achievement of one group or even of one generation. Inevitably it was the work of many hands extending back over many generations. In the same way, the economic explanation is also dependent on the notion of gradual maturation which initially fostered slavery but ultimately created a conjunction of interests which destroyed it. In each case abolition is seen as the result of an extended chain of events which by the late eighteenth and early nineteenth centuries had created a situation in which the slave trade, and later slavery itself, could no longer be regarded as acceptable.

Comparing these two explanations, it may be noted that in one respect at least the economic view scores over what, for want of a better term, we may call the intellectual diffusionist account in that it is more firmly rooted in what are commonly regarded as the major developments of the period. Much of the plausibility of Williams's account, indeed, derives from the fact that Britain, the first nation to industrialize, also took the lead in the campaigns to abolish the slave trade and slavery. This is a development which the intellectual diffusionist account virtually ignores. Moreover, there is something patently unsatisfactory about any explanation of a historical event, particularly a historical event as important as the abolition of the slave trade and slavery, which is based on developments in the realm of ideas and which fails, at least in any detailed way, to relate those ideas to the actual lives of people of the period. Most ideas, as we know, have long pedigrees. Often, too, they are capable of acquiring a momentum of their own and can develop, almost regardless of changes in the material world, according to an inner logic of their own. But equally plainly ideas are shaped by circumstance, and the longer the time span the greater the likelihood of this happening. Thus in accounting for the attack on slavery we need to know not simply when ideas originated and who first formulated them, but what it was at a certain point in time that made man choose, out of all the ideas available, those particular ideas, and furthermore to act on them. To assume, as the abolitionists frequently did, that their ideas were right and that virtue requires no explanation is inadequate, since plainly not everyone agreed with them. We still need to be shown why what seemed right to the abolitionists—and, more to the point, to an increasingly large proportion of their contemporaries—had not seemed right to their predecessors.

Yet, if the intellectual diffusionist account has its pitfalls, so also does the economic explanation, the principal one being that it is exceedingly difficult to show that the overthrow of either the slave trade or slavery would actually have influenced the material interests of those who pressed for it, except, in some cases, adversely. So far as the attack on the British slave trade is concerned, as Seymour Drescher has recently argued in *Econocide: British Slavery in the Era of Abolition* (1977), the whole theory of West Indian decline upon which Williams bases his thesis is without foundation. West Indian decline was the result, rather than the cause, of abolition. Much the same may be said of the abolition of slavery itself, which further accelerated the decline process. As I attempted to show in an appendix to *British Antislavery, 1833–1870* (1972), the attack on West Indian slavery could not have been an attack on monopoly, since before 1833 a large proportion of the West Indian sugar crop was sold on the world market, which determined the price. Rather, it was the abolition of slavery, which reduced production below that necessary to supply British needs, that created a monopoly, thus driving up prices and creating a demand for an end to differential tariffs. Nor is it easy to fall back on the alternative argument, often used in such cases, and say that what mattered were not economic realities but how men perceived them, since in each instance the results that ensued were widely predicted. Plausible though it might appear at first sight, and attractive though it might remain in theory, the truth is that the economic explanation fails to take account of the fact that slavery was itself very much a capitalist institution, that in general it offered a good return on investment, that it provided a plentiful supply of cheap raw materials, and that the usual effect of emancipation was to drive up the price of the products upon which the burgeoning industries of Europe and America depended.

But if neither the economic nor the intellectual diffusionist accounts provide a satisfactory explanation, what alternatives are there? One obvious tactic, of course, is to try to link the two together. The problem here is that simple mixing does nothing to improve the quality of the initial ingredients. If both are defective, the same will inevitably be true of the final mixture. In the present instance, however, there is a special difficulty in that the two accounts are based not only on different but largely on diametrically opposing views of human nature. The intellectual diffusionists, in their explanation, place a high premium on disinterested benevolence and on the instinctive desire of those who were not themselves victims of, or indeed in any way implicated in, the practice of slaveholding to alleviate the sufferings of others. Williams, for his part, does not entirely discount this element. The abolitionists were "a brilliant band" and they, or at all events some of them, were genuine idealists. Nevertheless, their role has been "seriously misunderstood and grossly exaggerated," for what really destroyed the slave system was not altruism but greed, self-interest, and the lust for power—in other words, the same motives which had built it up in the first place. So unless we suppose, as Williams does, that there were two quite separate groups involved, it is hard to see how the two views can be reconciled. That there *were* two groups is a theoretical possibility, but this is a view which, on the basis of the available evidence, it has so far proved impossible to substantiate, and in any case it is hard to see where the profit motive lay.

One possible way of getting out of this impasse, however, is to look again at the conceptual framework which historians have used. And here we may begin by noting that there is something essentially artificial about the way in which altruism and self-interest have been juxtaposed, as if they were the only motives from which the participants acted. Williams is plainly guilty of this, but so also are the traditionalists in their emphasis on those elements of right thinking and self-dedication which led W. E. H. Lecky in his *History of European Morals* (1884) to describe the crusade against slavery as "among the three or four perfectly virtuous pages comprised in the history of nations." Large numbers of people, and certainly groups as large and variegated as those responsible for the overthrow of the slave trade and slavery, which of course included not only the abolitionists but all those who voted against these practices in Parliament and Congress, together with those who supported them in their efforts, are simply not moved, or at least not entirely moved, by abstract benevolence. Nor, for that matter, is economics, Adam Smith notwithstanding, merely the pursuit of individual self-interest. Adam Smith himself, significantly enough, disapproved of slavery for reasons which turn out on examination to have nothing to do with its immediate cost-effectiveness. Thus even in his system, and no less strikingly in those of his successors, economics in this broader sense is seen as being concerned not merely, or even primarily, with how best to pursue short-term individual gains, but with the way in which societies actually do, or in theory should, order their affairs. Viewed in this way economics and benevolence no longer appear as opposing principles. As the Victorians in particular were well aware, the two could not only be reconciled but were often mutually supportive. Thus, whether we look at economic thought or at the possible range of motives which led large numbers of individuals, the great majority of whom were not abolitionists in the narrow sense, to turn against the slave trade and slavery, we find ourselves dealing with large-scale, and in many respects overlapping, systems of belief which are far too complex to be categorized in terms of either self-interest or benevolence.

To call these systems ideologies is, perhaps, to invite misunderstanding, although it is not clear what other word will suffice. Certainly it is not intended here to postulate a rigid set of assumptions which everyone opposed to slavery shared. Perhaps the word could be used in that sense with regard to some antislavery groups which expected a strict orthodoxy of belief on the part of their members, although even then there are distinctions that would need to be recognized. But if we take ideology to mean an assortment of beliefs and values shared by the members of a society and used by them to explain and guide social action, no such rigidity need be assumed. Such an ideology would be expected to change along with the society that produced it, and whose aspirations and beliefs it reflected. Nor should we expect that it would be logically consistent. Much of the impulse for change would come, in fact, from attempts to reconcile internal contradictions. Not surprisingly, many within the society would claim that their beliefs were not simply personal, or for that matter social, but represented universal truths. But whether they did or not is a question which might appropriately be left to philosophers or theologians; for present purposes they should be regarded as social products.

So how might such a concept be used to explain the development of the antislavery movement? One way to begin is to examine the character of the two societies, Britain and the northern United States, which found themselves in the forefront of the struggle. And here we may start by noting that both had experienced remarkable rates of economic growth in the course of the eighteenth century. Probably nowhere else in the world was the relative increase in wealth and population more striking than in the thirteen colonies. This, as we all know, was one of the factors which persuaded the British government to attempt to tighten its hold on the colonists, and so helped to precipitate the break with the mother country. Yet Britain's own rate of growth during these years, although less marked in relative terms, was also impressive, whether we compare it with what had happened in previous centuries or with the experiences of her political rivals. This was, as economic historians continually remind us, a period of crucial importance for the Western world. Instead of the rhythmic expansion and contraction of populations and their products which had taken place over the previous millennium, the gains of the eighteenth century represented the departure point from which began the sustained growth that has characterized the modern world. Britain and her ex-colonies were in the forefront of this development. Materially speaking, they had reason to feel proud of their achievement.

A second characteristic that Britain and the northern states (as opposed to the South) shared was the fact that they had achieved this prosperity without direct recourse to slave labor, at least on any significant scale. To be sure, there was slavery in Britain right up to the end of the eighteenth century (the Somerset decision notwithstanding), and it lingered on in the northern states even longer. As late as 1820 there were still eighteen thousand slaves in the northeastern United States, and at the time of the first census in 1790 the figure was more than double that; but compared with the situation south of the Mason-Dixon line this represented a relatively modest stake in the institution. It must also be remembered that both Britain and the northern states had profited, and were continuing to profit on an ever-increasing scale, from the employment of slaves elsewhere. Nevertheless, the fact remains that, so far as their domestic arrangements were concerned, both were committed to an essentially free-labor system.

These points are too obvious to dwell on. Yet they are worth emphasizing if only because they help to explain why men in these two societies were so ready to accept ideas of progress, and in particular ideas of progress which linked individual freedom to material prosperity. The two, needless to say, are not necessarily connected. More often than not they have been seen as opposing principles, the assumption being that the pursuit of the one must necessarily entail the sacrifice of the other. Implicit in the whole idea of government is the belief that individual freedom must be given up to secure the benefits of an ordered society, among which must be included a measure of material satisfaction. How much freedom needs to be sacrificed is a matter of opinion, but history is not wanting in examples of societies welcoming tyrants because the alternatives of anarchy and lawlessness were regarded as even less acceptable. So the commonly expressed eighteenth century view that freedom and prosperity were not only reconcilable but mutually supportive, and that the more you had of the one the more you could expect of the other, is something that needs explaining. The explanation, I suggest, is to be found not in the ideas of the philosophers, still less in theories about the general progress of the human mind, but in the immediate lives of people of the period.

This, then, is one way of relating material and intellectual developments, and one that throws a good deal of light on the thinking of such figures as Adam Smith and the exponents of the secular antislavery argument generally. For what is striking about the secular case against slavery is the *assumption* that slavery was an economic anachronism. Smith's own attitudes are particularly revealing, because of all eighteenth century commentators he was probably the one best qualified to argue the case against it on strictly economic grounds. Yet, as already noted, the case he actually presents is not based on economics at all, at least not in any cost-accounting sense, but on the general proposition that greater freedom would lead to greater prosperity. Like other eighteenth century thinkers he expresses himself in terms of universal principles, but at bottom it is a historical argument, derived from his own beliefs about the nature of the historical process. Whatever the objective truths of Smith's arguments, the fact remains that they are very much the product of one kind of society, and indeed of one particular class within that society.

An obvious objection to this argument is that, while it may very well be true that Adam Smith rejected slavery for the reasons suggested, it is by no means clear that other people did. Very few, after all, were Smithians. The point that is being made here, however, is not that Smith was important for his teachings (although Clarkson was happy to cite him) so much as for what he reflected about the continuing processes that characterized the age in which he lived. Of course, not even Smith himself realized that the Western world was entering a new economic era. Nevertheless, it is evident that substantial increases in trade and improvements in agriculture had begun to be made long before Smith's time and so were readily observable by his contemporaries. Furthermore, if what is at issue here is the origin of the Western idea of progress, it should be borne in mind that this owed at least as much to developments in the field of knowledge as to material changes. Certainly by the end of the seventeenth century men not only knew more than their predecessors but knew that they knew more.

Yet even if we grant that these developments go some way toward explaining the secular case against slavery, it by no means follows that they motivated the early leaders of the antislavery movement, most of whom, if we may judge by the arguments they used, believed that they were acting out of religious principles. This is a tricky problem because by and large these principles stem directly from the Christian tradition. But if, instead of following the Clarkson method of attempting to trace them back to their origins, we ask simply what it was that brought them to the fore at this particular point in time, we can perhaps make a start by observing that what was fundamental to the whole attack on slavery was the belief that it was removable. Politics, we are continually reminded, is the art of the practical, but so also are ethics practical in the sense that what is irremovable may be deplorable, inconvenient, or embarrassing, but can scarcely be unethical. Ethics, in other words, implies optionality. Moralists may be more stringent in their views than politicians, but in this respect at least the underlying considerations are the same.

In a sense, of course, slavery always was removable to the extent that institutions men establish they can, given an adequate stimulus, usually get around to disestablishing. But until the eighteenth century that stimulus was generally lacking, with the result that slavery was accepted with that fatalism which men commonly reserve for aspects of nature which, whether they are to be celebrated or deplored, have to be borne. To argue against slavery was to argue against the facts of life. Before slavery could become a political issue—or even, in the proper sense, a moral issue—what needed to be shown was that the world could get along without it. And what better demonstration could there be than the development, within the heartland of Western civilization, of societies which not only did without slavery but which did very well without it, and which furthermore appeared to owe their quite remarkable dynamism to the acceptance of principles which represented the direct negation of the assumptions upon which slavery was founded.

This was not, of course, a development particularly likely to impress the inhabitants of those societies which relied directly on slave labor. They knew perfectly well how much they owed to their slaves, not only in a strictly economic sense, but for the maintenance of their whole way of life. They also knew that they were contributing in no small way to the prosperity of the free-labor societies by providing them with cheap raw materials and foodstuffs. And, by virtue of their position, they were well placed to judge the revolutionary nature of the abolitionists' demands—what a rapid shift from slave to free labor would mean in terms of political and social power. Often what they said in this regard was a great deal more realistic than anything said by their opponents. Yet the fact remains that as societies they were overshadowed by cultures whose values, deriving from a quite different set of historical experiences, were in the process of changing in ways that made the justification of slavery, even on hardheaded economic grounds, increasingly difficult.

What I am suggesting, in other words, is that the attack on slavery can be seen as an attempt by a dominant metropolitan ideology to impose its values on the societies of the economic periphery. And what I am also suggesting is that this attack was the product of a widening ideological gap occasioned by the extraordinary success, not least in material terms, of those societies which practiced a free-labor system, among which Britain and the northern United States were outstanding examples. For if we suppose that the manner in which societies gain their existence helps to form the ideas of their members as to how people in general should live, we must also, I think, concede that there were very powerful reasons why men in these two societies (and one could add France as a third) should have come to regard slavery as not only immoral but anachronistic.

This, of course, is a very different thing from saying that the promotion of their own economic interests *required* the abolition of slavery, because in most cases it did not. Nor is it necessary to argue that relative to the slaveholding societies the free-labor societies were becoming more powerful, although sometimes this was so. It was much easier for Britain to attack slavery after the departure of the American colonies. But by the same token it became correspondingly more perilous for the Americans themselves to do anything about it, and in the event little was done to remove the institution until war made action possible. Thus any general account which attributes the rise of the antislavery movement to considerations of economic necessity is open to serious objections.

Slave Revolts and the End of Slavery

MICHAEL CRATON

On 22 March 1816, Matthew Gregory "Monk" Lewis, gothick novelist and absentee planter on his first visit to his Jamaican estates, recorded in his diary a kind of proto-calypso or revolutionary hymn, said to have been sung by some Ibo slaves plotting a rebellion under cover of a funeral in the neighbouring parish of St. Elizabeth. Allegedly, there were "above a thousand persons . . . engaged in the plot, three hundred of whom had been regularly sworn to assist in it with all the usual accompanying ceremonies of drinking human blood, eating earth from graves, &c." Among the would-be rebels were said to be "a *black* ascertained to have stolen into the island from St. Domingo, and a *brown* Anabaptist missionary." The latter was perhaps the author of the hymn, but the singing was led by the elected "King of the Eboes":

> *Oh me good friend, Mr. Wilberforce, make we free!*
> *God Almighty thank ye! God Almighty thank ye!*
> *God Almighty, make we free!*
> *Buckra in this country no make we free:*
> *What Negro for to do? What Negro for to do?*
> *Take force by force! Take force by force!*

What are we to make of this subversive ditty, which, significantly, was not published until 1834, after the Emancipation Act had come into effect, sixteen years after Lewis's own death by yellow fever, and a year after the death of Wilberforce himself? Provided that we are certain of its authenticity, it seems to indicate that the St. Elizabeth plotters believed that God had the power, and perhaps the will, to free them, that they could call upon certain godly allies in England—the chief of them being the chief of the Evangelical Saints—that, with or without external aid, the time was ripe for making a move, and that since they could not expect their immediate oppressors ever to relent, they had every justification and right to resort to armed rebellion.

Source: From Michael Craton in *Out of Slavery: Abolition and After*, ed. Jack Haywood, 1985, excerpts from pp. 110–22, 123–26. Reprinted by permission of Frank Cass & Co. Ltd.

I believe it to be axiomatic that all slaves wanted their freedom—that is, freedom to make a life of their own—and that all slaves resisted slavery in the ways best open to them, actually rebelling, if rarely, when they could or had to. In rebelling, they seized the weapons that were to hand and used the aid of whatever allies they could find. Perhaps, then, the Lewis ditty accurately reflected the resistant spirit of the British West Indian slaves when it was sung; their ideology of resistance.

Between the year that Lewis recorded the Ibo song and the year of its publication, not only did the emancipation movement come to fruition, but there was also a crescendo of slave unrest in the British West Indies, with highlights in three of the largest ever slave rebellions, in Barbados in April 1816, in Demerara in August and September 1823 and in Jamaica between December 1831 and February 1832. What this paper aims to do is to examine each of these major outbreaks, briefly describing the sequence of events, the causes alleged at the time and what I take to be the truer causes, and the outcome, both in the colonies and, even more important, in the metropole. It will try to establish the relative parts the principal actors played in the drama of British slave emancipation, which was enacted barely a year after the suppression of the Jamaican rebellion; the avowed Emancipationists, the British legislators, the West Indian planters, the missionaries and, above all, the British West Indian slaves themselves. My main purpose is to test the conclusions by Eric Williams, in 1944, that "the alternatives were clear: emancipation from above or emancipation from below," and of Richard Hart, in 1980, that British West Indian blacks were "slaves who abolished slavery."

The Barbados revolt began with thrilling suddenness on Easter Sunday night, 14 April 1816, at a time when the slaves were free from work and had ample opportunities to organise under the cover of the permitted festivities. What made the outbreak all the more shocking to the planters was that there had never been an actual slave rebellion in Barbados, and not even a plot had been uncovered to ruffle their complacency for 115 years. Indeed, so convinced were the Barbadian planters of their physical and psychological control over their slaves that they were certain that a rebellion could only have been generated by outside forces, namely the English Emancipationists, and fomented by local agents other than slaves, specifically a cabal of disaffected free coloureds under the leadership of one

Joseph Pitt Washington Franklin, "a person of loose morals and abandoned habits, but superior to those with whom he intimately associated."

Some 20,000 slaves were involved, from more than seventy-five estates, and within a few hours they had taken control of the whole south-eastern quarter of the island. They fired the cane-trash houses as beacons and drove most of the Whites into Town, but did not commit widespread destruction or kill any of the hundreds of Whites virtually at their mercy. Having reached within sight of Bridgetown, they set up defensive positions, hoping and expecting the regime to negotiate.

They were soon disabused. Martial law was declared by the Acting Governor and the military commandant, Colonel Codd, was placed at the head of a punitive column. This consisted of regular troops, including the black First West India Regiment, and the much less disciplined and more vindictive white parochial militiamen. Codd encouraged the killing of all slaves who resisted and authorised the burning of houses and destruction of gardens, but still had to report that "Under the irritation of the Moment and exasperated at the atrocity of the Insurgents, some of the Militia of the Parishes in Insurrection were induced to use their Arms rather too indiscriminately in pursuit of the Fugitives." Whereas one white civilian and one black soldier were killed, at least fifty slaves died in the fighting and seventy more were summarily executed in the field. Another 300 were carried to Bridgetown for more leisurely trial, of whom 144 were in due course put to death and 132 deported.

Once the revolt was suppressed, the regime was at pains to exculpate itself. Whites asserted that slaves never gave bad treatment as a cause of revolt, and masters were eager to demonstrate, against their metropolitan critics, that Barbadian slaves were well fed, clothed and housed, were not cruelly punished, received good medical treatment and had opportunities to grow their own provisions and raise livestock, even to sell their surpluses. The official Assembly Report, not published until 1818, echoed the statement made by Colonel Codd as early as 25 April 1816: "The general opinion which has persuaded the minds of these misguided people since the proposed Introduction of the Registry Bill [is] that their Emancipation was decreed by the British Parliament. And the idea seems to have been conveyed by mischievous persons, and the indiscreet conversation of Individuals."

However, such a spontaneous rebellion could not have occurred without widespread disaffection, organisation and leadership among the slaves themselves, and concerted, if unrealistic, aims. The local equivalent of the authors of the subversive ditty from St. Elizabeth, Jamaica, seems to have been a remarkable woman called Nanny Grigg, a literate domestic from Simmons's estate. Nanny had been telling her fellow slaves during 1815 that they were to be freed on New Year's Day. She claimed to have read this in the newspapers and said that her master and the other planters were "very uneasy" about it. Accordingly, she urged strike action, telling the other slaves "that they were all damned fools to work, for that she would not, as freedom they were sure to get." When the New Year came and went without emancipation, Nanny's advice became more militant. "About a fortnight after New-year's Day," reported another slave, "she said the negroes were to be freed on Easter-Monday, and the only way to get it was to fight for it, otherwise they would not get it; and the way they were to do, was to set fire, as that was the way they did in Saint Domingo."

Yet Nanny Grigg was no more than a firebrand. The real leaders and organisers of the slaves were tightly-knit groups, cells, of elite creole slaves led by rangers—that is, slave drivers, chosen by the Whites for apparent reliability, with much more freedom of movement than most of their fellows. Chief of all these was Bussa, the ranger of Bailey's estate, after whom the revolt has always been popularly known. What motivated Bussa and his lieutenants, it seems, was a hatred of slavery made intolerable by even worse than average conditions, coupled with a misguided sense that because the plantocracy now had enemies in England the time was opportune to rise up and dictate the terms under which the Blacks would continue to work on the sugar plantations.

What makes Bussa's revolt all the more poignant is the evidence that the rebels felt that they had the right to negotiate because they, even more than the Whites, were now true Barbadians. As Colonel Codd put it, "they maintained to me that the island belonged to them, and not to white Men." In their attempts at mobilisation, the Barbadian rebels marched under certain banners or standards, carried by such persons as "Johnny the *standard bearer*" who came from Bussa's estate. One of these banners, since, unfortunately, lost, was forwarded to London. Reports of it differ. Some locals claimed that it depicted "the Union of a Black Man with a white Female," an accurate configuration of the planters' Freudian fears, while another account simply discerned that it showed a black Barbadian on terms of equality with a white. Perhaps even more significant was the fact that when the rebels took as their first objective the St. Philip's militia armoury, besides muskets they took away the standard of the parochial militia regiment, which they carried forward into the skirmish at Lowther's yard on Easter Monday. Thus, it could be maintained, the slaves saw themselves not as simple rebels but as the authentic black militia of their native parish.

The chief miscalculations of the Barbadian rebels lay in underestimating the power of the local regime, in vainly presuming that the imperial troops would not be used against them (particularly the black West India Regiment), and in overestimating the support they might get from metropolitan liberals. In fact, even those in the metropolis who blamed the white Barbadians for bringing the rebellion on themselves by complacency and loose talk—calling slave registration but the thin end of a wedge leading to slave emancipation, and talking of imperial dictation over a Registry Act as tyranny worthy of rebellion in the style of the Americans in 1776—were horrified by the slave uprising. Not a single white person anywhere, it seems, reckoned the deaths of 264 rebel slaves as overkill.

Wilberforce's own role was critical. Although he had supported the Corn Law in 1815 ostensibly in return for government support of the Slave Registry Bill, he was already wavering over the Bill before news of Bussa's revolt reached London at the end of May 1816. The news, though, seems to have convinced him that the Emancipationists had best "rest on their oars" for the moment. He did not oppose the address to the Prince Regent deploring the insurrection, and on 19 June made a speech so defensive and self-exculpatory that he came close to a rift with his brother-in-law, James Stephen. Clearly, Wilberforce was terrified by the thought that he might be held responsible for the Barbados slave revolt, and he may well have been influenced by none other than Monk Lewis himself, with whom he dined between Lewis's arrival in England on 5 June and his speech in the House on 19 June. Wilberforce's diary merely records that he and Lewis met "to talk over Jamaica," and discussed Lewis's plans "to secure the happiness of his slaves after his death," but it is inconceivable that Lewis did not tell Wilberforce of the St. Elizabeth plot less than three months before, including the fact that the plotters had so memorably invoked Wilberforce's name. The idea of popular insurrection was anathema to Wilberforce, in England even more so than in the West Indies. In the period 1817–19, indeed, he spent almost as much effort in supporting the government's repressive measures at home, as he did on the West Indian cause.

Just as Bussa's revolt came in conjunction with the dissensions over the Slave Registry Bill, so the Demerara rebellion of August 1823 followed close on the heels of the next great wave of Emancipationist activity: T. F. Buxton's assumption of the leadership from the ailing William Wilberforce, the founding of the new Anti-Slavery Society in January 1823, Buxton's unsuccessful motion for gradual emancipation and Canning's canny substitution of an ameliorationist policy in May, and the Colonial Secretary, Lord Bathurst's first amelioration circular, which reached Georgetown on 7 July 1823. As happened in Barbados, the Guiana plantocracy angrily complained of imperial interference and dragged its feet over the implementation of the Bathurst circular. What further provoked the planters was that in British Guiana, unlike Barbados in 1816, nonconformist missionaries were already active and rapidly gaining converts, the most effective being the Rev. John Smith of the London Missionary Society, pastor of Bethel chapel on Le Resouvenir estate.

When the revolt was found to have been preceded by exaggerated rumours of impending changes decreed from London, seemed to focus on Le Resouvenir and the adjacent Success estate (owned by the father of William Ewart Gladstone), and to have been inspired by Smith's chief deacon, Quamina, the planters naturally claimed that the Emancipationists, misguided imperial statesmen and meddling missionaries were chiefly to blame. A more careful analysis, however, shows that the causes were, at least, more complex and, maybe, basically other.

Despite the planters' disclaimers, the Demerara slaves had even more cause to rebel than the Barbados slaves in 1816. Sugar monoculture had intensified and the slaves were worked harder and punished cruelly, callously shifted around with family ties ignored. Quamina, for example, on the day that Peggy, his wife of thirty years, lay dying, was refused leave to return to his house before sundown, when he found Peggy dead. For Christian slaves, the refusal of the planters to grant more than Sunday free from estate labour was particularly irksome, since it led to a conflict between the will to worship in chapel and the need to work provision grounds and go to market.

Christianity undoubtedly provided solace for many slaves, but less encouragement for rebellion. The missionaries, including Smith, were scrupulous in following their instructions to spurn political issues and counsel hard work and obedience. Bethel chapel was undoubtedly an important meeting place for slaves from the entire East Coast of Demerara, but subversive discussions occurred outside rather than inside the building. Likewise, Quamina, though a revered figure, seems to have been drawn into the rebellion rather than leading it, carrying no arms and being absent from the fighting. A far more dangerous type of rebel was his son, Jack Gladstone, a backslider in chapel but an ardent and wily agitator who was later to give evidence against Parson Smith and got off with deportation to St. Lucia.

As far as the Whites were concerned, the revolt broke out with shocking suddenness on Monday 18 August. Nearly all the 30,000 slaves on the sixty estates over a thirty-mile stretch east of Georgetown were involved. Again, by a concerted policy, there was little property damage, and the Whites held captive were merely placed in the slave punishment stocks. Governor Murray, himself a planter, on the first morning confronted a party of rebels and asked them what they wanted. "Our rights," he was told. When Murray told them of the forthcoming Bathurst reforms, the rebels replied, in Murray's account, that "these things . . . were no comfort to them. God had made them of the same flesh and blood as the whites, that they were tired of being Slaves to them, that their good King had sent Orders that they should be free and they would not work any more." Murray then said that he would only negotiate once the rebels laid down their arms, at which the crowd grew ugly. Murray thereupon turned tail, galloped into Georgetown and ordered a general mobilisation.

The slaves were no match for the forces of the regime under Colonel Leahy, which, contrary to the slaves' wishful expectation, included well-drilled regulars, black and white, and Amerindians, as well as the local white militia. The only serious clash was at Bachelor's Adventure plantation, halfway down the coast, on 20 August, where 2000 slaves met with Leahy's 300 redcoats. "Some of the insurgents called out that they wanted lands and three days in the week for themselves, besides Sunday, and that they would not give up their arms till they were satisfied," wrote a militia rifleman. "They then said that they wanted their freedom," went another account, "that the King had sent it out—and that they *would* be free." Leahy did give the rebels three chances to lay down their arms, but when their leaders announced that "the negroes were determined to have nothing more or less than their freedom," and one prominent rebel waved a cutlass and dared the troops "to come on," Leahy gave the order to fire. The first volley scattered the rebels and in the ensuing orgy of hunting and shooting, particularly enjoyed by the militia, between 100 and 150 rebels were killed or wounded, at the cost of two wounded soldiers. The rest of the campaign was simply mopping up.

Besides the slaves killed in resistance, Leahy himself admitted that some sixty were shot out of hand, while an equal number were more ceremonially executed after military trials, a total of 250 slaves killed in all, compared with three Whites killed and a handful wounded. Quamina was hunted down and shot by Amerindians on 16 September, his body being hung in chains close to Bethel chapel, where it was left for months. Parson Smith was arrested and charged with complicity and incitement, tried under martial law, found guilty and condemned to death—with a recommendation for mercy—on 19 November. Suffering from galloping consumption, he died in his prison cell on 6 February 1824, a week before King George IV signed a reprieve with an order for deportation.

When the news of the Demerara revolt reached England in early October, it was a great disappointment for the Emancipationists but provided fresh ammunition for the pro-slavery lobby. Both sides were initially convinced that it was the timing of the Bathurst circular which had triggered the revolt, and even Zachary Macaulay went so far in attempting to reassure Buxton and Wilberforce as to maintain that the insurrection was "the work of Canning, Bathurst and Co. and not of your firm." Canning and the government duly reneged on their promise to impose the amelioration measures, except in Trinidad, and when Buxton opposed this in Parliament he felt himself to be "the most unpopular man in the House."

No one dared to defend in public the actions of the slaves. However, as the details of Smith's trial reached England, along with the news of the concurrent wrecking of Shrewsbury's Methodist chapel in Barbados and the Jamaican planters' over-reaction to a threatened revolt in Hanover parish, a more effective line of attack presented itself to the Emancipationists. Clearly, the West Indian Whites could be held chiefly to blame; not just for agitating the slaves by their repressions, resistance to reform and loose talk of secession, but, even more, for their lawless godlessness in attacking the Christian church and its adherents. Lord Brougham, in a four-hour attack on the colonial plantocracies on 1 June 1824, virtually, in Charles Buxton's phrase "changed the current of public opinion." John Smith, rather than any of the 250 dead rebels, was styled "the Demerara Martyr"; not just because of what was described as his Christ-like forbearance and fate, but because his teaching had actually prevented the slaves from greater excesses. In perhaps the most telling passage of his marathon speech, Brougham quoted the Rev. W. S. Austin, the Anglican rector of Georgetown who had been deported for daring to defend Smith at his trial, that "he shuddered to write that the planters were seeking the life of the man whose teaching had saved theirs." A fortnight later, in his last ever speech before Parliament, Wilberforce castigated the government for believing that such a body as the Guianese planters would ever reform itself, and helped wrest the minor concession that the Bathurst measures would be imposed on Demerara and St. Lucia as well as Trinidad.

The period between 1824 and 1832 saw a steadily widening gulf between the metropolis—Colonial Office, public and even Parliament—on the one hand, and the colonial plantocracies on the other. The Emancipationists, gaining confidence, made the crucial transition from gradualism to immediatism in May 1830, while, for their part, the colonial slaves increasingly took advantage of developing conditions. Slave unrest was wide-spread, almost endemic. Even in a non-plantation colony like the Bahamas, where the slaves were healthier, less hard worked and less supervised than elsewhere, dissatisfactions with slavery fed on rumours of imperial change. For example, the largest holding of Bahamian slaves, Lord Rolle's in Exuma Island, fearing a transfer to Trinidad and loss of their lifestyle, rose up early in 1830. A group of forty-four led by one Pompey, seized their master's boat and sailed to Nassau to lay their case before a governor, Carmichael Smyth, who enjoyed an exaggerated reputation for favouring slaves over their masters—being flogged for their rebellion but at least ensuring that they would not be moved from their island home.

Fittingly, though, it was in Jamaica—the richest and most populous plantation colony, with the harshest regime and most turbulent history of slave resistance—that the climactic and largest ever British slave revolt erupted around Christmas 1831. Jamaica was also the colony in which Christianity had most firmly taken root, a development that the planters regarded as chancy at best, highly dangerous at worst. Cautious proselytising by the established church or by the more "respectable" and regime-supporting sects—such as Moravians or Methodists—might usefully socialise the slaves. Yet the most ardent converts were the followers of "Native Baptist" preachers, who had originally come to Jamaica with the Loyalists in the 1780s, more than twenty-five years before the first white Baptist missionaries arrived in the colony. Obviously, the "brown Anabaptist priest" mentioned by Monk Lewis in 1816 was such a person. Another was Sam Sharpe, the pre-eminent leader of the 1831 rebellion, though he, like most of his kind, had more or less been subsumed into a white missionary's chapel as a deacon.

So many black deacons and their followers were to be involved in the Christmas rebellion that it was popularly known as the Baptist War—a fact that was initially a great embarrassment and only retrospectively useful to the white ministers who, like John Smith in 1823, were largely ignorant of what went on beyond their notice or understanding. From an extreme point of view, the preferred kind of "native" Christianity was quasi-millenarian, and thus politically explosive. Evidence garnered after the rebellion described "the rebel churchgoers' emphasis on membership and leadership, their fervent secret meetings, their use of dream, trance and oaths, their almost cabalistic reverence for the Holy Bible, [and] their choice of biblical texts stressing redemption, regeneration and apocalypse." Undoubtedly there was intrinsic tinder in the Native Baptist style, but a careful examination of the actions and aims of Sam Sharpe and his coterie of leaders suggests a close affinity to those of the vanguard led by Bussa in Barbados—who were, of course, not Christians—and that which included Jack Gladstone, Sandy and Telemachus in Demerara. The slaves' more or less authorised Sunday activities and the chapels provided cover for organisation and planning, chapel services contributed to rebel rhetoric and contact with missionaries even provided a sense that the slaves were linked with sympathetic allies overseas. But Christianity was not essential to the slaves' resistance.

Consider the best evidence of Sam Sharpe's activities in the latter part of 1831. Though he was a slave and based in Montego Bay, Sharpe was practically free to roam far inland on the pretext of preaching. A favourite meeting place was the home of a senior slave called Johnson (later to die at the head of an armed body of slaves some have called the Black Regiment), on Retrieve estate, a dozen miles up the Great River valley. One condemned rebel called Hylton later described how the charismatic Sharpe

> referred to the manifold evils and injustices of slavery: asserted the natural equality of man with regard to freedom ... that because the King had made them free, or resolved upon it, the whites ... were holding secret meetings with the doors shut close ... and had determined ... to kill all the black men, and save all the women and children and keep them in slavery; and if the black men did not stand up for themselves, and take their freedom, the whites would put them at the muzzles of their guns and shoot them like pigeons.

The slaves, said Sharpe, should be ready to fight, but merely threaten force while engaging in strike action, binding "themselves by oath not to work after Christmas as slaves, but to assert their claim to freedom, and to be faithful to each other." A rebel slave called Rose testified that Sharpe asked him to take the oath. "I said Yes. The oath was if we should agree to sit down & I said Yes & so did every body in the house say Yes. Must not trouble anybody or raise any rebellion." Another rebel called Barrett testified that, "Sharpe said that we must sit down. We are free. Must not work again unless we got half pay. He took a Bible out of his pocket. Made me swear that I would not work again until we got half pay."

The Whites had some premonition of the drift of events as early as 15 December but largely ignored the signs, so that the uprising that began with the refusal of thousands of slaves to go back to work after the Christmas holiday ended on Tuesday 27 December, and the firing of Kensington estate high above Montego Bay that night, was a stunning shock. Almost immediately, the revolt spread over an area of 750 square miles centred on the Great River valley, involving more than 200 estates and perhaps 60,000 slaves. The Whites, including a militia regiment defeated at a skirmish at Montpelier on 29 December, were driven into the coastal towns, and the rebels controlled the western interior of the island for nearly three weeks. Their hopes of bringing the regime to terms, with the imperial government as mediator and the imperial troops standing aside, turned out (as in 1816 and 1823) to be a cruel delusion. The Governor, Lord Belmore, promptly declared martial law, the military commander, General Sir Willoughby Cotton, acted with ruthless efficiency, while the white militia exacted savage retribution for their earlier setback.

This time, however, the regime's response was undoubtedly over-kill. Though the planters later claimed damages of over a million pounds (including the valuation of the slaves and the crops they had lost), no one computed the damage to the slaves whose huts and provision grounds were burned. Some 200 slaves were killed in the fighting (for less than a dozen killed by them), while no less than 340 were executed, including more than a hundred after civil trials once martial law was lifted on 5 February 1832. Beyond this, the local Whites, largely under the aegis of an Anglican organisation called the Colonial Church Union, carried out a veritable pogrom against the nonconformist missionaries and their congregations, burning down virtually every chapel in Western Jamaica. Sam Sharpe himself was one of the last to die, being hanged in Montego Bay on 23 May 1832; his last statement being, in the words of an admiring Methodist missionary, "I would rather die on yonder gallows than live in slavery."

Had Sam Sharpe known what had already happened in England, and what was about to happen, he might have died happier. When the first news of the Jamaican rebellion reached England in mid-February, it found the country in the throes of the complex political ferment that accompanied the reform of Parliament itself. . . .

. . .[T]he very day after Sam Sharpe's execution in distant Jamaica, [T. F.] Buxton made his crucial speech in the Commons pressing for the appointment of a select committee, not just a committee of inquiry like that of the Lords, but one that would "consider and report upon the Measures which it may be expedient to adopt for the purpose of effecting the Extinction of Slavery throughout the British Dominions, at the earliest period compatible with the safety of all Classes in the Colonies." Buxton's motion was defeated, by 136 to 90, but a committee was appointed, although with a mandate far short of discussing the means of emancipation. And the evidence that the committee heard over the next six months, in conjunction with the rising wave of anti-slavery agitation throughout the country, made it inevitable that the Whig government would be bound to pass an Emancipation Act within eighteen months. Key actors in this phase were the refugee missionaries, especially William Knibb (who, on hearing as his ship came up the Channel that the Reform Bill had passed, is alleged to have said, "Thank God! Now I will have slavery down!"); though another important witness was the same Rev. W. S. Austin who had been deported from Demerara eight years before.

Even the English public, it seems, was far more easily stirred up by the evidence of the persecution of white missionaries than by the slaughter of slave rebels—and in this sense the missionaries, as in 1823, stole the martyrs' crown. But the missionaries would not have had a case to make without the actions of the slaves, whether the rebels were their parishioners or not. As far as Parliament was concerned, however, neither slaughtered slaves nor missionaries tarred and feathered were as effective as the general threat posed to the imperial economy—to the empire itself—by the virtual civil war between the slaves and their masters. The question for Parliament was essentially a political one; it was a matter of morality only in the sense that, in a liberal world, empire can only be maintained if its morality is justified. What Buxton was able to show in his great speech of 24 May, was that the actions of the slaves and the planters' counter attack showed up both slavery's immorality and its political impracticality. "Was it certain," asked Buxton, "that the colonies would remain to the country if we were resolved to retain slavery? . . . How was the government prepared to act, in case of a general insurrection of the negroes? . . . a war against people struggling for their rights would be the falsest position in which it was possible for England to be placed. And did the noble Lords think that the people *out of doors* would be content to see their resources exhausted for the purpose of resisting the inalienable rights of mankind?" In perhaps his most brilliant and telling passage, Buxton then quoted Thomas Jefferson, a statesman by then universally respected but one of the most tortured of slavery's defenders. "A [slave] revolution is among possible events; the Almighty has no attributes which would side with us in [such a] struggle."

In sum, then, slave resistance and emancipationism were clearly intertwined in British slavery's final phase. News of slave resistance was disseminated more quickly, more widely and more thoroughly than ever before, while more and more slaves heard, if not always accurately, about Emancipationist activity in Britain. Moreover, slave resistance rose to a climax, in Jamaica, at the very point that the process was set in motion which led to the passing of the Emancipation Act on 31 July 1833. It remains to be decided, though, to what degree slave resistance and emancipationism, respectively, actually caused or speeded each other.

At the most obvious level, the Emancipation Act of 1833 was simply the political culmination of a widespread movement or campaign in the metropole. In conjunction with the general movement towards liberal reform, the small nucleus of convinced Emancipationists were able to carry the country towards a conviction that colonial slavery must be abolished. Through the interweaving of events—some of them, such as the victory of the Whigs and the passage of the Great Reform Bill, almost fortuitous—this popular conviction became translated into legislative fiat. This interpretation naturally plays down—if not actually denies—the effect of the actions of the slaves themselves in swaying first the British populace and then a sufficient majority in Parliament.

In an immediate sense, all the slave protests were certainly failures, and the slave rebellions of 1816 and 1823 actually set back the Emancipationist cause. Yet the slave resistance, not only rising to a crescendo but increasingly well publicised, gradually drove home the realisation both of the falsity of the assertion that the slaves were contented and of the plantocracy's claim to enjoy effective control. More than this, the increasingly paranoid behaviour of the colonial Whites both outraged and dismayed all levels of metropolitan opinion. . . .

At least some of the slave leaders—including the authors of the subversive slave ditty of 1816 with which we began—saw the political problem in its full dimensions. To achieve the aim of freedom, they realised, the slaves needed not only solidarity among themselves, but the strengthening of links with metropolitan allies against their immediate oppressors. Christianity was, at the least, a universalising medium, with the white missionaries as messengers and mediators; mediators not so much with God, or even that other Big Massa, the English king, but with the larger congregation of fellow Christians among the British populace. And, in the event, what was most impressive of all to this larger constituency (though the pro-slavery forces did their utmost to mask it) was that the rebel slaves, though resolute in their aims, were initially more pacific in their means than the plantocratic regimes which they confronted, only resorting to force (as the 1816 ditty had it) when met by actual force.

Thus, the resistance of the slaves unequivocally contributed—if not only in direct and obvious ways—to the fact that the slave system was increasingly seen in Britain to be not only morally wrong and economically inefficient, but also politically unwise. So, in assessing the contribution of the slaves themselves to the achievement of emancipation in 1833, one can conclude that while Richard Hart's 1980 claim that British West Indian blacks were "slaves who abolished slavery" is rather overstated, the earlier contention of Eric Williams that "the alternatives were clear: emancipation from above or emancipation from below" is much more than simply plausible.

Suggestions for Further Reading

For a comprehensive bibliography of the slave trade and slavery, see Joseph C. Miller, *Slavery: A Worldwide Bibliography, 1900–1982* (1985). Peter C. Hogg, *The African Slave Trade and Its Suppression: A Classified and Annotated Bibliography of Books, Pamphlets and Published Articles* (1973) is very useful for older sources.

General surveys of the Atlantic slave trade include Philip D. Curtin, *The Rise and Fall of the Plantation Complex: Essays in Atlantic History* (1990); Edward Reynolds, *Stand the Storm: A History of the Atlantic Slave Trade* (1985); James A. Rawley, *The Transatlantic Slave Trade* (1981); and Basil Davidson, *The African Slave Trade* (rev. ed., 1980). The early Atlantic slave trade is examined by John Thornton, *Africa and Africans in the Making of the Atlantic World, 1400–1680* (1992).

For further discussion of the size and distribution of the slave trade, see the articles by David Richardson, David Geggus, and Paul Lovejoy in the *Journal of African History* 30 (1989). Herbert S. Klein, *The Middle Passage: Comparative Studies in the Atlantic Slave Trade* (1978) applies quantitative data to particular issues.

Collections of primary sources include Elizabeth Donnan, ed., *Documents Illustrative of the History of the Slave Trade to America*, 4 vols. (1930–1935), especially the first two volumes, which are not confined to the United States. Michael Craton, James Walvin, and David Wright, eds., *Slavery, Abolition and Emancipation: Black Slaves and the British Empire* (1976) has a strong focus on the Caribbean. On the African side, see Philip D. Curtin, ed., *Africa Remembered: Narratives by West Africans from the Era of the Slave Trade* (1967). A modern critical edition of Equiano is Paul Edwards, ed., *The Life of Olaudah Equiano, or Gustavus Vassa the African* (rev. ed., 1989).

General collections of studies include Joseph E. Inikori and Stanley L. Engerman, eds., *The Atlantic Slave Trade: Effects on Economies, Societies, and Peoples in Africa, the Americas, and Europe* (1992); Barbara L. Solow, ed., *Slavery and the Rise of the Atlantic System* (1991); Barbara Solow and Stanley L. Engerman, eds., *British Capitalism and Caribbean Slavery: The Legacy of Eric Williams* (1987); Paul E. Lovejoy, ed., *Africans in Bondage: Studies in Slavery and the Slave Trade* (1986); Joseph E. Inikori, ed., *Forced Migration: The Impact of the Export Slave Trade on African Societies* (1982); and Henry A. Gemery and Jan S. Hogendorn, eds., *The Uncommon Market: Essays in the Economic History of the Atlantic Slave Trade* (1979).

Some national histories of the slave trade and its abolition are Johannes M. Postma, *The Dutch in the Atlantic Slave Trade 1600–1815* (1990); Jay Coughtry, *The Notorious Triangle: Rhode Island and the African Slave Trade, 1700–1807* (1981); Colin A. Palmer, *The British Slave Trade to Spanish America, 1700–1739* (1981); David R. Murray, *Odious Commerce: Britain, Spain, and the Abolition of the Cuban Slave Trade* (1980); Robert Louis Stein, *The French Slave Trade in the Eighteenth Century: An Old Regime Business* (1979); and Leslie Bethell, *The Abolition of the Brazilian Slave Trade: Britain, Brazil and the Slave Trade Question, 1807–1869* (1970).

Brief overviews of the effects of the slave trade in Africa are presented by John D. Fage, "African Societies and the Atlantic Slave Trade," in *Past and Present* 125 (1989): 97–115; Joseph E. Inikori, "Africa in World History: The Export Slave Trade from Africa and the Emergence of the Atlantic Economic Order," B. A. Ogot, ed., UNESCO *General History of Africa*, vol. 5, *Africa from the Sixteenth to the Eighteenth Century* (1992); and Jacob F. Ade Ajayi and B. O. Oloruntimehin, "West Africa in the Anti-Slave Trade Era," pp. 200–221 in John D. Fage and Roland Oliver, eds., *Cambridge History of Africa*, vol. 5. *c. 1790 to c. 1870*, ed. John E. Flint (1976). More detailed surveys of the various trades in African slaves are Patrick Manning, *Slavery and African Life: Occidental, Oriental, and African Slave Trades* (1990) and Paul E. Lovejoy, *Transformations in Slavery: A History of Slavery in Africa* (1983).

Studies of different parts of Africa during the era of the slave trade include Robin C. C. Law, *The Slave Coast of West Africa 1550–1750: The Impact of the Atlantic Slave Trade on an African Society* (1991); Joseph C. Miller, *Way of Death: Merchant Capitalism and the Angolan Slave Trade, 1730–1830* (1988); Richard L. Roberts, *Warriors, Merchants, and Slaves: The State and the Economy in the Middle Niger Valley, 1700–1914* (1987); Patrick Manning, *Slavery, Colonialism and Economic Growth in Dahomey, 1640–1960* (1982); Robert W. Harms, *River of Wealth, River of Sorrow: The Central Zaire Basin in the Era of the Slave and Ivory Trade, 1500–1891* (1981); David Northrup, *Trade Without Rulers: Precolonial Economic Development in South-Eastern Nigeria* (1978); Edward A. Alpers, *Ivory and Slaves in East Central Africa: Changing Patterns of International Trade to the Later 19th Century* (1975); Philip D. Curtin, *Economic Change in Precolonial Africa: Senegambia in the Era of the Slave Trade* (1975); Ivor Wilks, *Asante in the Nineteenth Century* (1976); A. J. H. Latham, *Old Calabar, 1600–1891: The Impact of the International Economy upon a Traditional Society* (1973); Phyllis M. Martin, *The External Trade of the Loango Coast* (1972); Kwame Daaku, *Trade and Politics on the Gold Coast, 1600–1720* (1970); Walter Rodney, *A History of the Upper Guinea Coast, 1545–1800* (1970); and I. A. Akinjogbin, *Dahomey and Its Neighbours, 1708–1818* (1967).

The end of the slave trade is discussed in David Eltis, *Economic Growth and the Ending of the Transatlantic Slave Trade* (1987); Seymour Drescher, *Capitalism and Antislavery: British Mobilization in Comparative Perspective* (1987); David Eltis and James Walvin, eds., *The Abolition of the Atlantic Slave Trade: Origins and Effects in Europe, Africa, and the Americas* (1981); Seymour Drescher, *Econocide: British Slavery in the Era of Abolition* (1977); Roger Anstey, *The Atlantic Slave Trade and British Abolition, 1760–1810* (1975); Johnson U. J. Asiegbu, *Slavery and the Politics of Liberation, 1787–1861: A Study of Liberated African Migration and British Anti-slavery Policy* (1969); and Christopher Lloyd, *The Navy and the Slave Trade* (1949).

For the role of slave revolts in ending slavery, see Michael Craton, *Testing the Chains: Resistance to Slavery in the British West Indies* (1982) and C. L. R. James, *Black Jocobins: Toussaint L'Ouverture and the San Domingo Revolution* (2d ed., 1963).